ENGLISH AS A LINGUA FRANCA

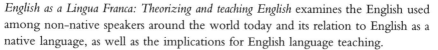

English as a Lingua Franca: Theorizing and teaching English examines the English used among non-native speakers around the world today and its relation to English as a native language, as well as the implications for English language teaching.

Challenging and incisive, this book analyses positive and negative accounts of English as a lingua franca, and its linguistic features, within the context of:

- native and World Englishes
- multilingualism and intercultural communication
- sociolinguistic issues including accent and identity
- classroom teaching and learning.

English as a Lingua Franca is a useful guide for teachers and trainee teachers, and is essential reading for advanced students and linguists concerned with multilingualism, language contact, language learning, language change, and the place of English in the world today.

Ian MacKenzie teaches English, linguistics and translation in the Faculty of Translation and Interpreting at the University of Geneva.

ENGLISH AS A LINGUA FRANCA

Theorizing and teaching English

Ian MacKenzie

Routledge
Taylor & Francis Group

LONDON AND NEW YORK

First published 2014
by Routledge
2 Park Square, Milton Park, Abingdon, Oxon OX14 4RN

Simultaneously published in the USA and Canada
by Routledge
711 Third Avenue, New York, NY 10017

Routledge is an imprint of the Taylor & Francis Group, an informa business

British Library Cataloguing in Publication Data
A catalogue record for this book is available from the British Library

Library of Congress Cataloguing in Publication Data
MacKenzie, Ian, 1954–
English as a lingua franca : theorizing and teaching English / Ian MacKenzie.
pages cm
Includes bibliographical references and index.
1. English language–Variation–Foreign countries. 2. English language–
Globalization. I. Title.
PE2751.M33 2013
418–dc23
2013010913

ISBN: 978-0-415-80990-0 (hbk)
ISBN: 978-0-415-80991-7 (pbk)
ISBN: 978-1-315-89008-1 (ebk)

Typeset in Bembo
by Taylor & Francis Books

Printed and bound by CPI Group (UK) Ltd, Croydon, CR0 4YY

CONTENTS

PREFACE

When, not so many decades ago, during the glory days of communicative language teaching, I began teaching English as a foreign language in a friendly school in a large suburban house in the transpontine backwoods of South London, I soon decided that I preferred upper-intermediate and advanced classes. There are young teachers who prefer beginners – there's so much to teach them, and they progress so rapidly! – and there are those who like advanced learners, because you can speak more naturally and discuss interesting topics (it's not really a job, is it?). The downside is that progress is less visible. With the benefit of hindsight – and, I have to concede, the writings of Barbara Seidlhofer, Anna Mauranen, Jennifer Jenkins, Andy Kirkpatrick *et al.* – it is easy to see that one of the reasons why progress was slow was that I wasted time attempting to correct the more intractable 'errors' being committed by rather fluent speakers. Today, I would describe many of those 'errors' as natural developments of English used as an additional language or a lingua franca by non-native speakers around the world, simplifications and adaptations of the more incongruous and idiosyncratic elements of English grammar (and pronunciation). And I would ponder the question as to whether speakers of English as a lingua franca (or ELF) need to worry about these niceties of native English usage.

Yet my reassessment of 'errors' as 'natural developments' has occurred in the past few years. Research into ELF is burgeoning, but as many of the leading researchers like to point out, it is all rather recent. My own acceptance of some of the arguments put forward by ELF researchers is more recent still, but over the past few years I have found myself explaining the incontrovertible *logic* of ELF – that versions of a language used among non-native speakers clearly do not need to resemble any given native speaker variety – to hostile or aghast translation students, virtually all of whom protest that they want to speak and write English (almost) as well as its native speakers. On the other hand I still find implausible some of the more extreme claims made by various ELF theorists (the native speaker is irrelevant to the future of English; native speakers are numerically insignificant in global English usage; many ELF users will never even encounter a native speaker, etc.).

In the preface to a previous book (MacKenzie 2002) that outlined opposing positions (pragmatic linguistics and deconstructionist literary theory) I wrote that I didn't expect it to lead to any Damascene conversions, in that instance of deconstructionists. This book is not intended to convert anyone to anything either; it merely tries to describe English as it is used as a lingua franca, to set out various arguments relating to ELF usage and English teaching, and to draw some plausible conclusions. Consequently in the following chapters I consider ELF in relation to native and nativized varieties of English, and examine its linguistic elements (lexicogrammar, phraseology, phonology, pragmatics, etc.) and related sociolinguistic factors (accent, identity, uses, variability, and so on). The book also considers ELF in relation to bilingualism and intercultural communication. It analyses ELF in relation to classroom teaching and learning, and suggests that there are advantages to being able to understand and use more than one variety of English in the world today.

Being, (almost) by definition, a non-native use of language, ELF presents something of a challenge to 'nativist' and formalist linguistics, and it should be of particular interest to theorists of second language acquisition. But the unstable nature of ELF should also make it particularly interesting to proponents of usage-based theories of language. This book takes an essentially usage-based and emergent view of language, but the fluidity of the grammar, lexis and phraseology of ELF require a reconciliation of usage-based approaches to cognitive processing with a radically variationist account of language.

Because prefaces are the place to be pretentious and presumptuous, I will quote Milroy and Muysken (1995: 11), who describe 'a linguistics text which systematically deals with a single issue' from a wide 'range of subdisciplinary perspectives' as being 'as rare as a pink rhinoceros,' and bemoan 'the trend of hyperspecialism which increasingly isolates linguists from other practitioners of the *sciences humaines* as well as from each other.' The following pages necessarily cover a wide range of linguistic topics – multilingualism, language contact, sociolinguistic variation, language and identity, usage-based theories of lexicogrammar and phraseology, second language acquisition, phonology and pragmatics – all of which have a bearing on ELF, and some of which may in turn be affected by ELF. Chapters on language policy, and translation and interpreting unfortunately had to be cut for reasons of space.

Synopsis

Chapter 1 offers a definition of ELF, discusses the notion of the native speaker, and situates ELF in relation to World Englishes. Chapter 2 discusses ELF in relation to bi- and multilingualism, given that all ELF speakers are by definition at least bilingual. Chapter 3 outlines the effects of language contact and adolescent and adult second-language learning, and the theory of usage-based linguistics and emergent grammar. Chapter 4 looks at specific identifiable characteristics of the grammar of ELF, of which there are not a great many, given that English has made the transition from being a synthetic language to a largely analytic (and greatly simplified) one due to its having been learned and used by non-native speakers for hundreds of years. Chapter 5 looks at the lexical aspect of ELF. Chapter 6, the longest chapter, considers the language processing strategies of L1 and L2 speakers, and the phraseological nature of native English, as well as examining the phraseology of ELF, in which speakers have the choice of adopting ENL (English as a native language) idioms, adapting them, constructing their utterances analytically without recourse to formulaic language, or inventing their own formulaic sequences and idioms. Contrary to the logic of entrenchment discussed in Chapter 3, ELF seems to show a huge range of phraseological variation. Chapter 7 considers the role of language, and especially accent, in the construction of individual and group identity, and to what extent speakers identify with an additional or auxiliary language. It also discusses Jenkins' proposed Lingua Franca Core for pronunciation. Chapter 8 examines widely attested pragmatic processes used in ELF but also contests some of the more angelic accounts of ELF put forward by its proponents, such that everyone is always trying to be maximally communicative and converge on shared meaning in a shared affective space: if ELF is used in a full range of functions, there will also be somewhat less consensual contexts involving obfuscation, deception, hostility, contempt, and so on. The final chapter considers the implications of all that has gone before for language teaching: which models and what content are appropriate to the teaching of English today?

ACKNOWLEDGEMENTS

This book has benefited from the kindness of several people. Kirsten Stirling showed me where I failed to come up to the standards of first year BA 'English Composition' students. Nadia Seemungal at Routledge showed admirable forbearance when sent a manuscript that was 66 per cent longer than commissioned. A happy compromise ensued.

I'd like to thank Anna Mauranen for letting me a read a proof copy of *Exploring ELF*. Margie Berns and Barbara Seidlhofer kindly sent me hard-to-find articles. We all need to thank Seidlhofer and Mauranen for instigating the compilation and publication of million-word corpora of spoken ELF; anyone who has recorded and transcribed as little as a minute or two of spoken discourse will have a sense of how much work this involves.

Rebecca Cupit and Tessa Carroll did what copy editors and proofreaders do, which is to save authors from great embarrassment.

An earlier version of Chapter 2 appeared in the *International Journal of Multilingualism*. Bits of an article that appeared in the *European Journal of English Studies* are spread over several chapters.

For a change, I won't dedicate this book to Kirsten (*sine quo non*), though we *can* now revert to an unELFy existence, but instead to 'Robert,' Hubert, Jan, Rogier, Hans, Gerard, Dieric, Quinten, Joachim, Hieronymous and Pieter. And to Stelios, who changed the world (or at least Europe), and made it possible to go and see them all at will.

LIST OF ABBREVIATIONS

AmE	American English
BrE	British English
EFL	English as a foreign language
EIL	English as an international language
ELF	English as a lingua franca
ELFA	The English as a Lingua Franca in Academic Settings corpus
ELT	English language teaching
ENL	English as a native language
ESL	English as a second language
GA	General American
IaEs	Interactions across Englishes
L1	First language
L2	Second language
LFC	Lingua Franca Core (for pronunciation)
MICASE	The Michigan Corpus of Academic Spoken English
NES	Native English speaker
NNES	Non-native English speaker
NNS	Non-native speaker
NS	Native speaker
RP	Received Pronunciation
SLA	Second language acquisition
StE	Standard English
VOICE	The Vienna-Oxford International Corpus of English

1

WHAT IS ELF?

Se ti sabir,
Ti respondir;
Se non sabir,
Tazir, tazir.

Molière, Le bourgeois gentilhomme (4.5)[1]

The new language which is rapidly ousting the language of Shakespeare as the world's lingua franca is English itself – English in its new global form.

Graddol (2006: 11)

A character in Julian Barnes' novel *Talking It Over* working as an EFL teacher in London has a revelation: the reason his former students can't even buy a bus ticket is that they were taught English as a Foreign Language – 'Why don't they teach English as English, that's what I want to know' (1992: 122). After all, who wants to learn to speak English like a foreigner? Little did Barnes (or at least his character, Oliver) know that a decade or two later, some people would consider a non-native English speaker (NNES) speaking like a native English speaker (NES), or even attempting to do so, to be a Bad Thing.

This is because many NNESs use English as a language of wider communication, or as a lingua franca, largely in order to communicate with other NNESs, and it is argued that English teaching should reflect this state of affairs. If people learn English for use as a lingua franca, the language need no longer be related to a particular native 'target culture' in which certain ways of speaking and behaving are appropriate. On the contrary, rather than imitating the norms of NESs, users of English as a lingua franca (ELF) should adopt ways of speaking (with their bi- or multilingual English-speaking interlocutors) which aid mutual intelligibility and successful communication. Such is the logic underlying ELF.

This chapter sketches out what is generally meant by the term ELF and the claims its supporters make for it. It then considers the notion of the native speaker, and the position of NESs in ELF, and seeks to distinguish ELF from World Englishes or New Englishes – the nativized or indigenized varieties used in former British colonial territories. Unlike nativized World Englishes, ELF is not, and will almost certainly never become, a stable variety, because of the range of participants in the international use of English.

English as a lingua franca

The term 'lingua franca' comes from a contact language used in the eastern Mediterranean from the eleventh to the early nineteenth centuries.[2] Today, the term 'English as a lingua franca' is used to refer to 'any use of English among speakers of different first languages for whom English is the communicative medium of choice, and often the only option' (Seidlhofer 2011: 7). ELF is an alternative term for English as an international/global/world language, and International English (see Seidlhofer 2004: 210).[3] Of course ELF is an applied linguists' term; most users probably just think they are speaking English.

As well as being used – often in a very simple form – by tourists, ELF is prominent in international politics and diplomacy, international law, business, the media, and in tertiary education and scientific research – which Yamuna Kachru and Larry Smith (2008: 3) call ELF's 'mathetic function' – so it is clearly not a reduced lingua franca in the term's original (Frankish) sense. Yet it usually differs from English as a native language (ENL), the language used by NESs. Spoken ELF contains a huge amount of linguistic variation and non-standard forms (although formal written ELF tends to resemble ENL to a much greater extent). To use Noam Chomsky's (1986: 20) term, in ELF there is no fixed or shared E-language (external language) as such.

This could result from the fact that ELF users – 'different constellations of speakers of diverse individual Englishes in every single interaction' (Meierkord 2004: 115) – are uninterested in the lexicogrammatical norms of any particular NES speech community (Seidlhofer 2001b, 2009a, 2011), or simply from the 'shaky entrenchment' (Mauranen 2006: 138) or the fuzzy processing (Mauranen 2012: 41), or – from another perspective – the imperfect learning to be expected in a second language (L2). Either way, the leitmotif of the proponents of ELF is that it is different from but not inferior to ENL. Henry Widdowson (2003: 48–49) describes 'the *virtual* language, that resource for making meaning immanent in the language which simply has not hitherto been encoded and so is not, so to speak, given official recognition,' and Barbara Seidlhofer (2011: 120) describes ELF as 'a different but not a deficient way of realizing the virtual language, or playing the English language game': instead of restricting themselves to the realizations of NESs, ELF speakers exploit unused latent possibilities of English morphology, syntax and phraseology.

Dell Hymes (1972: 286) described 'communicative competence' in terms of 'the systematically possible, the feasible, and the appropriate,' but in relation to native speaker (NS) norms; ELF speakers expand what is possible, feasible, and appropriate. As Widdowson (2004: 361) puts it, the ELF perspective is that

> the modified forms of the language which are actually in use should be recognized as a legitimate development of English as an international means of communication. The functional range of the language is not thereby restricted, but on the contrary enhanced, for it enables its users to express themselves more freely without having to conform to norms which represent the sociocultural identity of other people.

Not everybody shares this perspective, of course; for example, conference interpreters, who in general view ELF very negatively, often use the acronym BSE, for 'bad simple English' (Reithofer 2010: 144). From a *formal* point of view, one might agree with Michael Swan (2012: 387), who argues that

> The most appropriate conceptualisation of ELF is surely a negative one. It is not that its speakers conform to identifiable ELF norms; it is that, like the speakers of all foreign languages, they do *not* conform to all NS norms; and this in various and largely uncodifiable ways.

But from a *functional* point of view, what is intrinsic to ELF – what Alan Firth (2009: 150) calls the 'lingua franca factor' – is not any specific language or discourse forms, but rather 'the inherent interactional and linguistic variability that lingua franca interactions entail,' and a 'lingua franca outlook' on language that ELF users adopt. As Seidlhofer (2011: 77) puts it, ELF should be 'functionally not formally defined; it is not a variety of English but a variable way of using it.'[4]

However, stress on the inherent variability of ELF, and on function rather than form, is a recent development.[5] Previous work suggested that ELF could be codified and taught. For example, Seidlhofer (2001b: 150) floated 'the possibility of a codification of ELF with a conceivable ultimate objective of making it a feasible, acceptable and respected alternative to ENL in appropriate contexts of use.' She suggested that a codified ELF could be 'a possible first step for learners in building up a basis from which they can pursue their own learning in directions (ELF or ENL) which it may be impossible, and unwise, to determine from the outset' (p. 151).[6] More recently, Jennifer Jenkins *et al.* (2011: 287) have written that

> in line with increasing evidence of the fluidity and flexibility of ELF communication, the focus of research has shifted from an orientation to features and the ultimate aim of some kind of codification (an aim which, nevertheless, has not been dismissed out of hand), to an interest in the processes underlying and determining the choice of features used in any given ELF interaction.

Yet a few pages later they also state that 'we can identify emerging patterns of lexical and grammatical forms' (pp. 288–89) and that there is 'a certain degree of typicality in the more salient features that occur in lingua franca interactions' (p. 289), meaning that there *are* features that could be codified and taught. Similarly, Seidlhofer (2009b: 239) writes about how ELF speakers are making a significant contribution to norm development, so that ELF could become 'endonormative' or in Braj Kachru's (1985: 16ff) terms, norm-developing or (ultimately) norm-providing rather than norm-dependent. Drawing on Ayo Bamgboṣe (1998), she compares ELF with endonormative World Englishes, stating that 'codification is recognized as a crucial requirement in this process, and one that does not deny the inherent fluidity of ELF' (p. 240). At first glance this seems contradictory, but Seidlhofer stresses that Bamgboṣe discusses *behavioural norms* as well as code norms and feature norms, and argues that these are compatible with a focus on the underlying significance and functional motivation of particular ELF forms.

A further reason for the linguistic variation and non-standard forms found in ELF is that English is in contact with the majority of the world's languages, so there are ELF speakers whose English is influenced by (and contains recognizable transfer features from) a great many first languages (L1s). Given that all ELF speakers are bi- or multilingual, ELF interactions are likely to include borrowing, code-switching, and other types of crosslinguistic interaction. Transfer leads to people of many different typologically diverse L1s speaking recognizable varieties or 'lects.' These lects differ from regional dialects, which arise in local communities of speakers talking to each other, as, e.g. Japanese speakers do not normally need to speak to other Japanese speakers in English; they speak English to people with different L1s. So these lects come into prolonged contact with each other in ELF, in linguistically heterogeneous situations. Because 'they arise in parallel, not in mutual interaction,' Anna Mauranen (2012: 29) describes these hybrid variants as 'similects,' and says[7] that ELF can be characterised as 'second-order language contact' – a contact between hybrids:

> Second-order contact means that instead of a typical contact situation where speakers of two different languages use one of them in communication ('first-order contact'), a large number of languages are each in contact with English, and it is these contact varieties (similects) that are, in turn, in contact with each other. Their special features, resulting from crosslinguistic transfer, come together much like dialects in contact.
>
> *(p. 30)*

Because speakers have a natural tendency to adapt to variability and to accommodate to each other's uses, Mauranen suggests that second-order language contact will lead to the spread of innovations inspired by different L1s. Certain hybrid forms will diffuse into common usage, so that ELF will become more stable (p. 32). The features likely to be diffused are those that are widely shared among the world's English speakers, because they are common in other languages, and therefore acquired comparatively easily in English as an additional language.[8] As in all language contact, there is also likely to be simplification, and a convergence or levelling of phonological and grammatical systems, so that irregular and marked features are replaced by regular, unmarked alternatives (see Trudgill 1986; Thomason and Kaufman 1988; Thomason 2001; Winford 2003). These processes will be examined in Chapters 3–6.

ELF researchers insist that ELF speakers are *users* and not *learners*. As Mauranen (2006: 147) puts it, we need to

> stop considering second and foreign language users as eternal 'learners' on an interminable journey toward perfection in a target language. Speakers may opt out of the role of learner at any stage, and take on the identity of language users, who successfully manage demanding discourses despite imperfections in the code.

Consequently many orthodox second language acquisition (SLA) and English as a foreign language (EFL) concepts are not relevant to ELF. Beyza Björkman (2008b: 36) says that 'the terms "interlanguage" and "language errors" do not apply in the ELF context. [...] ELF research in general, unlike SLA, treats these non-standard forms not as errors but divergent forms or "features."' The same applies to 'interference,' 'fossilization,' 'overuse,' 'underuse,' etc.: Seidlhofer (2001b: 144) argues that the ways in which NNESs simplify, overuse, underuse or avoid certain expressions or structures, compared to ENL, should not be regarded as learning strategies – 'a constructive way of making do with the limited resources available at a particular stage of interlanguage' – but rather as 'communication strategies: evidence not of a linguistic deficit, but, if intelligible, of successful communication.' As Jenkins (2007: 238) puts it, in international communication, 'the ability to accommodate to interlocutors with other first languages than one's own (regardless of whether the result is an "error" in ENL) is a far more important skill than the ability to imitate the English of a native speaker.'

Mauranen (2003: 517) offers what could almost be a manifesto for ELF:

> it is important for people to feel comfortable and appreciated when speaking a foreign language. Speakers should feel they can express their identities and be themselves in L2 contexts without being marginalised on account of features like foreign accents, lack of idiom, or culture-specific communicative styles as long as they can negotiate and manage communicative situations successfully and fluently. An international language can be seen as a legitimate learning target, a variety belonging to its speakers. Thus, *deficiency models,* that is, those stressing the gap that distinguishes NNSs from NSs, should be seen as inadequate for the description of fluent L2 speakers and discarded as the sole basis of language education in English.

Yet the gap that separates NNESs from NESs can be overstated. Some of the proponents of ELF criticize those who compare fluent ELF speakers to fluent NESs (see, e.g. Seidlhofer 2010: 366; and Jenkins 2007: 35), as if fluent non-native English could be wholly different from native English and still remain the same language. Yet as ELF corpora show, fluent ELF necessarily has many similarities with ENL.[9] In a study of international university students in Britain, Christiane Meierkord (2004) found that 94–95 per cent of utterances by NNESs were syntactically regular according to ENL norms (after discounting the less competent speakers and their learner errors). As Peter Trudgill (2005b: 87) says, 'Discussions about using native speaker models in ELT are thus not really about *whether* to use native speaker models but about *how far* to use such models.' Jenkins (2007: 38) describes ELF as being 'self-determining and independent of Anglo-American English,' as if there was no overlap with ENL, but both ELF and postcolonial World Englishes have largely appropriated the grammatical core of ENL, at least in their written forms, and there is also a great deal of lexis common to all varieties – not unlike the way humans share 99 per cent of their DNA with chimpanzees and 97.5 per cent with mice (and 50 per cent with bananas)![10] Another way of putting this is that English is English. There *are* means of communication that are radically different from native English – such as the one on the planet Margo, as reported in Kurt Vonnegut's novel *Breakfast of Champions* (1973), which is a combination of farting and tap dancing – but ELF is not one of them.

On the other hand, ELF speakers do not share a cultural background and what Seidlhofer (2011: 16) calls 'conventions and markers of in-group membership' such as 'idiomatic phraseology, and references and allusions to shared experience.' Instead, as Luke Prodromou (2008: 88) puts it, they 'belong to the more disparate and diverse culture of the global village.' Thus Meierkord (2002: 128–29) describes 'lingua franca communication' as 'both a linguistic masala' of numerous codes 'and a language "stripped bare" of its cultural roots.' All this means that rather than being an easy option, communicating in ELF can be hard work; as Mauranen (2012: 7) says, 'The cognitive load in ELF is unusually heavy on account of the variety and unpredictability of language parameters: interlocutors' accents, transfer features, and proficiency levels.' Like speakers of World Englishes, ELF speakers often do not want or need to master the entire language; Shikaripur Sridhar (1994: 802) calls this 'the composite pragmatic model of bilingualism, one that recognizes that a bilingual acquires as much competence in the two (or more) languages as is needed and that all of the languages together serve the full range of communicative needs.'[11] All of this will be expanded in the following chapters.

ELF and native speakers

Native speakers tend to get a bad press in work on bilingualism and ELF. They also regularly acquire scare quotes – 'native speakers.' Vivian Cook (1999: 185) complains that 'It is often taken for granted that the only rightful speakers of a language are its native speakers,' but in fact the only thing that can be taken for granted is that the only *native* speakers of a language are its native speakers, because most of the other claims for NSs do not stand up to scrutiny.

Cook summarizes characteristics of NSs, according to various sources (Stern 1983; Davies 1996; Johnson and Johnson 1998). Apart from being brought up in a specific speech community, NSs are said to have:

  (i)   a subconscious knowledge of rules,
 (ii)   an intuitive grasp of meanings,
(iii)   the ability to communicate within social settings,
 (iv)   a range of language skills,
  (v)   creativity of language use,
 (vi)   an identification with a language community,
(vii)   the ability to produce fluent discourse,
(viii) knowledge of differences between their own speech and that of the 'standard' form of the language, and
 (ix)   the ability to interpret and translate into the L1 of which they are a native speaker.

But Cook points out that some NSs function poorly in social settings; they may be far from fluent in speech, for mental or physical reasons; they may be unaware how their speech variety or dialect differs from the standard form;[12] they are free to disassociate themselves completely from their L1 community without thereby giving up their native speaker status; and they can only interpret and translate if they know at least one other language.[13]

It *does* seem to be true that NSs have a subconscious (procedural) knowledge of the 'rules' of the language they grew up with, an intuitive grasp of meanings, and of the limits of acceptability and productivity (according to other NSs in the same speech community), and a range of language skills. Why try to deny this? (The converse, as Seidlhofer (2001b: 149) rightly says, is that NESs cannot have *intuitions* about ELF, or experience it as a foreign language; they can only have *impressions*.) Non-native speakers (NNSs) can acquire a declarative knowledge of an L2, but this rarely matches the intuitive knowledge of the NS.[14] As Mauranen (2012: 4) says, it is 'a reasonable guess that a speaker's later languages are less well-entrenched than their first,' and one would 'expect that things like ease and speed of retrieval, access to alternative expressions, or mapping linguistic and social repertoires routinely onto each other operate differently in a speaker's first and other languages.'

The NS has a linguistic code acquired in early childhood in conjunction with lived experience of the culture attached to the language. The code acquired is generally a particular sociolect of a particular dialect, but NSs can also develop an ear for other sociolects and dialects. Many people, including David Bellos (2011: 60), have pointed out that there is a splendid circularity to all this: to be a native speaker is to have complete possession of a language, and complete possession of a language is what a native speaker has. Children can of course acquire more than one language simultaneously, and so have two first languages or mother tongues (which will affect both languages; see Chapter 2). They can also emigrate into a new linguaculture during childhood, so that a new language becomes dominant and their mother tongue recedes. In short, as Trudgill (1995: 315) puts it, the concept of 'native-speaker,' like most sociolinguistic concepts, 'is not a matter of either-or' but 'a concept which admits of degrees of more or less,' so that 'some people are more native speakers than others.'[15]

But the fact remains that a post-adolescent or adult learner can never replicate childhood learning. However, as Davies (2004: 447) suggests, this is only a problem if (or when) the bio-developmental account of nativeness merges into the prescriptive and social view that the NS is the repository and guardian of the true language and the standard setter for all speakers.[16] ELF theorists almost unanimously point out the absurdity of setting NNSs the impossible target of becoming nativelike, and then defining them in terms of what they cannot be, as failed NSs. As David Graddol (2006: 83) puts it, 'Within traditional EFL methodology there is an inbuilt ideological positioning of the student as outsider and failure – however proficient they become.' EFL necessarily 'can and does tolerate high levels of failure' (p. 84); indeed it might even be said to be 'designed to produce failure' (p. 83).

It is a sociolinguistic commonplace that it is iniquitous to measure one group of speakers against the norms of another group – blacks against whites, working-class against middle-class, etc. (see Labov 1972a). As Michael Halliday (1968: 165) puts it, anyone who is 'made ashamed of his own language habits suffers a basic injury as a human being: to make anyone, especially a child, feel so ashamed is as indefensible as to make him feel ashamed of the color of his skin.'

Yet, as Cook, Graddol and most ELF researchers point out, this is precisely how most L2 users have long been treated. Cook (2002: 335) argues that L2 speakers need to be seen as people in their own right: 'The crucial implication for education is ensuring that the standards against which L2 users are measured should be L2 user standards, not L1 native speaker standards. Success should be measured by the ability to use the second language effectively.'

It is also worth pointing out that the standard model for EFL is not any old native speaker, but rather an 'educated native speaker.' Moreover, although Standard English (StE) is often defined as that which is spoken by an educated native speaker, 'educated' is usually left undefined (see Trudgill 1999). Widdowson (2012: 13) points out that the educated native speaker is just as much of 'an idealized construct, a convenient abstraction' as Chomsky's (1965: 3) ideal speaker-listener, the difference being that 'Chomsky is quite explicit that his speaker-listener is indeed a non-existent ideal abstraction, accessible only to intuition,' whereas many language teachers and linguists assume educated native speakers to exist as a observable group. As Claire Kramsch (1997: 363) puts it, more aggressively, 'The native speaker is in fact an imaginary construct – a canonically literate monolingual middle-class member of a largely fictional national community whose citizens share a belief in a common history and a common destiny.'

Even if we accept Cook and Kramsch's account of 'the privilege of the non-native speaker,' the question remains as to the place of the native speaker in English as an international language (EIL). Alessia Cogo (2010: 295) states that

'ELF communication may include native speakers of English, though the majority of exchanges take place among bilingual users of English.' She also asserts that

> ELF and ENL are different and, consequently, a NS of English is not a NS of ELF. That is, if a NS of English is involved in ELF communication she or he will have to negotiate the communicative norms operating in the context, rather than transposing her or his ENL norms.

If we define ELF and ENL as being different, it is trivially true that a NS of English is not a NS of ELF, but they are still not different languages. An ENL/ELF speaker is *not* bilingual. And an ENL speaker who thinks, as many do, that English is English, does not *have to* negotiate communicative norms when interacting with ELF speakers. More interculturally competent speakers of course do so, using the subconscious accommodation skills most speakers develop; less interculturally competent speakers do not, or not so much. There is little evidence that the majority of users of English in political, economic or academic settings around the world (e.g. the UN, the EU, the G8, the G20, the OECD, OPEC, the IMF, the WTO, the Davos forum, multinational companies, CERN, the Max Planck Institute, etc.) think of themselves as speaking ELF. For the moment, it is largely applied linguists who talk about ELF, and until such time as users recognize their own or other people's language as ELF, not much is going to change.

Following Juliane House (2003), it has become conventional to describe ELF users in terms of Etienne Wenger's (1998) concept of 'communities of practice.' These are often not (local) 'speech communities' but international 'discourse communities' (Swales 1990) with a common communicative purpose, possibly communicating by email and Skype rather than face-to-face. Communities of practice are, however, real communities, unlike what Benedict Anderson (1983/1991) called 'imagined communities' of people who may never meet but who have presumed or imagined affinities. Yet such communities of practice frequently include both NESs and NNESs. Karlfried Knapp (2002: 221) argues that ignoring the existence of NESs in ELF (and their sometimes uncooperative and non-consensual style) 'would simply mean ignoring the reality.' More recently (2009: 137), he has suggested that NESs 'will be present' in most professional communities of practice, 'and determine what counts as the norm.' If the native speaker is 'an imaginary construct,' as Kramsch puts it, so is the native speaker who *has to* abandon his or her ENL norms when participating in international communication with ELF speakers.

ELF and World Englishes

It must also be remembered that EIL is not only used by NESs and ELF speakers, but also by many millions of speakers of English as a second language (ESL), or indigenized World Englishes.

Following Kachru (1985: 12), it has become conventional to talk about three circles of English.[17] In the inner circle countries, English is used (by native speakers) as a primary language. In the outer circle countries, mostly former British colonies in Africa and Asia, English has an official second-language role in a multilingual setting, and is often used by an economic elite as a lingua franca for major *intra*national functions (politics, administration, legislation, education, etc.). For many educated people in these countries, even though English is not, chronologically, their first language, is it their primary or dominant language – 'the one they use most, and perhaps are most comfortable and fluent in for many or even most purposes' (Trudgill 1995: 314).[18] But English speakers are still a minority in outer circle countries – 'at best between 20% and 30% of the total population' (Mufwene 2010: 57). In the expanding circle – which is the rest of the world – English is learnt and used as a foreign (or additional) language, for communication with speakers from all three circles.[19] Although Seidlhofer (2009b: 240) says that 'obviously communication via ELF frequently happens in and across all three of Kachru's circles,' the bulk of ELF research (as well as proposals to replace the EFL paradigm with ELF) has concerned speakers from expanding circle countries.

World Englishes, or 'New Englishes,'[20] share a number of characteristics. They often have high status, and are used in the education system as both a subject and a medium of instruction, as well as for a range of other purposes (Platt *et al.* 1984: 6). They have undergone 'focusing' and become nativized by developing characteristic local features of grammar, lexis, phraseology and pronunciation, frequently induced by transfer from local L1s. As indeed do most languages: Salikoko Mufwene (2001: 113) argues that 'native Englishes, indigenised Englishes and English pidgins and creoles have all developed by the same kind of natural restructuring processes,' while Andy Kirkpatrick (2007: 5–7) argues that British varieties of English were also influenced by local languages and cultures, and are consequently nativized or indigenized, while American and Australian varieties were influenced by both the earlier British English and by local languages and cultures. As a result, New Englishes can be regarded as stable or stabilizing linguistic varieties with regular, standardized, codified patterns of use that have become normative, including for use in writing.[21]

Some commentators, notably Robert Phillipson (1992), describe English as an alien influence in postcolonial societies, the result of dominance, hegemony, subjugation, imposition, and so on. Other scholars (including Pennycook 1994, 1998, 2010a; Canagarajah 1999; and Brutt-Griffler 2002) have argued for the *agency* of the speakers of World Englishes. Brutt-Griffler shows that 'the spread of English involved a contested terrain in which English was not unilaterally *imposed on* passive subjects, but *wrested from* an unwilling imperial authority as part of the struggle by them against colonialism' (p. 31). Similarly, Suresh Canagarajah argues that postcolonial communities can 'find ways to negotiate, alter and oppose political structures, and reconstruct their languages, cultures and identities to their advantage. The intention is not to reject English, but to reconstitute it in more inclusive, ethical, and democratic terms' (p. 2). Speakers appropriate from English what is needed locally, so that indigenized varieties come to express the values and linguistic and sociolinguistic identities of postcolonial countries.

Local needs lead World Englishes to add to the inner circle varieties from which they derive. As Rajend Mesthrie and Rakesh Bhatt (2008: 110) point out, the use of the term 'borrowing' for local L2 words transferred to English is not entirely appropriate as speakers are neither adopting a new word nor acquiring a new concept; 'These items are therefore better characterized as "retentions" from the ancestral languages of a territory.' As Alastair Pennycook (2010a: 71) puts it, 'The issue is not one of English spreading and being locally appropriated but of English bringing back old things, and reappropriating them.' After all, the *British* in India mainly continued to speak British English. Consequently, 'Global Englishes are not what they are because English has spread and been adapted, but because local practices have been relocalized in English' (p. 74).

The Nigerian novelist Chinua Achebe's conclusion to his essay 'The African Writer and the English Language' (1975: 61–62) is widely quoted:

> I feel that the English language will be able to carry the weight of my African experience. But it will have to be a new English, still in full communion with its ancestral home but altered to suit its new African surroundings.

Pennycook wants to give less importance to the ancestral home, but his focus on local practices of adoption, adaptation, transformation, rearticulation, refashioning, resistance to homogenizing forces, etc., are a refreshing counterpoint to one-dimensional accounts of 'linguistic imperialism.'

What is the relation of ELF to World Englishes? Various linguists (including Graddol 1997: 11; Mesthrie and Bhatt 2008: 211–12; and Meierkord 2012: 5) have suggested that the extensive use of English in some expanding circle countries, particularly in higher education and business, e.g. in northern Europe and Central America, might require them to be recategorized as outer circle countries. Against this, Martin Schell (2008: 120) argues that unlike in outer circle countries, people in expanding circle countries very rarely speak English to each other when no foreigners are present (they are not 'colinguals'), certainly not enough to generate new national varieties with their own norms. Yet many Europeans *do* use English intranationally, in business, in universities, etc., albeit generally in the presence of foreigners, and some *international* norms may well develop in the fullness of time, drawing on features common to the majority of 'similects.' Margie Berns – who had previously argued that English could be a means of expression of European identity (1995a), and that Europe constitutes a 'sociolinguistic unit' (1995b) – distances herself from what she calls the 'Lingua Franca Movement' (2009: 193), because she says English in Europe 'functions as more than an international lingua franca, serving interpersonal, instrumental, creative, and administrative functions as well' (p. 198). Besides what might be called 'ELF interactions' (the interpersonal function), English is widely used in education (thus fulfilling the instrumental function); it is one of the official languages of the EU, and an increasingly dominant one at that (the institutional or administrative function); and it is pervasive in the media and in advertising (which incorporates the innovative function).

In short, 'English is used locally, as an additional language, for intra-regional communication in the multilingual community that constitutes the European Union,' and 'European English is not unlike South Asian English, or the other world Englishes used in multilingual linguistic areas' (p. 196).

For reasons like these, Manfred Görlach (2002: 114) suggests that we should adopt the term (long used by Fishman, e.g. 1992) 'English as an additional language,' which collapses the distinction between ESL and EFL. Yet Berns insists that Europe is an expanding circle territory *par excellence*, having backtracked from her earlier description of Germany, Luxembourg and the Netherlands as 'dual circle' countries, overlapping the outer and expanding circles (1995b: 9).

Moreover European English is but one regional English; Yasukata Yano (2001: 126) suggests that because there is much more intra- than inter-regional use, English will converge into six major regional standard Englishes – European, Asian, Latin, Arab, African and Anglo-American, 'leagues of varieties' sharing cross-national intelligibility within the region while keeping local lingua cultural characteristics and identities. This logic collapses Kachru's three circles, as Asian and African regional varieties would necessarily contain both outer and expanding circle countries. However, Kachru himself has proposed that the 'inner circle' should now be thought of as the group of highly proficient speakers of English (maybe half a billion strong) who have 'functional nativeness' regardless of which circle they come from. Around this circle are other concentric ones with speakers of lessening proficiency (see Graddol 2006: 110).[22]

Jenkins (2009: 32) argues that Kachru's revised model fits in well with the concept of ELF, as it uncouples proficiency from nativeness, and defines it in terms of international communication, which requires 'an internationally intelligible accent and good accommodation skills.' Consequently the new inner circle excludes 'many NSs of English, who are not able to communicate successfully in international communication.'[23] Yet Jenkins (2007: 14) also seeks to incorporate ELF into the (outer circle) World Englishes paradigm. She quotes Susan Butler's (1997: 106) set of criteria for determining a variety of World English:

> A standard and recognizable pattern of pronunciation handed down from one generation to another [...] particular words and phrases which spring up usually to express key features of the physical and social environment and which are peculiar to the variety [...] a history – a sense that this variety of English is the way it is because of the history of the language community [...] a literature written without apology in that variety of English [...] reference works – dictionaries and style guides – which show that people in that language community look to themselves, not some outside authority, to decide what is right and wrong in terms of how they speak and write their English.

Jenkins suggests that 'with slight adjustments to the criteria in order to embrace its international character, it could be predicted that ELF will eventually fit all these criteria' (2007: 14–15). Yet this sits badly with most recent accounts of ELF in terms of fluidity, flexibility and variability, as well as with accounts of a global inner circle of competent users who know how to accommodate to a broad range of speakers. If ELF speakers come from lots of different L1s, there is unlikely to be a 'standard and recognizable pattern of pronunciation,' and unless we are explicitly talking about a localized ELF (or localized ELFs), 'the physical and social environment' responsible for the appearance of particular words and phrases would be the entire planet, and 'the history of the language community' would be the history of mankind.

Edgar Schneider (2007) proposes a 'Dynamic Model' showing how New Englishes, which begin as a second language imported by colonists, pass through different evolutionary phases, becoming nativized by way of the growth of indigenous linguistic forms and habits, until they move towards endonormativity (i.e. become norm-developing). Schneider (2012: 87–88) suggests that in specific types of ELF communication – 'contexts where interaction remains stable in similar constellations over a longer period' – the 'stabilizing effects of mutual accommodation between the speakers and speaker groups involved' *may* lead to 'increased conformity via negotiation' and, ultimately, the kind of 'stable communal varieties' found among ESL speakers in New Englishes.

Perhaps. But stable long-term interaction among similar constellations of speakers is only a part of ELF. Knapp (2009) argues that professional communities account for less spoken ELF than random encounters involving infrequent users such as tourists. Users like these, he says, 'normally do not memorize the linguistic means they employed more or less successfully,' so that 'if a similar situation arises, they have to reinvent their lingua franca English' (p. 133). Such reinventions will be similar, as L2 users typically employ similar communication strategies, but they will not lead to a stable set of linguistic forms or a group or community that shares them. Moreover, Schneider's logic goes against both Firth's 'lingua franca factor,' defined in terms of 'inherent interactional and linguistic variability,' and Knapp's perception of the non-negligible role of NESs. Yet even if ELF never stabilizes in the way that New Englishes have, individual ELF speakers do adapt the language in similar ways to speakers of New Englishes, as will be seen in various chapters in this book.

Interactions across Englishes

Predictions concerning stable varieties of ELF, free from exogenous NES norms, appear to underestimate the participation of both the 'small minority' of NESs (Jenkins 2006a: 161) in global English use – 375 million of them alive today, quite apart from all those who have left their mark on the language in the past – and the speakers of indigenized outer circle varieties.[24] Seidlhofer (2009b: 237) describes ELF as 'the most widespread contemporary use of English – that which from a global perspective actually constitutes the prevailing reality of English, with the largest number of speakers, in interactions in which more often than not no native speakers participate.' But this is tendentious. The 'prevailing reality of English' also includes native speakers and the speakers of World Englishes, and 'a global perspective' of the movie and music industries, among many others, needs to make room for a lot of inner circle speakers and products. Even if schools and other educational institutions turned their backs on books and other teaching materials using ENL (which is unlikely), many English users in the outer and expanding circles would continue to 'consume' cultural offerings of some form or another produced by NESs according to inner circle norms (books, TV series, films, music, etc.), and many professional people would continue to need to read texts in native English.

Other linguists are rather more sceptical about the very notion of ELF, and the possibility of 'endonormative' standards for expanding circle speakers. For example Mufwene (2012: 368) says of such speakers:

> Their interactions with each other in English take place in settings where they interact concurrently with nationals of other countries, who might give up on you if they are from the Inner (or Outer) Circle and you do not satisfy the standards that they find acceptable. The choice is between approximating standards from the Inner Circle and ignoring them, and therefore narrowing one's range of competitiveness. In fact, I wonder who learns another group's language not caring at all about being understood (and being accepted) by the native-speaking community.

Mufwene suggests that ELF speakers setting up their own standards, and diverging from the target models would risk 'defeating the very reason why they invest so much energy and money to learn the language' (p. 369). ELF theorists, in contrast, deny that ENL varieties are the target models for ELF, and that diverging from them slightly will lead to speakers not being understood by NESs. But Mufwene continues:

> Are there many native speakers who accommodate non-native speakers other than by being patient, unless they evolve in the Outer Circle and know that the host's standards prevail or become acceptable? And what will happen if the local or regional ELF standards impede international communication not only with Inner and Outer Circle speakers, but also among the ELF speakers themselves?
>
> *(p. 369)*

This is a chastening reminder that the proponents of ELF do not necessarily constitute a majority amongst linguists working in the fields of language contact and evolution. Because of ELF theorists' dogged insistence on the numerical importance of ELF speakers and the statistical insignificance of NESs, various authors on the international use of English (including Kachru and Smith 2008; Prodromou 2008; Berns 2008; Mesthrie and Bhatt 2008; Maley 2009; and Meierkord 2012) give short shrift to the ELF position. Meierkord (2012: 2) suggests that ELF should be subsumed into a broader category, 'Interactions across Englishes' (IaEs), arguing that different Englishes potentially merge in these interactions, possibly resulting in new emergent varieties, or rather, 'a heterogeneous array of new linguistic systems,' but ones which do not exclude inner and outer circle speakers. However, expanding circle ELF users and ELF discourse communities *do* exist, and this book will seek to outline the major characteristics of the language used in such contexts (lexicogrammar, phraseology, pronunciation, pragmatic strategies, etc.).

Given my use of Englishes in the plural, and my leitmotif that 'English is English,' it is clear that I do not subscribe to the belief that separate languages do not in fact exist. It is one thing to argue – as I do, in Chapter 3 – that 'grammatical rules' might better be thought of as routinized or sedimented ways of saying things, resulting from the repetition of frequently used forms in discourse; it is another to say that separate languages, as such, are inventions, as is argued, e.g. by Makoni and Pennycook (2007). Integrational linguists (notably Harris 1981, 1997, 1998; and Toolan 1996) describe languages as the cumulative product of communication situations, rather than pre-determined, static, autonomous 'rules' or 'codes' or systems of context- and user-independent signs that exist in advance of our acquiring (or learning or internalizing or assimilating) them. But in a foreign language classroom, at least at lower levels, one generally needs to teach the 'pre-determined' forms and lexis of a specific language.

Once a language has been acquired, it does indeed become part of a repertoire combining semiotic devices from different languages, but that does not prevent it being described on its own.[25] I prefer to believe that the English language does exist, albeit in an immense range of varieties and uses. Yet the heterogeneity of ELF speakers and the range of linguistic variation they produce require us to stretch many basic linguistic concepts, such as those concerning speech communities, linguistic identities, shared internalized rules, shared lexis and phraseology, shared phonology, competence levels, etc. ELF does not show that languages do not exist, but that the notion of what constitutes a language probably needs to be expanded and revised.

Notes

1 In Molière's comedy, a false Mufti speaks in Sabir (or Lingua Franca) and says 'If you know Sabir, You will reply; If you do not know it, Be silent, be silent.'

2 Lingua Franca was largely based on languages from northern Italy and southern France, with elements from Arabic, Spanish, Portuguese, Greek, Turkish, Persian, etc. It was also called Sabir, from the Italian *sapere*, to know (Kahane and Kahane 1976; Dakhlia 2008). *Franc* or *Franci* originally meant 'French,' of whom there were many in the Crusades. The Byzantine Greeks called the occident *Phrángia* and westerners in general (and Francs in particular) *Phrángoi*. In Arabic, the language of the Francs was called *lisan-al-farang*, which in the thirteenth century was translated into Latin and Italian as *lingua franca*. The plural could be *lingue franche* or *linguae francae*, but in English it is clearly *lingua francas*.

3 Canagarajah (2007) chooses to use the term 'lingua franca English.' Dröschel (2011: 22) uses 'Lingua Franca English' in a different sense, to describe 'the formal properties of the

language as opposed to the functional aspects English as a Lingua Franca has for its users.' Kecskes (2007) and Mesthrie and Bhatt (2008) opt for 'English Lingua Franca,' but English as a lingua franca has become the preferred term.

4 Cf. Smith (1983c: vi): '*English as an International Language* refers to functions of English, not to any given form of the language.'

5 Only Berns (2009) explicitly relates this to the architectural slogan 'form follows function.'

6 Seidlhofer also wrote (2001a: 43), in a splendidly hedged sentence, 'I do not wish to deny that there may be learning purposes for which adhering to native speaker English models is a valid, or at least arguable, option.'

7 I regularly use the word 'says' instead of 'writes' because it sounds more natural.

8 The same process of second-order language contact has clearly occurred in American English. Seidlhofer and Widdowson (2007: 367) point out that histories of American English strangely play down the fact that it was used as a lingua franca by huge numbers of immigrant NNESs, particularly in the nineteenth century, though Trudgill (2010: Chapter 5) gives some examples of what seem to be the results of large-scale contact with German, Yiddish and other European languages, including the grammatical constructions *I like to skate* (as opposed to *I like skating*) and *Are you coming with?* (as opposed to *Are you coming?*), and restricted collocations of verbs like *have* and *take* compared with British English.

9 In transcripts of academic users of English in VOICE and ELFA (see Chapters 2–6), you can find paragraphs or pages at a time which give no indication as to the speaker's origin before you come to a minor non-standard (or ELF) use. Even if fluent ELF speakers are not aspiring to ENL norms, proficient non-native English is necessarily similar and hence comparable to proficient native English, just as violins can be compared with violas, or German shepherd dogs with wolves, even though the former are not aspiring to native viola-ness or imitating wolf norms.

10 As Prodromou (2008: 248) puts it, 'the grammatical core of Standard English has already been appropriated by users of English in Asia and Africa and is indeed no longer the property of the "native speaker." As many core elements of Standard English are already an integral part of World Englishes and EIL, especially in the written medium, the question of imposing its "norms" does not arise: the horse has bolted.'

11 Similarly, Schneider (2012: 75) writes about the properties of English which 'may make the language difficult for learners (and possibly constrain their ultimate level of attainment).' Yet ELF researchers regularly insist that the notion of deficiency has no place in the ELF paradigm.

12 Cf. Lady Chatterley talking to her gamekeeper in a well-known bad novel: 'Why don't you speak ordinary English?' she said coldly. 'Me! Ah thowt it wor ordinary' (Lawrence 1960).

13 Cook also offers two opposing arguments against the 'creativity of native speakers' claim. Firstly, in a traditional literary sense, creativity belongs to only a small percentage of NSs. Secondly, there is the Chomskyan claim that the ordinary everyday use of language is a matter of 'rule-governed creativity' (see, e.g. Chomsky 1964: 22), so that any novel sentence uttered or comprehended is creative – although this is almost as lame as the ELFish argument that any approximately grammatical (or ungrammatical) utterance is inherently innovative, creative, and the precursor of language change.

14 Ullman (2001, 2007) distinguishes between *declarative memory*, implicated in the learning (or storage) and use of knowledge of facts and events, and *procedural memory*, which is implicated in the acquisition and expression of motor and cognitive skills and habits. He argues that in an L1, declarative memory contains a lexicon of memorized words (and longer idiosyncratic expressions), while procedural memory contains a combinatorial mental grammar that allows the composition of sentences. Thus grammatical rules are learned implicitly or non-consciously. In an L2 (learned by post-adolescents), however, grammatical forms and rules (which depend upon procedural memory in an L1) are often dependent on declarative (or lexical) memory, or explicit memorization.

15 Trudgill (2005b: 84) also points out, however, that 'Linguists engaged in that most important of all linguistic tasks, the writing of grammars of threatened languages, need to find, recognize and work with native speakers of those languages. No linguist in their right mind would work with a non-native speaker unless there were no natives left.'

16 Some people would also object to the gender ideology underlying the concept of the mother tongue.

17 Kachru's model derives from the three-way distinction between English as a native language, an official second language, and a foreign language in Quirk *et al.* (1972: 3).

18 In some outer circle countries, particularly Singapore, there are an increasing number of families using English as an L1 at home, and consequently an increasing number of NESs.

19 There are problems with Kachru's three circles model (which combines classifications of countries, types of speakers, types of variety, and functions of English), and there have been many pertinent critiques, notably Bruthiaux (2003), as well as suggestions for rival models, including McArthur (1998: 97), Yano (2001: 126), Graddol (2006: 110), Prodromou (2008: xiv), and Pennycook (2009: 204), which I do not have space to discuss here.

20 This term seems to originate in Pride (1982) and Platt *et al.* (1984). See also Mufwene (1994: 21), who argues in favour of the term New Englishes, rather than non-native, nativized or indigenized. However I use most of these terms synonymously.

21 A huge amount has been written about World Englishes. For overviews, see Crystal (1997, 2003), McArthur (1998), Melchers and Shaw (2003), Mesthrie and Bhatt (2008), Kachru and Smith (2008). For models of their development see Kachru (1992) and Schneider (2003, 2007, 2011). For descriptions of varieties see Görlach (1991, 1995, 1998, 2002); Kortmann *et al.* (2004), and Schneider *et al.* (2004).

22 Graddol does not give a source for Kachru's revised view.

23 House (2006: 89) puts this differently: 'in ELF all speakers of English – as first, second or foreign language – are in a sense in the same expanding circle.'

24 Jenkins' mention of the 'small minority' appears in this sentence: 'The majority of ELF researchers nevertheless accept that speakers of English from both inner and outer circles also participate in intercultural communication (albeit as a small minority in the case of inner circle speakers),' although Graddol (1997: 11) gives an identical (and equally 'small') number for inner and outer circle speakers – 375 million. That makes 750 million inner and outer circle speakers potentially participating in intercultural communication, which may be a minority, but not an especially small one.

25 Chapter 2 discusses bilingualism and crosslinguistic interaction. Rampton (2005) and Jørgensen (2008), among others, give examples of 'crossing' and 'polylingual languaging' among urban youth groups, and Pennycook (2007: 126ff) gives fine examples of mixed languages from hip-hop. Meanwhile Blommaert (2010: 102) and Blackledge and Creese (2010: 122) recommend the Bakhtinian concept of heteroglossia and plurilingual resources. But outside of immigrant communities and multi-ethnic urban teenage peer groups there still remain hundreds of millions of children in western countries who are brought up speaking one language, and not understanding any others, give or take a few words, until they begin learning an L2 at school.

2

ELF, BILINGUALISM AND MULTICOMPETENCE

Wer fremde Sprachen nicht kennt, weiß nichts von seiner eigenen.

Goethe, *Maximen und Reflexionen* 91

Monolingualism can be considered as a widespread form of language deprivation.

Cook (2009: 57)

ELF could be viewed, not as a set of varieties but as a fluid cluster of communicative practices where speakers draw on a wide, not clearly bounded range of linguistic features – some standard, some non-standard, and others not English at all (at least according to the conventional view)

Ferguson (2009: 129)

English as a lingua franca is widely described (though not usually all in one sentence) as an adaptive, contingent, creative, changing, diverse, dynamic, flexible, fluid, fragmented, fuzzy, heterogeneous, hybrid, indeterminate, mutable, open, shifting, unbounded, unpredictable, unstable, variable but self-regulating system (see, e.g. Ferguson 2009; Firth 2009; Seidlhofer 2009c), and a 'particularly ad hoc and emergent form of everyday communication' (James 2000: 34) involving a virtual speech community, or 'different constellations of speakers of diverse individual Englishes in every single interaction' (Meierkord 2004: 115). It embraces the dimensions that Wenger (1998: 76) describes as characterizing a 'community of practice,' namely 'mutual engagement, a joint negotiated enterprise, and a shared repertoire of negotiable resources.' Crucially, most ELF users are not emulating the idealized competence of native speakers, or moving, in a more or less linear progression, towards someone else's target, as in the SLA concept of an interlanguage or approximate system (Selinker 1972). Furthermore, they are all, by definition, bi- or multilingual.[1]

Canagarajah (2007) compares the use of what he calls 'lingua franca English' (LFE) with language use by radically multilingual communities in South Asia and

Africa, where simultaneous childhood acquisition makes it hard to say which language comes first, or to identify a mother tongue or native language. This leads him to question whether languages are actually 'separated from each other, even at the most abstract level of grammatical form' (p. 923), and to suggest that 'LFE raises serious questions about the concept of language system' (p. 926). Canagarajah states that

> LFE's form is hybrid in nature. The language features words, grammatical patterns, and discourse conventions from diverse languages and English varieties that speakers bring to the interaction. Participants borrow from each other freely and adopt the other's language in their interaction with that participant.
>
> *(p. 926)*

This chapter will suggest that many of the linguistic strategies attributed to LFE (or ELF) users, including language mixing, are actually common to most bilinguals and multilinguals, even though the type of multilingualism described by Canagarajah is relatively uncommon.

Most writers on multilingualism claim, like François Grosjean (2010: 13), that 'half of the world's population, if not more, is bilingual,' and as Philippe Van Parijs (2011: 2) says,

> more and more countries all over the world face the immigration of large numbers of native speakers of a wide variety of languages that are being maintained and transmitted to the next generation more than was ever the case before. As a result, permanent linguistic diversity has become a common experience in many places essentially devoid of it so far.[2]

Despite this, few multilinguals acquire all their languages in early childhood: Grosjean states that 'Simultaneous bilinguals are less numerous than children who acquire their two languages successively (certainly less than 20 percent of bilingual children)' (2010: 178), though he is obliged to add in a footnote 'Unfortunately no good statistics exist on this point' (p. 261). Certainly there are fewer radically multilingual communities in Europe than in South Asia and Africa, and it is more common to talk about people coming from specific linguacultures (or linguacultural backgrounds).[3]

Yet there *are* a great many bi- and multilingual speakers in Europe for whom English is a second or third language.[4] Moreover, there are also often similarities among neighbouring languages, so it is in Europe, rather than in Africa or Asia, that ELF most readily allows multilinguals to exploit what Cook (1991) calls 'multicompetence,' or a dynamic multilingual system in which mental representations from different languages interact, and more than one language can be activated at the same time. What might be considered, in the use of a native language, as accidental transfer lapses, erroneous words, deviant idioms and collocations, unconscious calques, or even evidence of language attrition, can equally be seen as signs of linguistic awareness and enhanced communicative competence when used in ELF.

Bilingualism and code-switching

Grosjean (2010: 75) has long insisted on what he calls

> the bilingual or holistic view of bilingualism, which proposes that the bilingual is an integrated whole who cannot easily be decomposed into two separate parts. The bilingual is not the sum of two (or more) complete or incomplete monolinguals; rather, he or she has a unique and specific linguistic configuration. The coexistence and constant interaction of the languages in the bilingual have produced a different but complete language system.[5]

Cook (1991: 112) makes a more radical argument, describing 'the compound state of a mind with two grammars' as 'multicompetence,' in which the two languages are integrated, as opposed to coexisting. Importantly, a multicompetent speaker's knowledge of his or her second language is typically not identical to that of a NS, while the L2 will also have an effect on the multicompetent speaker's L1, which will thus differ from that of a monolingual. This is because bilinguals – after a certain threshold is reached – have a conjoined system with a partially integrated mental lexicon, or a 'common underlying proficiency' (Cummins 1984, 2000), or a 'common underlying conceptual base' (Kecskes and Papp 2000). Philip Herdina and Ulrike Jessner (2002: 27) go further:

> we would rather see the two languages as two liquids, which, when mixed, acquire properties (such as explosiveness in the case of nitroglycerine) that neither of the liquids had. So these new properties constitute a complete metamorphosis of the substances involved and not merely an overlap between two systems.

They call this 'crosslinguistic interaction,' and propose a 'Dynamic Model of Multilingualism.' A similar set of analogies, from chaos and complexity theory, are proposed by Diane Larsen-Freeman (1997) and Larsen-Freeman and Lynne Cameron (2008): languages are self-organizing, complex, adaptive, open systems arising from the interactions of their components, which continually change in dynamic and sometimes chaotic ways.

Grosjean (2008: 38) further describes bilinguals' 'language modes': states of activation of languages and language processing mechanisms at any given time. There is a continuum going from 'the monolingual speech mode,' in which 'the bilingual deactivates one language (but never totally)' to 'the bilingual mode' in which 'the bilingual speaker chooses a base language, activates the other language, and calls on it from time to time in the form of code-switches and borrowings.'[6] Grosjean insists (and most bilinguals would agree) that their languages are never totally deactivated, and that there is constant interaction between or among them: 'bilinguals make dynamic interferences (ephemeral deviations due to the influence of the other deactivated language) even in the most monolingual of situations' (p. 46).

Code-switching, once considered an alarming symptom of 'double semi-lingualism,'[7] has of course acquired its *lettres de noblesse*: as Shana Poplack (1980: 615) argues, it is 'a verbal skill requiring a large degree of linguistic competence in more than one language, rather than a defect arising from insufficient knowledge of one or the other.'[8] Or to put it more poetically, 'it is helpful to imagine that when bilinguals code-switch, they are in fact using a twelve-string guitar, rather than limiting themselves to two six-string instruments' (Valdés 1988: 126). Borrowing and code-switching do, however, normally require the interlocutors to share the same languages, which is not necessarily the case with ELF: as Theresa Klimpfinger (2009: 348) puts it, 'ELF, *per definition*, involves typically three languages: the speakers' first languages and English.' Yet as suggested above, many European ELF users speak (or at least understand) several languages, and if they don't share their interlocutor's L1, they may speak a typologically similar language. Many Europeans are capable of understanding a large amount of cognate lexis, as a result of either multilingualism or what Rita Franceschini (2009) calls 'unfocussed acquisition' – picking up a language through direct contact without any overt, conscious effort.[9]

Although it is a Germanic language, English has so much Latin and French lexis (as well, of course, as other loanwords from all around the world) that it has been called a 'semi-Romance language' and (facetiously) 'French badly pronounced.'[10] Consequently, an English speaker has some familiarity with about 40 per cent of the lemmas in ten national languages – French, Italian, Spanish, Portuguese, Romanian, German, Dutch, Danish, Swedish and Norwegian – as well as various other languages (e.g. Catalan) and dialects.[11] There is an old joke, 'I speak ten languages – all of them in Yiddish,'[12] but – Yiddish-shmiddish – this might equally apply to English. Marcus Ravage, an early twentieth-century Romanian immigrant to the US wrote (1917: 103) that 'My friends were finding English contemptibly easy' because of their 'partly justified' notion 'that it was a mixture of Yiddish and Rumanian'! (quoted in Jarvis and Pavlenko 2007: 2). Thus it is hard for an English speaker *not* to instantly recognize a great many words in western European languages, even if they are often spelled differently than in English (*établissement, innocenza, insecto, Mekaniker, midnatt, Musik, natuur, organización*, etc.). This applies even more so to bi- or multilingual European ELF users, which often renders code-switching and borrowing viable communicative strategies even when speakers do not share the same L1s.

Clearly, most ELF speakers know less than linguists and language teachers about language families, but a lot of experimental evidence shows that language learners do have a strong sense of typological (or psychotypological, or crosslinguistic) similarities and congruities among languages. For example, Håkan Ringbom (1987, 2001, 2007) shows that Swedish-speaking Finns borrow Swedish rather than

Finnish words when speaking English, and Jasone Cenoz (2001) offers a similar demonstration of Basque speakers borrowing from Spanish rather than Basque. Where languages are similar, learners understand the L2 (or L3, etc.) more easily, and perceive genuine similarities, which leads to positive L1 or 'substrate' transfer. On the other hand, they are also often inclined to assume nonexistent similarities, which leads – from a mainstream SLA perspective, but less so from an ELF perspective – to negative transfer.

Transfer and crosslinguistic influence

Quite apart from intentional transfer and code-switching, multilinguals experience non-intentional, automatic transfer or crosslinguistic influence from not-totally-deactivated languages.[13] A great deal of research suggests that bilinguals establish mental links between stored representations of words in different languages, and that there is a semantic influence of one language on the processing of others. This suggests, as Kees De Bot (2004: 23) puts it, that 'access to words in the lexicon is non-selective, i.e. words from more than one language compete for activation both in production and perception.' The standard account (e.g. Jarvis 2009: 105) is that an activated word in one language can co-activate a word in another language which has a similar form, resulting in unintentional lexical errors or intrusions.[14] Yet given the lexical overlap across western European languages, and the fact that ELF is not dependent on NS norms, it seems that 'error' and 'intrusion' are not always the appropriate concepts in European ELF. There is a huge literature on transfer and crosslinguistic influence (e.g. Kellerman and Sharwood Smith (eds) 1986; Odlin 1989; Ringbom 2007; Jarvis and Pavlenko 2007), largely concerned with identifying sources and types of transfer, and developing pedagogical techniques to moderate their effects in both learning and performance. For example, Scott Jarvis (2009: 113) isolates four types of lemmatic transfers, involving the violation of semantic, collocational, morphological and syntactic constraints on words, namely:

1 semantic extensions,
2 calques (literal translations of idioms and fixed expressions),
3 collocational transfer, and
4 subcategorization transfer.

Admirable as these attempts are in a standard SLA perspective, they have less pertinence in relation to a language spoken among non-native speakers.

Standard examples of erroneous semantic extensions are false friends or false cognates, generally in closely related languages. There are thousands of false friends between English and European languages, most of which are likely to lead to miscomprehension among people not sharing the same L1, such as saying *offers of violence* using the Swedish word for *victims*, or saying *embarrassed* to mean pregnant, translating the Spanish *embarazada*, or using the German or Scandinavian *gift* to mean poison, and so on. On the other hand, there are a number of French words that have been borrowed in most Germanic and Slavic languages, but which are used in English with changed meanings. Well known examples include *actual* (meaning current or topical), *eventual* (possible), *possibility* (opportunity), *fabric* (factory), *concurrence* (competition, competitors), and *sympathetic* (friendly). All of these are false cognates in native English, but would probably be comprehensible in context to the vast majority of European ELF users. Alternatively, one could argue that these are, quite simply, true ELF cognates.[15] ELF speakers use them confidently, generally with an English pronunciation.[16] There seems little point in describing uses such as these as 'transfer errors,' given that 'The English of multilingual LFE speakers is not used in deference to the norms of prestige varieties such as British or American English' (Canagarajah 2007: 927). Clearly a handful of shared French loanwords do not make the whole of Continental Europe a *Sprachbund* or convergence area, but they do suggest that describing all semantic extensions as errors is not appropriate to European ELF.[17] There are many semantic extensions that are better regarded as European English lexical items, which NESs will need to recategorize as polysemous.

Calques – literally translated or transferred idioms and fixed expressions – are willed interlingual associations between languages which need not be typologically related. Most writers on bilingualism frown on calqued fixed expressions: e.g. Grosjean (2010: 71–72) states that 'He was laughing in his fist,' translated from the German, 'comes close but isn't quite right' as 'the correct English expression is "He was laughing up his sleeve."'[18] However the line usually taken in ELF research is that calques of idioms and fixed expressions are signs of idiomatic creativity rather than errors: in a hybrid variety and speech community, there is no need to use standardized ENL formulaic sequences, and every reason to calque or translate useful expressions and idioms that you think will be understood (i.e. not totally opaque ones). As Prodromou (2008: 251–52) says,

> when idioms do appear, they will appear in modified form, taking on the shape of the mother tongue of the speaker and the pluralistic nature of the speech encounter. [...] ELF speakers will poach on L1 linguistic territory when it suits them and when they are able to do so. Their use of phraseology will be different from, but on an equal footing with, their L1-user counterparts.

This will be discussed in Chapter 6.

Similarly, although collocational transfer is often considered to be a sign of imperfect language learning, it is not linked to proficiency, and can just as easily occur as reverse (L2-L1) transfer (see Jarvis 2003: 91). In such cases one can either evoke language loss, deterioration or attrition ... or perhaps just recognize the typical speech patterns of a bilingual. We may indeed 'know a word by the company it keeps' (Firth 1957/1968: 179), but for bilinguals, words sometimes keep the same company as translation equivalents in another language.

What Jarvis (2009: 117) calls subcategorization transfer errors are syntactic, involving the erroneous use of a complement with a headword, e.g. *late from* instead of *late for*, and *kissed with* instead of just *kissed*. Yet in ELF research, as in work on New Englishes, Jarvis' 'subcategorization errors' are usually described neutrally as 'a shift in preposition use,' or 'the use of redundant prepositions' or 'new prepositional verbs,' often used for the sake of explicitness, and in analogy with other verb or noun constructions. They in no way impede communication (see Chapter 4).

Language mixing

Conscious borrowing, calquing and code-switching by fluent bilinguals are generally the result of semantic decisions: one language seems to express something better than the other, possessing the right turn of phrase or *le mot juste*. The other language is introduced into the discourse because it adds something. A more radically multi- or plurilingual view of ELF endorses the use of words from other languages (or Anglicized versions of them) in any given interaction, without there being any noticeable semantic or conceptual payoff. For example, Cornelia Hülmbauer (2009: 340) analyses an interaction from VOICE (the Vienna-Oxford International Corpus of English) in which a Greek L1 speaker, speaking to a German speaker and an Italian speaker in Vienna, says 'here on my card,' indicating a street map.[19] Since these three languages have the cognate words *chartis* (χάρτης), *Karte* and *carta* (for *map*), Hülmbauer suggests that from the interlocutors' interlingual perspectives, '*map* could even seem to be the "odd one out"' (p. 341). Hülmbauer is not recommending the arbitrary mixing of languages – 'card' in this example was probably a performance error – but she rightly emphasises the 'situationality factor' (p. 324) in ELF, and the 'situational resource pool which changes as speaker constellations change' (p. 325).[20] ELF speakers have a plurilingual repertoire which can consciously or unconsciously enhance comprehension.

Hülmbauer's argument recalls Alan Firth and Johannes Wagner's (1997: 293) assertion that

> Anomalous forms of talk may be accounted for not by incompetence but by the notion of recipient design, that is, speakers purposively designing their talk in anomalous ways in response to their specific, local circumstances, for this coparticipant, at this particular sequential moment […] Features of talk that are initially perceived and categorized as interference or fossilizations may be more appropriately viewed as adroit, local responses to practical and discursive exigencies that have arisen in the unfolding talk, resulting, on occasions, in purposive 'codeswitching.'

Firth and Wagner then quote Ben Rampton's (1987: 55) remark that identical linguistic phenomena can be interpreted in different ways, so that 'Code-switching in sociolinguistics winds up as interference in SLA.' As Nanda Poulisse (1997: 326) points out, Firth and Wagner – who stress the social, discursive, contextual and interactional dimensions of language, and deem L2 speakers to be, at all times, users rather than learners (as there can be no acquisition without use) – do not distinguish between strategic (intentional) transfer and automatic (unintentional) transfer.[21] Yet if Hülmbauer's example was not a performance error, its adroitness and strategic value are open to question.

Cognates of *card* (for *map*) are not as widespread as, say, the Continental use of *actual* and *eventual*. Most European languages have more than one word for *map* (depending on whether it is a street map or plan, a map of a larger area, a naval chart, etc.), many of them cognate with *map* (Czech, Polish, Portuguese, Serbian, Slovak, Spanish *mapa*; Italian *mappa;* etc.), many of them cognate with *card* (French *carte*; Italian, Spanish *carta*; Norwegian *kart*; German *Karte*; Latvian *karte*; Dutch, Estonian *kaart*; Finnish *kartta*; Serbian, Swedish *karta*; Danish, Icelandic *kort*), and many cognate with *plan* (German *Plan*; Czech, French, Polish, Romanian, Serbian, Turkish *plan*; Slovak *plán*; Estonian *plaan*; Latvian *plāns*; Italian *piano*; Portuguese *planta*, etc.). If you spoke more than one of these languages, you *could* make the effort to vary the noun you used according to your ELF interlocutors, although this would take some effort and require some speedy accessing of the multilingual lexicon. Alternatively, of course, you could speak *English* – as a lingua franca – and use the word *map*, on the reasonable assumption that a competent ELF user from Europe, Asia, Africa, etc. would understand the word. *Map* is the kind of word you might expect a university-level English speaker to know; it comes quite high in word frequency lists, and is even to be found in Jean-Paul Nerrière's 'Globish' (2004), a basic form of English of his own devising that uses only 1500 words.[22]

Another reason to borrow or code-switch would be a lack of vocabulary in English. As Grosjean (2010: 29) points out, 'Bilinguals usually acquire and use their languages for different purposes, in different domains of life, with different people. Different aspects of life often require different languages.' He describes this as the 'complementarity principle,' adding 'If all languages were used in all domains, there would probably be much less reason to be bilingual. Just one language would normally be sufficient' (p. 30). A speaker not used to using English for a particular domain may lack the domain-specific vocabulary.[23] Bilinguals are probably 'in an intermediary mode on the continuum […] when they are talking about a subject in the "wrong" language (their other language is probably activated in such a situation, even if they do not use it)' (p. 42). However this state of affairs is generally neglected by ELF researchers, who often take a decidedly angelic view of the language, disregarding the very possibility of a lack of linguistic competence, or of communicative failure. For example, Canagarajah (2007: 925) is confident that 'speakers are able to monitor each other's language proficiency, to determine mutually the appropriate grammar, phonology, lexical range and pragmatic conventions that would ensure intelligibility,' while House (2003: 557) states (with two negatives) that 'a lingua franca speaker is not *per definitionem* not fully competent in the part of his/her linguistic knowledge under study,' and only found instances of miscommunication when ELF speakers were interacting with monolingual NESs.

A negative account of examples like Hülmbauer's would be that relying on the multicompetence deriving from a knowledge of more than one Romance or Germanic language may work in most of western Europe, but could also be seen as a narcissistic local or regional indulgence: borrowing from, say, Basque or Hungarian or Gaelic will not be productive, and relying on a recognition of Romance and Germanic cognates, and typological similarities, is unlikely to be useful in lingua franca communication with people from, e.g. Asia, where the languages do *not* exhibit such overlaps. For example, Kirkpatrick (2010: 91), discusses the 'use of lexical items and idioms with meanings specific to a language variety' and 'code-mixing,' and states categorically that

> One would not expect their use to be effective in lingua franca communication, as the specific lexical meanings would often be unknown to at least some of the participants. Code-mixing would be an unlikely phenomenon in lingua franca communication because its use requires proficiency in specific languages, and in lingua franca communication one could never anticipate that all participants could possibly be familiar with all the possible languages. After all, that is precisely why the participants in lingua franca communication choose a lingua franca in the first place.

However this merely underlines the difference between the linguistic make-up of Asia and that of Europe. The 'situationality factor' comes into play in ELF.[24] Just as bilinguals are not in the bilingual mode when speaking with monolinguals, ELF speakers will not deliberately draw on languages their interlocutors do not understand But in the right language combinations, these resources are there to be used.

On the other hand, if you take Eurocentric language mixing to an extreme, you might abandon ELF for Diego Marani's ludic concept of 'Europanto,' a mixture of words and grammatical structures borrowed from various Romance and Germanic languages, with English providing the basic structure and filling in the gaps:

> Europanto: eine lingua por spiel
>
> Por speak Europanto tu basta mix parolas from differente linguas. Keine study, keine grammatica, just improviste, und voilà que tu esse perfecte Europanto speakante.
>
> Erodant habe keine grammatica. Better dixit, grammatica habe, aber tu can liberamente und instinctivamente invente.
>
> Aquì tambien, der gutte rezipe esse de mix maxime common grammaticale elementos from differente linguas.
>
> *(Marani 2009)*

In real life, however, using language like this – which Peter Auer (1999) would describe as no longer language mixing but as a case of 'fused lects' – removes the possibility of creating specific meanings or effects by way of sporadic, well-chosen code-switches.

A further argument against such language mixing might be that Europeans in general do not manifest any desire to speak 'Euro-English.' For example, Sandra Mollin (2006b) – in a book that begins with a splendid sceptical flourish: 'Euro-English seems to be the Yeti of English varieties: everyone has heard of it, but no one has ever seen it' (p. 1) – argues that 'Europeans do not want a Euro-English. Near-native competence in English is a status symbol that European speakers wish to achieve' (p. 200). This conclusion is based on questionnaire responses from nearly 4,000 educated informants across the continent and, conveniently, it seems to accord with Mollin's extensive corpus data, which appear to show that no such thing as Euro-English exists. However, Mollin's corpus largely consists of speeches, briefings, discussion groups and press conferences at the European Commission, formal situations in which the participants knew they were being recorded for the EU audio archive. Such data is rather less likely than, say, ordinary conversation to reveal spontaneous English use (see, e.g. Labov 1972b; and Jarvis and Pavlenko 2007: 208). One can also contest Mollin's questionnaire results: while they may accurately express speakers' *desires*, they reveal nothing about their actual *use* of English. People's stated attitudes towards English do not necessarily reflect the English they actually speak. There is clearly a huge conceptual difference between mixing languages intentionally and accidentally, and those who do it intentionally are likely to do it more frequently than those for whom it is accidental, but the resulting language use can sound much the same.

A final argument against language mixing is that there seems less *imperative* for European ELF speakers to do it than people in genuinely bilingual and bicultural communities, since for most Europeans, English remains an additional language (or 'another tongue'), rather than a language of culture and identity, and bilingualism is achieved through schooling much more than natural acquisition.[25] There is very little evidence of identification with a set of linguistic forms that are indigenous to ELF, and that might lead to nativization, or the development of a stable endonormative variety, as has happened with the postcolonial outer circle varieties or World Englishes (see Schneider 2003: 249–50). The linguistic situation of Europeans is not the same as that of, e.g. bicultural Hispanics in the USA, who live in two languages and often mix English and Spanish in what has come to be known as Spanglish.[26] For example, Gloria Anzaldúa insists that

> Until I am free to write bilingually and to switch codes without having always to translate, while I still have to speak English or Spanish when I would rather speak Spanglish, and as long as I have to accommodate to English speakers rather than having them accommodate to me, my tongue will be illegitimate.
>
> I will no longer be made to feel ashamed of existing. I will have my voice.
>
> *(Anzaldúa 1987: 81; excerpted in Stavans (ed.) 2008: 124)*

And Susana Chávez-Silverman (2004: 75) writes like this:

> Cuando tenía 17 años, maybe 18, me mudé a la casa de mi novio de entonces, a British-born Kawasaki off-road team mechanic and part-time racer. Yeah, I moved in con él, y con sus 2 male roommates. I didn't have a job for that summer en Santa Cruz so me fui con todo y mis $400.00 para vivir en esa bland, one-story, all-male house en los suburbs de Orange County ... [27]

This is a rather different sort of language mixing from a Greek in Austria using an English cognate of the word *chartis*. While Chávez-Silverman simply mixes or alternates the two languages, much of the joy of everyday spoken Spanglish lies in its dynamism, playfulness and creativity, and the invention of calques such as *grocerías* to mean groceries (as opposed to *grosería,* rudeness), and *jaiscul* (high school), *troquero* (truckdriver), *huayfa* (wife), *quechear* (to catch), *huachear* (to watch), and *tener un buen tiempo* (to have a good time, rather than *divertise*), and so on. This process broadens semantic fields, and gives new connotations or meanings to words that are widely used in the speech community. A similar process marks the history of Yiddish. This kind of language mixing is spontaneous and widely attested, unlike Marani's Europanto, which is merely a diverting pastime, and a very clever way of selling the same, untranslated article to newspapers in half a dozen countries.

As Stavans (2008: x) puts it, 'Spanglish, I'm convinced, is a frame of mind,'[28] but there is of course also a contrary frame of mind that reverts to complaints about 'double semi-lingualism,' and sees Spanglish as a threat. For example, US English Inc., who sell bumper stickers reading 'The United States of America – built, powered and made great by immigrants *who learned English*,' live in mortal fear of (imagined) texts like 'I pledge allegiance de la bandera de los Estados Unidos de Amerika und der republik ... '[29]

Even though most ELF-using Europeans are not as bicultural as many of the US's 40 million plus Hispanics, the lexical similarities across European languages might indeed make Europe the ideal environment in which to exploit cross-linguistic interaction. Canagarajah (2007: 924) argues that recent research related to LFE is 'radically reconfiguring the new models of language usage and acquisition being constructed in our field.' As suggested above, however, many of the features of ELF/LFE have previously been described by researchers into language contact, bilingualism and second language acquisition. The difference is that most SLA researchers write about 'transfer errors' and 'intrusions' rather than, say, the inter-subjective construction of each specific interaction, complete with borrowings, code-switchings and transfer. What is new about ELF/LFE research is a frame of mind, or a positive attitude to crosslinguistic influence. All bi- and multilinguals have a certain language awareness and competence, whether they are bicultural and speak two languages natively, or whether they only use one as a (multicultural) lingua franca, and Canagarajah concedes that 'it is possible that multilinguals already come with this competence and do not wait for their interactions in English to develop [the] ability' to handle diverse communicative situations (p. 928). But the 'new models of language usage' valorize language mixing, or at least crosslinguistic influence.[30]

Language awareness and multilingual competence

Many ELF speakers in Europe grew up bilingually, and learned English as a third (or fourth) language. Some speak two (or more) languages that have either typological or lexical similarities with English (e.g. in Belgium, Catalonia, the Italian South Tyrol, Luxembourg, Switzerland, etc.), while others speak one similar and one wholly dissimilar language (e.g. in the Basque Country and the Swedish-speaking parts of Finland, and in millions of families originally from Algeria, Morocco, Turkey, and many other African and Asian countries). Many more Europeans learn two languages at school, one of which is almost invariably English. Hence many European speakers of English are multilingual, and as Jessner argues in *Linguistic Awareness in Multilinguals: English as a third language* (2006), multilinguals tend to have a well-developed metalinguistic awareness, which increases with the number of languages spoken, and has a catalytic effect on further language acquisition.

Metalinguistic awareness is essentially the ability to think about the form and structure of a language, and of an utterance to be produced or understood. Multi-lingual or multicompetent speakers bring broader linguistic and grammatical knowledge to the process of language learning and language use, which gives them crosslingual receptive strategies for inferring word meanings, and a variety of compensatory strategies when faced with productive difficulties, including activating cognates, borrowing, transferring, switching, calquing, approximating, coining words, and generally experimenting with language. For example, Jessner (2003a: 51) argues that trilingual learners improve their phrasing by comparing crosslinguistic equivalents, which implies that 'the use of two or more languages results in the development of metalinguistic abilities, i.e. an increased monitoring system for all the languages known by the multilingual speaker, which thus enhances metalinguistic awareness per se.'

Whereas less proficient learners are more likely to transfer from the L1 – although some researchers have found what Jürgen Meisel (1983) called a 'foreign language effect,' resulting in the L2 rather than the L1 being activated in an L3 – more proficient multilingual speakers tend to transfer from typologically closer languages. Where many less-confident L2 learners use avoidance and simplification strategies to compensate for their lack of knowledge, and over-monitor and avoid cognate words that are in fact correct, more-confident multilingual speakers are likely to avoid avoidance strategies, and to hazard a guess. Such strategies may result in approximate grammar or lexical oddities, or what in an SLA framework, as opposed to a multilingualism or multicompetence framework, has traditionally been called negative transfer. However multilinguals themselves tend to be less disturbed by inaccuracies. As Helmut Zobl (1992: 193) has argued, there seems to be 'an inverse relationship between the conservatism of the learning procedure and the pool of linguistic knowledge available': people learning an L3 or an L4 are less likely to worry about ungrammaticality than people learning an L2.

This attitude to formal accuracy may be one facet of the many cognitive advantages that are now widely attributed to multilinguals, such as creative or divergent thinking, mental flexibility, superior concept formation, abstract language use, enhanced linguistic originality and playfulness, empathy, communicative sensitivity, and so on.[31] Consequently Jessner (2006: 120) argues that 'one of the main goals of future language teaching should be to foster linguistic awareness, one of the key factors of multilingual proficiency, in the classroom.'[32] Learners need to be encouraged to think about the forms of language and to recognize similarities and differences among languages. If this resourceful attitude to transfer and accuracy is advantageous in learning, acquiring and producing any language, it is all the more appropriate to ELF, a hybrid language used by a heterogeneous speech community without any native speakers. The multilingual approach to ELF suggests that European ELF speakers would do better not to over-monitor or censor themselves, but rather use lexis and phraseology that may not be perfect NS English, but which they can reasonably expect their ELF interlocutors to understand.

Yet although Jessner plays up multilinguals' metalinguistic awareness, she also asserts categorically that they will use their languages less well than monolinguals: 'there is ample evidence that bilinguals do not generally achieve the same levels of competence as monolingual speakers. [...] monolinguals speak one language very well and bilinguals tend to speak two languages, but these somewhat less well' (Herdina and Jessner 2002: 13).

Multilingual competence requires a lot of language management, and the more languages spoken, the more maintenance needed to guarantee homeostasis, and 'Multilinguals (particularly these are taken to include second language learners) appear to find maintaining and managing more than one language quite a challenge' (p. 60). Thus, 'In the case of multilinguals we are frequently confronted with the phenomenon of language loss, language deterioration and/or attrition' (p. 93), so the Dynamic Model of Multilingualism 'does not regard the absolute command of a language as a realistic perspective. A certain degree of under-achievement is to be expected' (p. 101).[33] Another way of putting this, given the assumption that over half the world's population is bilingual, is that 'Some L1 attrition [...] is a small price to pay for achieving the ordinary state of mankind' (Laufer 2003: 30). Yet the difficulties of language maintenance lead Herdina and Jessner (2002: 103) to 'a new interpretation' of code-switching, such that it 'might be employed because a single system in isolation no longer suffices to cover the communicative needs of the individual and therefore the second(ary) LS [language system] has to help out.'

However, whether or not one concurs with Herdina and Jessner's redefinition of multilingual competence as partial incompetence, the particular nature of ELF, above all in the linguistic environment of western Europe, lends itself to borrowing, code-switching and other forms of transfer. The typological and lexical similarities among many European languages, and the large number of cognates, allow European ELF users to draw on their plurilinguistic resources. They can often operate in what Grosjean calls the 'bilingual language mode' even if they do not share exactly the same language(s) as all their interlocutors. Yaron Matras (2009: 4) argues that

> Mature multilingual speakers face a constant challenge to maintain control over their complex repertoire of forms and structures and to select those forms that are context appropriate. Context appropriate selection does not necessarily conform to a separation of 'languages': In some contexts, certain types of crosslinguistic 'mixing' and 'inserting' may be socially acceptable and may constitute effective goal-oriented communication.

European ELF seems to be a context in which certain types of crosslinguistic mixing and inserting may indeed be socially acceptable and effective. This does *not* furnish a global lingua franca – mixing western European languages is unlikely to be an effective strategy with Chinese, Iranian and Japanese ELF speakers – but it *does* facilitate a situationally appropriate one. Rather than call European ELF a kind of performance without competence, as Allan James (2000: 27) does, it might be better to describe it as a widespread instantiation of what Cook calls multi-competence. The precise nature of the grammar, lexis and phraseology of ELF is the subject of the following chapters.

Notes

1 As Grosjean (2010: 4) states, 'There is a long tradition in the field of extending the notion of bilingualism to those who use two or more languages on a regular basis,' but I will use both the terms 'bilingual' and 'multilingual.' I also use 'multilingual' and 'pluri-lingual' more or less interchangeably. The European Council for Cultural Co-operation's *Common European Framework of Reference for Languages* (2001: 4) uses 'multilingualism' to refer to societies, or simply to 'the knowledge of a number of languages,' and 'pluri-lingualism' to refer to 'a communicative competence to which all knowledge and experience of language contributes and in which languages interrelate and interact.' However this distinction is not widely shared.

2 See also Blommaert's account of the 'super-diversity' (2010: 7) in many multilingual urban areas in western countries, where new migrants have fragmented, incomplete and truncated language repertoires (p. 9), and 'Heteroglossia is the default mode of occurrence of communication' (p. 181).

3 Moreover, as Trudgill (1986: 85–86) puts it, 'The better-known European languages tend to be of the focused type: the language is felt to be clearly distinct from other languages; its "boundaries" are clearly delineated; and members of the speech community show a high level of agreement as to what does and does not constitute "the language."'

4 And as Mesthrie and Bhatt (2008: 213) put it, 'where northern Europe is concerned (especially parts of Scandinavia and northern Germany) Anglo-Saxon is coming back home – much changed, of course, and much more refined via contacts with Latin and French, not to mention its enrichment by the languages of the colonies.'

5 See also Grosjean (1985).

6 These two terms can be differentiated as follows: 'A code switch is a complete shift to the other language for a word, a phrase or a sentence whereas a borrowing is a

morpheme, word or short expression taken from the less activated language and adapted morpho-syntactically (and sometimes phonologically) to the base language' (Grosjean 2008: 44).

7 This unlovely concept is discussed in Skutnabb-Kangas (1984).

8 Gardner-Chloros (1995: 68), however, criticizes the attempt to demarcate 'code-switching as a special form of skilled bilingual behaviour [...] from the aberrant manifestations of bilingualism which involve one language influencing another', arguing that 'this new type of ideal speaker-listener, whose existence depends on such discrete alternation, is as much a rare bird as Chomsky's monolingual original.'

9 Franceschini's examples concern Swiss-Germans in Zürich picking up some Italian. Rampton's (2005) account of the more radical practice of 'crossing' was mentioned in Chapter 1. However these instances are more deliberate acts of group identification and affiliation than communication strategies.

10 Barfield (1962: 59), quoted in O'Laoire and Singleton (2009), who also quote Pei's (1967: 92) assertion that 12,000 of the 20,000 words in 'full use' in English are of Latin, Greek and French origin.

11 See, e.g. the 'Language museum' – long appendices of Teutonic (English-Swedish-Danish-Dutch-German) and Romance (English-French-Spanish-Portuguese-Italian) cognates – at the end of Bodmer (1944/1985).

12 Attributed to the journalist Charles Rappaport (Rosten 2001: xvii).

13 'Crosslinguistic influence' was proposed by Kellerman and Sharwood Smith (1986) as a neutral term, as opposed to the negative 'interference.' As mentioned above, Herdina and Jessner (2002) prefer the term 'crosslinguistic interaction.' There is as yet no accepted collective English term to cover both willed and unwilled, positive and negative features of interaction (borrowing, code-switching, transfer, interference, etc.), but in French Lüdi (1987: 2) has proposed *marque transcodique*.

14 Although he focuses on errors, Jarvis (2009: 106) adds 'However, it is important to acknowledge that lexemic transfer can be and often is positive, especially in the case of closely related languages and especially during comprehension.'

15 Obviously the spelling changes across languages, e.g. *aktuálni, aktualnie, aktuell; eventuálně, ewentualnie, eventuell, eventuale; sympatický, sympatyczny, sympathisch, simpático, sympatisk, sympathiek*, etc. Ferguson (1982/1992: xvii) commented on the 'Continental meanings of *eventual* and *actual*' long before recent interest in ELF.

16 Where speakers are less confident that they are using a target language word, and feel they may be borrowing, they may use a source language pronunciation; as Gardner-Chloros (1995: 71) points out, 'switching can take place at the phonological level only.'

17 Lexical transfers such as these need to be distinguished from inappropriate *conceptual* transfers in L2 performance, or more importantly, from the intermittent conceptual restructuring and conceptual development necessary in the learning of an L2 to be used with its NSs. Language learners tend to link L2 word forms to already established lexical concepts in their L1, but where concepts differ their translation equivalents will not be perfect conceptual equivalents. (See, e.g. Wierzbicka (2006) on the semantics of *fair, evidence, reasonable*, etc. and Pavlenko (2009: 138) on *privacy* and *personal space*.) As Pavlenko puts it, 'Eventually L2 learners will need to adjust the boundaries of their linguistic categories, either expanding or narrowing them in accordance with L2 constraints. Failure to readjust the boundaries appropriately would lead to instances of L1 conceptual transfer. [...] In the case of successful restructuring, the boundaries of the L2 category are modified without changing the boundaries of the corresponding L1 category. As a result, speakers perform in accordance with the constraints of each language' (p. 136). This is the conventional account of language learning, but if the target is not NSs, but other bi- or multilinguals using a lingua franca, monolingual target-like performance is not necessarily an issue.

18 Although he uses the negative term *interference* rather than the more neutral *interaction*, Grosjean (2010: 76) does concede that interferences 'do not usually affect

communication. I would even suggest that they may render what is said more original and less stereotypical.'

19 The million-word VOICE is at http://www.univie.ac.at/voice/. The 'O' (without which the corpus would merely be Barbara Seidlhofer's vice) is due to financial support from Oxford University Press's dictionary department; there is a short section on ELF at the back of the 2005 edition of the *Oxford Advanced Learner's Dictionary of Current English* (p. R92ff.), though this is not in the 2010 edition.

20 Cf. Wenger's (1988: 76) 'shared repertoire of negotiable resources.'

21 Firth and Wagner's article, four responses to it, and a response to the responses, are reprinted in Seidlhofer (ed.) (2003).

22 But see Hülmbauer (2011) for a spirited defence of the meaning potential of cognates, a nascent 'plurilingual resource model,' and the confident assertion that 'a notion of plurilingualism which is still defined as using "one language at a time" (OLAAT) is clearly outdated. […] what seems to be more appropriate is an "all language at all times" (ALAAT) approach, taking language in a holistic sense, which involves linguistic elements from all sources' (p. 154).

23 The levels of the Common European Framework of Reference for Languages (CEFR) presuppose that speakers have differing abilities in productive and receptive skills in different languages.

24 Kirkpatrick's statement about code-mixing in Asia does however show that Cogo's (2009: 264) claim that 'use of languages other than English is so intrinsic to ELF as to be seen as a constituted and constitutive part of it' is Eurocentric and overstated.

25 See Hoffman (1996). James (2000: 31) contests this opinion, arguing that the distinction between achieved (institutionally learned) and ascribed (naturally acquired) bilingualism dissipates with English in Europe today, where the underlay of school English later tends to develop naturally.

26 See, however, Alptekin (2010) who argues that rather than being a unique case of bilingualism without biculturalism, ELF necessarily fosters a *multicultural* identity and some degree of intercultural competence.

27 For examples of equally intensive *oral* code-switching, see Gardner-Chloros (1991). Some of the Alsatian (*Elsässisch*)/French speech she reports seems to be a truly mixed code, rather than a base or matrix language alternating with a guest or embedded one. It has been suggested (see Kemp 2009) that multilinguals process psychotypologically similar languages as different varieties of the same language (e.g. French, Catalan and Spanish, or Danish, Norwegian and Swedish), but Gardner-Chloros' data and the example of Chávez-Silverman suggest that this can also be the case with less similar languages.

28 On the other hand, various linguists have objected to the part of Stavans' Spanglish 'data' that comes from contrived classroom exercises in language mixing and is consequently unlike anything found in naturalistic corpora. For example, Lipski (2004: 12) says of Stavans' own Spanglish version of the beginning of *Don Quijote*, 'This grotesque creation not only contains numerous syntactic violations of code-switching, but also phonotactically unlikely combinations in either language.' Almeida Jacqueline Toribio (personal communication) says that in this respect, it is not unlike the 'mock Spanish' described as 'covert rascist discourse' by Jane Hill. See Chapter 5 of Hill (2008), and Bullock and Toribio (2009).

29 An advertisement reproduced in Berthele (2008: 310).

30 The fact that SLA and ELF researchers come to antithetical conclusions about the same data does not diminish the scientific rigour of linguistics: a century ago the French physicist Pierre Duhem argued that that there can be an innumerable number of explanations for any given set of observations, depending on the background assumptions in play. To put this another way, theories are always underdetermined by facts. This is known as the 'Duhem thesis' (Duhem 1914/1991), though it is more often quoted subsumed into the 'Duhem-Quine thesis' (Quine 1953).

31 See, e.g. Jessner (2006: 38), who draws on Peal and Lambert (1962) and Vygotsky (1934/1962). See also Hamers and Blanc (1989). This valorization of bilingualism is relatively recent; it was previously believed to cause intellectual deterioration, mental conflict, conceptual poverty, moral deprivation, emotional difficulties, superficiality, laziness, etc; see Weinreich (1953/1968: 119–29), and Pavlenko (2011a).
32 Seidlhofer (2002, 2003) makes a similar argument.
33 See also Jessner (2003b).

3

ANALYTIC STRUCTURES AND EMERGENT GRAMMAR

> Unfortunately, or luckily, no language is tyrannically consistent. All grammars leak.
>
> Sapir (1921: 38)

This chapter is about the grammar of English, whether used as a native language, a nativized language, or a lingua franca. It seeks to explain English grammar today by way of two separate arguments about language change, one socio-historical, the other theoretical and 'usage-based.' Chapter 4 considers specific grammatical uses found in ELF corpora. However it will soon be seen (or at least argued) that the lexical, phraseological and grammatical resources of a language form a continuum, and combine in the realization of meaning. Thus the discussion of the grammar of ELF will necessarily spill over into Chapters 5 and 6, which nominally concern lexis and phraseology. Readers more interested in the nitty-gritty of ELF data than linguistic theory might prefer to go straight to Chapter 4.

The first argument is that high-contact language varieties like lingua francas, pidgins and creoles, and any other varieties involving adolescent and adult second-language learning, tend over time to replace synthetic structures with analytic ones, to show a reduction in redundancy, and to increase in regularity. A fully analytic construction has a transparent, one-to-one mapping of meaning units and forms. In other words, it uses independent words to express different concepts, along with fixed word order, rather than inflections (such as the conjugation of verbs and the declension of nouns, adjectives and pronouns), derivations, modifications of roots, etc. For example, *I will go* is more analytic than the Italian *andrò*; *more lovely* is more analytic than *lovelier*; *eye-doctor* is more analytic and compositional than *optometrist* or *ophthalmologist*, and – to take an ELF example (from Hülmbauer 2009: 338) – *over-fulled* (calqued from the German *überfüllt*) is more analytic than *crowded*.[1]

Native English has been in contact with other languages for centuries, and English is the most widely learned language in the world today (Graddol

2006: 96ff.). It is used globally, and is in regular contact with all the world's major languages. It has consequently already undergone a great deal of simplification. Thus we should not anticipate many *major* grammatical innovations in ELF, but rather simplifications of the enduring 'difficult' or 'idiosyncratic' aspects of English grammar that differ from the majority of natural languages. So we should expect to find things like zero marking of the third person singular present tense, the use of articles and plurals with what in ENL are non-count nouns, different uses of progressive and present perfect aspectual forms, and different patterns of verb complementation (infinitives instead of gerunds, different prepositions, etc.) – simplifications that are also widespread in the nativized World Englishes in Africa and Asia.

Mauranen (2012: 31) says 'one might assume that those aspects of a language that are already simple will remain intact if it is learned as a foreign language on a large scale,' but what looks simple to linguists sometimes appears less so to language learners, so we should also expect changes in less predictable areas of English lexicogrammar. Moreover there is also a difference between, on the one hand, ELF as used in the absence of a community of native speakers and, on the other, learner language and the English of ESL speakers in ENL countries. Most language learners in schools and migrants are, to a greater or lesser extent, attempting to imitate the target language of a native speech community; many ELF speakers, it appears, are not. Consequently, they have the freedom to change ENL constructions and patterns at will, for the sake of clarity, regularity and simplicity, and economy of processing effort.

The second main argument is that grammar is not a fixed set of rules that precedes language use, and can be logically detached from it, but rather, as Paul Hopper (1998: 156) puts it, just the name we give 'certain categories of observed repetitions in discourse.' Our utterances are based on previously heard utterances, rather than grammatical rules, and the ways people speak slowly change over time, according to needs and circumstances. Languages and their component parts are creatively stretched with use (so they change even when they are *not* being widely learned and used as L2s). Thus grammatical regularities 'are always provisional and are continually subject to negotiation, renovation and abandonment' (Hopper 1988: 120), and grammar is forever *emergent*. Importantly, *emergent*, referring to a perpetual process producing different forms, in which completion is always deferred, is to be distinguished from *emerging*, which implies an ultimate completion, perhaps by becoming part of an already existing grammar (Hopper 1998: 157).

If this is true of any speech community, it should be even truer of ELF, a hybrid language, or to quote Meierkord (2004: 115) once again, 'a variety in constant flux, involving different constellations of speakers of diverse individual Englishes in every single interaction.' If utterances are based on previously heard utterances, ELF users can be expected to speak differently from NESs. We should expect to find a potentially infinite number of emergent grammars in ELF interactions, with unpredictable, diverse, local grammatical – or lexicogrammatical, or phraseological – features deriving from contact with many other languages. On the other hand, as will be argued in Chapter 4, this lexicogrammatical variety comes up against a countervailing force – people's natural tendency to accommodate to and converge with their interlocutors' ways of speaking.

Between them, the socio-historical theory of language change induced by non-native learners, and the usage-based account of the emergent nature of grammar, combine to explain the formal lexicogrammatical features of ELF today.

Adult second-language learning, pidginization and simplification

The vast majority of ELF speakers begin learning the language at school, rather than acquiring it naturally in early childhood. And as everybody knows, there appears to be what Eric Lenneberg (1967: 175ff.) called a critical period for language acquisition.[2] Children acquire new dialects and languages perfectly up to the age of about eight, but there is very little chance of learning a language variety perfectly from mere exposure after the age of about fourteen. There is a gradual reduction in ability between eight and fourteen, depending on circumstances and the individual. Post-adolescent and adult learners prefer regularity and transparency to irregularity and opacity. They find things like inflections and grammatical gender and agreement hard to learn. So they tend to simplify the language. SLA theorists suggest that there are 'natural acquisitional processes' or 'acquisitional universals,' as there are 'types of errors that L2 learners from all L1 backgrounds make' (Jarvis and Pavlenko 2007: 192). For example, 'it has been found that learners from vastly different L1 backgrounds (though not necessarily all learners from those backgrounds) have the tendency to omit structures that are obligatory in the target language, such as inflectional affixes, articles, and prepositions,' as part of 'a universal tendency [...] often referred to as simplification, or more specifically as restrictive simplification' (p. 192). Another posited acquisitional universal is overgeneralization or elaborative simplification.

Trudgill (2011: 35) states that 'whenever adults and post-adolescents learn a new language, *pidginization* can be said to occur; and pidginization includes as a crucial component the process of simplification.' Pidginization is thus a common process which only very rarely leads to the development of an actual pidgin language.[3]

Simplification involves the regularization of irregularities (such as past tenses and plurals), an increase in lexical and morphological transparency, and a loss of redundancy (such as markers of verb agreement) and of what John McWhorter (2001: 132) calls 'baroque accretion' and 'ornamental elaboration.' Trudgill (2009: 101) argues that 'Pidginization involves simplification because high irregularity, low transparency, and high levels of redundancy make for difficulties of learning and remembering for adolescent and adult learner-speakers. Simplification is the direct result of the critical threshold.' The other two components of pidginization are reduction and admixture. Reduction means that in a pidginized form 'there is simply less of a language as compared to the form in which it is spoken by native speakers: the vocabulary is smaller, and there are fewer syntactic structures, a narrower range of styles, and so on' (Trudgill 2011: 67). Admixture refers to what in SLA theory is generally described as interference or transfer, although as outlined in the previous chapter, proponents of ELF and plurilingualism generally prefer to describe this in terms of multicompetence.

Trudgill suggests that any high-contact language variety that is widely learned by adolescents and adults is likely to change gradually from a synthetic to an analytic structure, and to become more regular. Given that high-contact situations have multiplied in recent centuries, *most* major contemporary languages bear the mark of post-adolescent second-variety acquisition. The histories of many Indo-European and Semitic languages reveal extensive syntactic regularization and the simplification of verbal morphology, such as reduction in conjugations, declensions and overt case-marking, an increase in the use of prepositions and auxiliaries and periphrastic verb forms, more restrictions on word order, and so on, resulting in regular, analysable, compositional and productive structures (Trudgill 1989: 231–32). Compare French with Latin, German with Old High German, or English with Old English or even Early Modern English – thou knowest it hath changed.[4]

Similarly, it seems entirely fair to say that postcolonial World Englishes or ESL varieties as well as ELF show the consequences of general principles (or limitations) of human cognition and second language production and perception, such as simplification, regularization, the minimization of redundancy, the reduction of potential ambiguity, and a tendency towards explicitness, or what Jessica Williams (1987: 166) calls 'hyperclarity' or maximum transparency. To explain the formal nature of ELF it helps to place it in a longer history of language change.

The theory of language change resulting from language contact means that 'the dominant standard modern languages in the world today are likely to be seriously atypical of how languages have been for nearly all of human history' (Trudgill 2011: 169).[5] For most of the 100,000 or so years that humans have used language, it was in small, dense, stable social networks (mainly of hunter-gatherers) in which everyone knew everyone else, and there was little contact with other language varieties. As Alison Wray and George Grace (2007) put it, languages that are used predominantly for esoteric or intra-group communication generally have features that are semantically and grammatically complex: 'much of what needs to be said can be said elliptically and formulaically, with huge reliance on shared knowledge, pragmatics and common practice' (p. 554). Languages used esoterically are, almost by definition, acquired in infancy, and so tend to abound in phonological complexities and morphological irregularities that are not easily learned by outsiders. As Wray has argued elsewhere (2002, 2008), children do not acquire language compositionally, with recourse to full systematicity, or process language analytically, but use lots of holistically processed formulaic sequences and idioms and fixed expressions which minimize processing effort in both production and comprehension. Such formulas might well be semantically opaque and impenetrable to adult outsiders. Wray and Grace suggest that esotericity is the natural default setting for human language, and that fully developed rule-based systematicity may be a cultural add-on, deriving from literacy, and from exoteric or inter-group communication: 'Languages used exoterically will tend to develop and maintain linguistic features that are logical, transparent, phonologically and morphologically simple, and (as a result) learnable by adult incomers' (Wray 2008: 56). But in historical terms, this is a relatively recent phenomenon; as Trudgill (2011: 152) puts it,

> simplification is actually not normal. If it were normal, all languages in the world would by now have been maximally regular and maximally transparent. I suggest that it is actually complexification that is, in an important sense, more normal. If languages are 'left alone,' the natural tendency is for them to accrue more and more complexity.

English used as a contact language or a lingua franca today is by definition exoteric, but given that the early history of England was one of repeated invasions, English has a long history of contact, and Trudgill argues that the remarkable simplification of Old English into Middle English resulted from language contact with the Brittonic Celtic language of the indigenous inhabitants (or the *wealas* or foreigners as the Anglo-Saxons tactfully called them). Although many of the Celts retreated to Wales, Scotland, Brittany and Galicia, some stayed in the south-west, west and north of England,[6] and (notwithstanding the well-known chorus of *Rule, Britannia*) were probably treated as slaves by the Anglo-Saxons, or at least as a lower 'caste' (Tristram 2004). They continued to speak Brittonic or Late British for several generations, before they shifted to Old English, somewhere between the sixth and ninth centuries.

Given that untutored adult learners tend to find inflections, grammatical gender and agreement difficult to learn and apply, the Celts dropped Old English case endings and used word order or prepositions (*to, with, from, at, in*) instead, and ignored grammatical gender. As Trudgill (2011: 54) puts it, 'children would have learned the imperfectly acquired L2 from their parents as their L1 and subsequently passed on their linguistic knowledge of the modified target language to their own children.' Thus it would appear that it was 'contact between a minority of Old English and a majority of socially inferior Late British speakers, in northern England, that set the process of simplification going, as Britons shifted to (their form of) English, and Late British was eventually lost' (p. 55). Eventually the simplified version became the dominant variety, as the native speakers of the language took up the simplified forms resulting from language contact.[7]

An alternative perspective is that this simplification should just be described as language change rather than imperfect learning. Janina Brutt-Griffler (2002: 129) argues that since 'any language is the linguistic expression of the speech community that speaks it,' it is 'contradictory to claim that a speech community can speak its own language in error. What holds for the individual speaker does not hold for the speech community.'

Brutt-Griffler describes second language acquisition (and indeed language shift) by speech communities as 'macroacquisition.' This redefines SLA as a social process, and a dynamic one: the language is no longer a static, fixed target, but something that alters as a result of its acquisition by a speech community. Brutt-Griffler asserts that 'There cannot be error as between two separate speech communities but, rather, difference' (p. 131). Hence the concepts of imperfect learning, interlanguage, error and fossilization do not apply to the results of macro-acquisition, whether by the Celts in England in the first millennium or by the speakers of New Englishes.[8]

Hence thanks to the Celts' macroacquisition, imperfect or otherwise, to which the Anglo-Saxons accommodated, modern English no longer has singular and plural nominative, accusative, genitive and dative endings for nouns, or masculine, feminine, neuter and plural adjectives, and so on.[9] In an article about pronunciation models and language teaching, Trudgill (2005b: 87) wrote, wryly, that 'even if native speakers do not "own" English, there is an importance sense in which it stems from them, especially historically' (!), although to the dismay of ELF theorists he continued 'and resides in them.' But it appears that English as we have it today also stems in part from the Celts, and other L2 learners. Yet the language, even though it has already been greatly simplified, is continuing to change, in both NS and NNS usage, because grammar appears to be forever *emergent*.

Emergent grammar and prior texts

The dominant paradigm in linguistics from approximately the late 1950s to the late 1980s was generative grammar, a 'formalist' approach associated with Chomsky. Chomsky (1977: 81) described a language as 'a set of structural descriptions of sentences,' which effectively equates language with (or reduces it to) grammar alone. He also (1981: 7) proudly proclaimed that in the study of generative grammar, 'the focus of attention was shifted from "language" to "grammar,"' and dismissed 'language' as 'an obscure and I believe ultimately unimportant notion.' Hopper (1988: 118) describes the Chomskyan approach as resting on the 'A Priori Grammar Postulate' (APGP), which is that grammar is 'a discrete set of rules which are logically and mentally presupposed by discourse.' According to the APGP, 'grammar is complete and predetermined and is a prerequisite for generating discourses.'

Hopper opposes this notion with what he calls the 'Emergence of Grammar' (EOG) attitude, which 'view[s] grammar as the name for a vaguely defined set of sedimented (i.e. grammaticized) recurrent partials whose status is constantly being renegotiated in speech and which cannot be distinguished *in principle* from strategies for building discourses' (p. 118). As the term 'recurrent partials' suggests, our primary discourse-building strategy, according to this view of language, is repeating or adapting things we have heard before: 'We say things that have been said before. Our speech is a vast collection of hand-me-downs that reaches back in time to the beginnings of language' (Hopper 1998: 159). Most of the time, 'utterances are closely similar to previous utterances,' and 'anything that is said has been said in something like that form before' (p. 165). Similarly, Alton Becker (1995: 15) describes previous utterances as 'prior texts,' and suggests that there is a 'pervasiveness of a kind of indirect quotation in all of our languaging. *Everything* anyone says has a history and hence is, in part, a quotation. *Everything* anyone says is also partly new, too' (p. 286). In this conception of language (or 'languaging'), grammar is redefined as 'meaningful repetition […] distributed among the various participants in a collaborative act of communication' (Hopper 1998: 162), or 'the set of sedimented conventions that have been routinized out of the more frequently occurring ways of saying things' (p. 163),[10] or 'an epiphenomenon of frequent combinations of constructions' (Hopper 2004: 153).

Hopper's account of emergent grammar is part of a broader group of 'usage-based' theories of language, a term introduced by the cognitive linguist Ronald Langacker (1987). The basic assumption underlying usage-based approaches is that rather than being innate, language structure and linguistic knowledge initially derive from the comprehension and production of specific utterances on specific occasions of use. This is in direct contrast to Chomsky's 'nativist' theory which sees children's capacity to acquire language as biologically determined, 'hardwired' in the brain in the form of a language instinct or a 'language-acquisition device' (LAD), without which language would be unlearnable. Chomsky originally postulated a 'universal grammar' consisting of 'rules.' In more recent incarnations of the theory, rules are replaced by a finite set of fundamental principles common to all languages and a finite set of parameters that determine syntactic variability among languages, and hence the grammaticality of a given language. Given the LAD, what a speaker actually needs to acquire is minimal, and Chomsky (1995) has developed what he calls a 'minimalist program.' The minimal amount of language acquisition is a theoretical necessity deriving from what is commonly referred to as the 'poverty of the stimulus' argument, the assumption, first expressed in Chomsky (1965), that the linguistic input children receive is of too poor a quality to explain the quantity and quality of their linguistic output after the age of two.

Usage-based approaches, in contrast, propose that languages consist of a conventional inventory of units or constructions (including units that convey grammatical patterns) that speakers assemble in order to communicate. As Michael Tomasello (2003: 5) puts it, 'When human beings use symbols to communicate with one another, stringing them together into sequences, patterns of use emerge and become consolidated into grammatical constructions.' This inventory of units, accumulated in the process of hearing and using the language, makes up a massive cognitive structure of linguistic constructions, concepts and cultural information. It reflects a huge amount of learning and memorization, which might be described as a maximalist program. A person's linguistic performance results from the accumulated experience of using language throughout a lifetime, but this skill is not separable from more general cognitive mechanisms – the ability to use symbols, to read intentions, to categorize, to make analogies and inferences, and to recognize, store and segment patterns (see Bybee 2010).

In this account of language, grammar emerges from patterns of use. Constructions that prove to be useful are regularly repeated in everyday conversational interactions and thus become 'entrenched' (Langacker 1987) or 'sedimented'

(Hopper 1988, 1992) or 'routinized' (Haiman 1994). Their regular use leaves a neuronal trace that facilitates their re-occurrence. Repetition of well-rehearsed routines leads to automatization and habit formation, so that constructions become easily elicited and reliably executed prefabricated units whose constituent parts do not require conscious attention. Such constructions include collocations, partially lexically filled phrases, and fully general phrasal patterns – 'types' that can be used with many different 'tokens' (Bybee 1985). Particular combinations of words become (provisionally) fixed or 'grammaticalized' (Hopper and Traugott 2003), and socially or institutionally codified.

From the perspective of 'construction grammar' (e.g. Fillmore *et al.* 1988; Goldberg 1995, 2006; Croft 2001), the basic units of language are constructions, or form and meaning pairings (or form and discourse function pairings), which are mentally stored along with information about register, formality and dialect variation. Combinations of words used in this way straddle the traditional linguistic demarcations between syntax and semantics, or grammar, lexis and phraseology.[11] Both types (constructions) and specific tokens (items) can become entrenched, and stored in people's minds as cognitive entities in their own right (see Dabrowska 2004); as Adele Goldberg (2006: 5) puts it, 'patterns are stored as constructions even if they are fully predictable as long as they occur with sufficient frequency.'[12] Indeed Tomasello (2003: 6) suggests that many constructions remain idiosyncratic and item-based into adulthood. This account contrasts with generative models of grammar which have no place for frequency effects, and only allow for the storage of irregular or idiosyncratic items, as regular forms are believed to be generated by rules at the time of use.[13]

Thus in contrast to the generative approach, which sees children adapting the principles of Universal Grammar so as to accommodate the 'syntactic structures' of the particular language to which they are exposed, the constructionist approach sees children as constructing the grammar of their language (or languages) from an input of constructions. Tomasello (2003: 6) argues that children 'construct an adult-like set of grammatical constructions (given several years in which they hear several million adult utterances).' The 'several million' is in direct contrast to the supposed 'poverty of the stimulus' in Chomskyan theory. As Goldberg (2006: 15) puts it, 'It turns out that the input is not nearly as impoverished as is sometimes assumed,' and, more plaintively:

> Surely it is premature to give up hope that humans, with our rich cognitive abilities, complex social skills, predilection to imitate, and 100-billion neurone brains, can learn a language from the available input. Children have ample motivation to learn language, hear thousands of utterances every day, and receive constant indirect statistical feedback.
>
> *(p. 69)*

On the other hand, classroom learners do not hear thousands of target language utterances every day, or have genuine socio-cultural experience of the use of the

L2. They cannot possibly replicate the same stages of language and communicative development and socialization as L1 speakers. They often have no access to authentic contexts in which to acquire forms and functions, and scant opportunities to use the target language in meaningful social interaction. Consequently they have to rely on their existing sociocultural knowledge – and on studying (or trying to infer) the 'rules' of the L2. As we have seen, this often leads to various simplifications, and usages which do not replicate those of NSs.

Patterns and idiosyncrasies

Susan Hunston and Gill Francis (1999) propose a lexical grammar of native English, based on patterns observed in the Bank of English, the large corpus on which the *COBUILD* dictionaries are based. Their purely descriptive 'pattern grammar' is 'an attempt to describe the whole of the language (or rather, all the frequently-occurring items in the language) in a principled way' (p. 14), analysing corpus data with minimal theoretical presuppositions about grammatical structure. Following on from John Sinclair's (1991) 'idiom principle,' and foreshadowing Michael Hoey's (2005) work on lexical priming (see Chapter 6), Hunston and Francis argue that all nouns (or rather, all individual senses of nouns) have attached phraseologies, and that all transitive verbs have complementation patterns – particular preposi-tions, groups or clauses that can follow them.[14] Hence patterns and lexis are mutually dependent in that – in nativelike production – each pattern occurs with a restricted set of lexical items, and each lexical item occurs with a restricted set of patterns. Different senses of words are distinguished by their typical occurrence in different patterns, while words which share a given pattern tend to share an aspect of meaning. The corpus data does however include idiosyncratic uses, and it will be seen that NNESs use patterns differently from NESs.

The patterns Hunston and Francis isolate go from the very general and simple, such as **V n** (a verb followed by a noun group), through more complex patterns like **V n wh-to-inf** (a verb followed by a noun group and a to-infinitive clause introduced by a wh-word, e.g. *I'll show you where to put it*), to the highly specific (but splendidly productive), such as **V way prep/adv**, in which the verb is fol-lowed by a noun group consisting of a possessive determiner, such as *my, his, her* or *their*, and the noun *way*, followed by a prepositional phrase or adverb group (e.g. *She ate her way through a pound of chocolate; We somehow talked our way out of it; He threaded his way among the desks, etc.*).[15]

As well as clearly demarcated patterns with lists of words that are used with them, Hunston and Francis give examples of 'non-core' words used with some patterns, which they describe in terms of creativity rather than error. When a pat-tern is used with words of a particular meaning, speakers begin, by a process of analogy, to use other words with a similar meaning with the same pattern, so that 'at any point in time, what words belong to a list is in a state of flux' (p. 96). For example, although *provide* is typically used with the pattern **V n with n** (e.g. *provide someone with something*), the corpus also contains examples of **V n *to* n** (*provide something to someone*), presumably by analogy with *give*. Another example concerns the patterns **V–ing** and **V to-inf**. There are verbs which are conventionally (and statistically) used in both of these patterns, and verbs that are only used in one of them, but the Bank of English corpus shows 'a certain amount of "leakage" across the two patterns' (p. 98), such as a few occurrences of *attempt/ confess/neglect doing* alongside thousands of occurrences of *attempt* and *neglect to do*, and *confess to +–ing*. There are also occasional uses of an intransitive verb with a direct object.

It is clearly impossible to tell from corpora whether such individual usages, stretching or breaking existing grammatical patterns, are intentional or accidental, although Pennycook (2007: 42) states that 'We do not live in a world where people conform mindlessly to the putative rules of language, we live in a world of language transgressions, impossible without some presumed order worth transgressing, and made possible by the desire for difference.' Certainly most people speak differently in different circumstances: sociolinguistic research has shown that there is variation in virtually any speech community, and that individual speakers use different variants in different social networks within a larger speech community (see, e.g. Weinreich *et al.* 1968; Labov 1972b; Milroy 1987). Although constructions or patterns are passed from speaker to speaker, rules are stretched and patterns adapted in face-to-face interaction according to the communicative needs of the present context, and to speakers' perceptions of their addressees' use of language. Most individual adaptations of patterns and linguistic idiosyncrasies have zero effect, but they can also lead, incrementally, to language change; as Hopper (2004: 153) puts it, 'These adaptations are microscopic [...] and either go unnoticed or are dismissed as "errors," but they provide the potential basis for future use and for the analogical spread of forms.' Which innovations are propagated probably largely depends on how many contacts (weak ties) the early adopters have (Milroy and Milroy 1985).

Although many sociolinguists and critical discourse analysts look for determinants in class, race, gender, sexuality, age, region, and so on, other linguists are more receptive to individual differences. For example Barbara Johnstone (1996: xi) states that while 'It is indisputable that speech is always multi-voiced, always drawing on other speech, and that the ways we talk are constrained, shaped, and dictated to us in more ways than we realize,' it is 'also indisputable that no two individuals always speak with the same voice'. Moreover, Johnstone argues,

> As it does the other things it does – refer to situations in the world, affirm people's connectedness, comment on itself, claim assent and adherence – talk always also shows who speakers take themselves to be, how they align themselves with others and how they differentiate themselves from others. All talk displays its speaker's individual voice. This is necessary because self-expression is necessary; no matter how much a society may value conformity or define people in relationship to others, individuals must on some level express individuated selves. In order to do this, speakers must do things with

language that other speakers do not do. Each speaker, must, quite literally, be idiosyncratic.

(p. 187)

Johnstone quotes R.B. Le Page and Andrée Tabouret-Keller (1985), who view discourse as a series of acts of identity performed by individual speakers, and argue that 'every use of language is a fresh application, a metaphorical extension of existing systems, made at risk' (p. 196).

Johnstone's account of individuality, and Hunston and Francis' description of analogical creativity, and of how pattern usage is always in a state of flux, are wholly compatible with Hopper's description of grammar as open-ended, provisional, and hence temporal, and with Larsen-Freeman's (1997) account of language as a complex system. Constructions or patterns are emergent, 'that is to say, their structure never reaches a point of closure and completion [...] They are intrinsically indeterminate' (Hopper 2004: 174). The rate of microscopic, analogical adaptation or change is sufficient for Joan Bybee and Paul Hopper (2001: 19) to state that 'grammar is not fixed and absolute with a little variation sprinkled on the top, but it is variable and probabilistic to its very core.' Individual speakers' linguistic choices and their intuitions about grammaticality derive from their experience with language, although 'the criteria for such comparisons with past experience are individual, inexact, and scarcely amenable to treatment in terms of precise objective categories.'

Yet notwithstanding regular invocations of variability, adaptation and flux, the way many usage-based linguists describe language clearly reveals what ELF theorists like to call 'NS ideology.' For example, Tomasello (2003: 5–6) states that

> competence with a natural language consists of a mastery of all its items and structures, and these constitute a much more complex set of linguistic representations than the 'core grammar' of formal approaches. They include the highly canonical (core), the highly idiosyncratic (periphery), and many things in between.[16]

This is unobjectionable as a description of NS competence (and as a piece of Chomsky-bashing), but it rather precludes the possibility of (multicompetent) L2 speakers who misuse or adapt (depending on your viewpoint) or, more likely, steer clear of highly idiosyncratic 'peripheral' phrases, being competent speakers in this sense. Despite Trudgill's and Wray and Grace's accounts of the regularized, rationalized nature of English, it still contains, like all languages, a lot of 'peripheral' item-based idiosyncratic constructions. Yet although native speech communities continue to use these forms, when interacting with outsiders they are more likely to express themselves the same way as the outsiders, which leads to the development of alternative rule-based, regular and semantically transparent forms that allow speakers to express much the same meaning, but which 'serve the needs of non-native to native, or non-native to non-native, communication' (Wray and Grace 2007: 557).

We will return to the use – or non-use – of idiosyncratic items and construc-tions by ELF speakers in Chapter 6. However NNSs also tend to 'misuse' (or adapt or creatively extend) transparent, regular constructions and patterns to a far greater extent than NSs, usually by a process of analogy. Wolfgang Teubert (2009: 82) asserts that 'Analogy goes together with language awareness and an intuition of what can be said and what cannot be said. It is the native speaker's refuge. Lan-guage learners have to fight against anomalies.' Again, this is the 'traditional' EFL or SLA position, which rather contrasts with the logic of fuzziness and flexibility that underlies ELF, in which what 'can' and 'cannot' be said does not conform to ENL conventions.

The closest forerunner to Hunston and Francis' book is a description of English usage designed for language teachers and L2 learners, A.S. Hornby's *A Guide to Patterns and Usage in English* (1954). Hornby detailed patterns (primarily verb pat-terns) and the words they could be used with, and warned that learners make false analogies.[17] For example, a learner 'may suppose that because he has heard and seen "I intend (want, propose) to come," he may say or write "I suggest to come," that because he has heard and seen "Please tell me the meaning," "Please show me the way," he can say or write "Please explain me this sentence"' (Hornby 1954: v). But of course many L2 speakers of English can and *do* say and write things like *suggest to do* and *explain me*, rather than 'fight against anomalies,' and these are the kind of usages that do not bother proponents of ELF or, as ELF corpora reveal, ELF users themselves.

It appears that the processes of repetition, routinization and sedimentation described by usage-based theorists largely occur in naturally acquired languages used by specific speech communities. Although migrants moving into a new speech community may hear thousands of utterances every day, they will lack the several million adult utterances that the local children have heard. On the other hand, schoolchildren being taught a language in order to communicate with its native speakers at some future date will be exposed to far fewer target utterances or prior texts than L1 speakers, and thus have a much smaller and probably more approximate inventory of constructions. They will typically hear and produce ungrammatical as well as grammatical utterances during classroom learning, with less exact repetition and consequently less feedback and routinization. Where English learners *do* have a 'collection of hand-me-downs' or 'frequently heard utterances' or 'prior texts,' they are likely to include phrases like the ones Hornby warns against, such as *Can you explain me this?* and *I suggest to do* and *This allows to make*, etc.

Yet we are likely to find even less routinization among many ELF speakers than among L2 learners. Given that the users of a lingua franca almost by definition come from a range of L1 backgrounds, we should expect all the effects of cross-linguistic interaction discussed in the previous chapter. As mentioned in Chapter 1, Mauranen (2012: 29) describes this as second-order language contact via English. While individual speakers, or a classroom of learners, are likely to show the effects of crosslinguistic influence from a particular language (or perhaps more than one language), any given configuration of adult ELF speakers is likely to hear the influence of several different L1s, perhaps more than in any other language ever used, leading to a broad range of variation, and possibly accommodation to or convergence with previously unheard ways of saying things.

Possibly as a result of hearing different L1-influenced loan translations of phrases and constructions, ELF speakers seem to tolerate variation or 'fuzziness' in frequent items. Verb constructions, and the use of articles, determiners and prepositions vary from speaker to speaker – or in the English used by the same speaker at different times. Various patterns or frames are 'overused' as compared with ENL, while at the same time the most common verbs in ENL uses of the patterns are 'underused.' Constructions and patterns often approximate rather than imitate NES usage, and there are many non-standard collocations and not quite nativelike phraseological units. All in all, meaning takes precedence over specific forms. Examples of all this will be given in the next chapter.

Becker (1983) argues that learning other languages should involve self-transformation and new ways of 'being in the world,' rather than merely expressing your existing self, and that a lot of listening, and recognition of 'prior texts,' should precede production. But users of English as a lingua franca are not necessarily trying to transform themselves or to assimilate another culture (that of NESs). Clearly, learning to speak fluently involves a lot of listening, but all the evidence suggests that ELF users tend to hear, accommodate to, and produce a variety of forms (and so are *not* obeying Oscar Wilde's dictum that 'One should never listen. To listen is a sign of indifference to one's hearers').[18] The more ELF speakers use a wide variety of constructions or patterns or phrases or collocations influenced by a number of languages, the less any particular ways of saying things – including those that are habitual and formulaic for native speakers – will become cognitively entrenched or routinized.

Mauranen (2005: 270) has also made the splendidly extravagant claim that because ELF 'offers an interactive situation stripped of the unnecessary decorations of established turns of phrase in a specific community, it sheds light on the most fundamental characteristics of human communication.'[19] As shown above, this statement does *not* apply to most of the past 100,000 years of human communication, from which the 'interactive situation' of ELF differs quite radically. From the usage-based perspective it is quite a remarkable assertion, because the entire logic of sedimented 'recurrent partials' and routinized 'prior texts' and entrenched 'constructions' is that 'established turns of phrase' are *not* 'unnecessary decorations' but the very essence of language, even if all patterns and turns of phrase are emergent and probabilistic and open to diachronic change. But it does indeed seem to apply to ELF, which clearly has fewer established turns of phrase.

Competence, variation, and performance

However despite the inherent variability of ELF, there are still limits as to what one can comprehensibly say (English is English), and it is unlikely that fluent speakers of any language construct all their expressions from scratch. The effects of repetition and memorization still hold, even though ELF speakers are likely to encounter and accommodate to 'prior texts' that are more diverse and heterogeneous and unstable than in less diffused languages. After all, Mauranen (2009: 218) also describes ELF speech as 'fundamentally normal language use despite some surface deviations from Standard English.'

It would appear that fluent language use (or performance) involves a certain competence in memorizing, and routinizing and/or adapting the forms of a language. Pennycook (2007), however, argues that the individual only comes to exist in a given utterance or in the performance of language. He allies Judith Butler's notion of gender as performance with Hopper's account of emergent grammar, and asserts that both individuals and language are called into social being by performance: 'we are the products of our performances,' and 'rather than an underlying competence driving our performance, it is the repeated performances of language and identity that produce the semblance of being' (p. 63). Just as for Butler the body has no 'prior ontological status outside its inscription into discourse' (Pennycook 2007: 70), and 'gender is always a doing, though not a doing by a subject who might be said to pre-exist the deed' (Butler 1990: 25), for Pennycook language, identity and linguistic competence do not pre-exist performance but are actually the by-product of performance.

Pennycook thus uses Hopper's account of speech as 'a vast collection of hand-me-downs' to 'challenge the centrality of competence (underlying system) over performance' (2007: 73). Yet 'underlying system' is an overly restrictive definition of competence. It is true that Chomsky (1965: 3) famously (or infamously) defined competence as the perfect knowledge of a language possessed by 'an ideal speaker-listener, in a completely homogeneous speech community,' two wholly imaginary constructs that do not exist with regard to native languages any more than to lingua francas. Yet Hymes' (1972: 286) 'communicative competence' is more broadly conceived as involving 'the systematically possible, the feasible, and the appropriate.' True, the notion of system is still there, but from an emergent grammar perspective, what is possible and feasible is clearly open to change. The question then becomes what is appropriate, which depends on the context and the interlocutors. How speakers perform linguistically (how they speak) does indeed depend on 'a wide array of social, cultural and discursive forces' (Pennycook: 2007: 60), but the way a speaker responds or adapts to these forces can still be conceived of as a form of linguistic competence; there is no reason to state that 'what ties performances together is not a competence that lies within each individual' (p. 60). Speaking appropriately to a context does not so much make competence 'the product of performance' (p. 59) as make it the ability that allows us to vary our performance according to circumstances.

Even if you believe, like Hopper (and the present author), that languages are 'the sedimented products of repeated acts of identity,' it is unnecessary to deny, as Pennycook does, that languages are 'entities that pre-exist our linguistic performances' (p. 13); it is precisely those sedimented products that pre-exist any particular utterance which uses or adapts them, and permit us to perform linguistically. It's all very well wishing to avoid 'foundationalist categories of language, identity, culture or gender' (p. 13), but the fact remains that you cannot speak at all without having some prior knowledge of a language – a repertoire (or foundation) of words, phrases and constructions (or alternatively, an ability to function – in either a conformist or transgressive way – in a repertoire of communicative contexts).[20] Pennycook himself states that the 'transgressive' theories and uses of language that he endorses would be 'impossible without some presumed order worth transgressing' (p. 42). That presumed order must include a language or languages that pre-exist our linguistic performances, although with ELF speakers it is often hard to know whether they are consciously or intentionally transgressing something, or whether they merely lack sufficient exposure to stable varieties of English for the constructions that make up the presumed order to have become entrenched.[21]

Hence linguistic competence can also be seen as choosing the right words (or the right 'sedimented products') for the right people in the right circumstances. As Valentin Voloshinov (1929/1973: 86) put it:

> The word [*slovo*] is a two-sided act. It is determined equally by *whose* word it is and *for whom* it is meant. As a word, it is precisely *the product of the reciprocal relationship between speaker and listener*, addresser and addressee. […] I give myself verbal shape from another's point of view, ultimately from the point of view of the community to which I belong. A word is a bridge thrown between myself and another. If one end of the bridge depends on me, then the other depends on my addressee. A word is territory shared.[22]

Both Voloshinov and Mikhail Bakhtin also point out the extent to which we use reported (and misreported) speech; as Bakhtin (1934–35/1981: 339) puts it:

> We need only keep our ears open to the speech sounding everywhere around us to reach such a conclusion: in the everyday speech of any person living in society, no less than half (on the average) of all the words uttered by him will be someone else's words (consciously someone else's) transmitted with varying degrees of precision and impartiality (or more precisely, partiality).

Other people's words are incontestably 'prior texts,' and as Becker (1994: 164) puts it, 'Appropriating prior text is a necessary, nonfaultable plagiarism […] that we all practice every time we speak or write. It's an ordinary thing.' While some people happily take over prior texts, others feel the need to individualize them; as Johnstone (1996: 19) puts it, 'linguistic idiosyncrasy is […] a cultural and psychological requirement for many speakers.' Repeated use of the same or similar linguistic idiosyncrasies by the same speaker, leading to an identifiable idiolect, rather suggests the existence of an individual or subject that precedes individual performances.

Voloshinov's arguments about utterances being two-sided acts or shared territory, and full of reported speech obviously apply to ELF just as much as, if not more than, 'ordinary' languages, with the apparent difference that in ELF, prior texts are likely to be reported or repeated with greater (grammatical and phraseological) variation. Once again, ELF does not need to be considered entirely separately from ENL. The next chapter will seek to give concrete examples of all the theoretical arguments presented in this one.

Notes

1 VOICE, LEcon418 transcribes this differently as *overfilled*.
2 Perhaps that should be 'as *almost* everybody knows'; although, as Trudgill (2011: 35) puts it, the inability of most adults to learn languages perfectly, especially in untutored situations, is a 'well-known fact, obvious to anyone who has been alive and present in normal human societies for a couple of decades or so,' there are some linguists who challenge the critical period hypothesis – see, e.g. Birdsong (ed.) (1999), and Pavlenko (2005: 10) who says, 'Rather there exists an age-of-acquisition effect that is mediated by the amount of exposure, interaction, motivation, and individual differences.'
3 See also Trudgill (1989, 2009, 2010).
4 Latin too changed to analyticity as it spread as an L2 in the Roman Empire; see Clackson and Horrocks (2007). Szmrecsanyi (2012) shows that the history of English is slightly more complex than this: there was a huge increase in analyticity in the thirteenth and fourteenth centuries, and stasis between the fourteenth and seventeenth centuries, with a steady drift toward more syntheticity and less analyticity since then. Szmrecsanyi (2009) shows that speech always tends to be more analytic and less synthetic than writing, and that written English has become more synthetic over the past forty or so years. Szmrecsanyi and Kortmann (2011) show that learner English is significantly more analytic than indigenized L2 varieties. They describe anti-syntheticity as an 'SLA universal' (see Klein and Perdue 1997). Comparing ELF corpora with learner English corpora has yet to be done.
5 Trudgill (2011: 67) goes as far as to describe 'most of the major standard language varieties in Europe today' as 'relatively high-contact *koinés* and *creoloids* which are the result of simplification resulting from dialect and language contact.' A *koiné* (Ancient Greek for *common*) is a variety resulting from dialect mixture, probably regularized and simplified but not reduced or limited in function, and a creoloid is a variety which has undergone admixture and simplification relative to a source language but without ever having been a reduced pidgin that expanded into a creole. Apart from modern English, a more extreme example of a simplified creoloid resulting from widespread language contact and non-native acquisition is Afrikaans in South Africa, compared with Dutch.
6 Specifically, Schrijver (2006) argues that Late British survived until at least the tenth century in the western half of England, the whole of Wales and much of Scotland.
7 Tristram (2004) suggests that morphological complexity disappeared from spoken English long before the written language, because a small literate elite deliberately preserved the 'correct' version (just as written Latin survived even when everyone was speaking one of the Romance languages that descended from it).
8 Winford (2003: 245) also argues that fossilization is an inappropriate term for group SLA as it assumes that the group is aiming at a faithful reproduction of the target language when they might in fact choose (at least subconsciously) to retain L1 features so as to preserve a group identity distinct from that of the target language group.
9 Not everyone is likely to be convinced by this theory. For example, Thomason and Kaufman (1988), attacking an earlier theory that Middle English was an Anglo-French creole, in a wonderfully combative style – 'The purpose of this book is to introduce

some *subtlety* into the thoughts and words of historical linguists' (p. 328) – insist that 'There does not seem to be any reason to believe that the degree of change exhibited in English between A.D. 900 and A.D. 1250 (350 years) is anything other than normal.' They argue instead that although Middle English underwent 'Norsification' (pp. 282ff.), 'From 900 to 1600 English overall shows no evidence of having undergone […] simplification due to language contact' (p. 331). They point out that many other European languages also lost the dative case and gender agreement (p. 320). The imperfect-learning-by-Celts argument also ticks *all* the boxes – namely causal, functional, genetic, abductive and teleological explanations – that irk Lass (1997), for whom language users 'have to make do with what's historically presented to them, and cope with it when it changes' (p. xviii).

10 In this article Hopper seems to wholly subsume grammar into discourse, but despite arguing that 'discourse in a broad sense provides the only motivation for grammar' (1992: 364), he concedes elsewhere (1988: 118) that both EOG and APGP as he describes them are extreme positions, and that 'many linguists in practice occupy a place somewhere between these two poles.'

11 The inseparability of grammar and lexicon led Bybee (1998/2007) to write 'The emergent lexicon' as a partner to Hopper's (1987) article 'Emergent grammar.'

12 For example, a NES might know the highly general, abstract, schematic, ditransitive construction **Subj V Obj$_1$ Obj$_2$**, e.g. *He gave her a book*, but also store many tokens of it such as *He gave her a break / a piece of his mind / a run for her money / a taste of her own medicine / a wide berth / as good as he got / hell / her head / his best shot / the boot / the cold shoulder / the creeps / the green light / the nod / the once-over / the push / the runaround / the silent treatment / the slip / the third degree*, etc.

13 This account of language also calls into question Levelt's (1989) language processing model, as well as De Bot's (1992) bilingual version, with a formulator (coming between the conceptualizer and the articulator) that separates lexical and grammatical processing.

14 Syntactic collocations (words that come with particular grammatical patterns) are also called *colligations*, a term coined by Firth (1957/1968: 182).

15 Hunston and Francis divide the verbs used with this pattern into eighteen different meaning groups, and give examples of common and rarely used verbs. However Israel (1996) shows the remarkable creativity of this construction, amply demonstrating that lists of verbs used with specific constructions can never be finite.

16 Indeed the genesis of Construction Grammar (capitalized by Fillmore *et al.* 1988) was an attempt to model idiosyncratic form and meaning pairings that cannot be derived from any general rules – opaque or arbitrary idiomatic expressions containing semantic, lexical and syntactic irregularities. Construction grammarians only later extended their account of form–meaning correspondences to the syntax and morphology of regular, rule-based structures.

17 There are also many more recent books for both learners and teachers similarly designed to highlight and correct common errors, false analogies and over-extended patterns, including Leech *et al.* (2001), Swan and Smith (2001), Swan (2005), Parrott (2010), as well as the *Oxford Advanced Learner's Dictionary*, 8th edn (2010).

18 From 'A few maxims for the instruction of the over-educated,' (1894/2000: 571).

19 In Mauranen (2012) this is rephrased as 'the notion of lingua franca use as focusing on what is most crucial to communication and most central to language […] stripped of its most contingent and volatile aspects' (pp. 100, 101).

20 Seidlhofer (2011: 97) puts it this way: 'It is obvious that when we perform, although we may not follow a pregiven script, we are prompted by some established framework of expectation, or otherwise the performance would be meaningless. Similarly, creativity presupposes the existence of conventional norms against which its non-conformity can be realized.' Hence 'competence serves as a prompt that inspires or gives rise to an expression, not as a script to be adhered to in every particular' (p. 110).

21 Pennycook (2007: 38, 43) also states rather wearily that it is time we took for granted the notions that interpretations are contingent, subjects are constructed, knowledge is

enmeshed in power, there is no position outside discourse, etc., and moved on. Yes indeed. But his accounts of performance and transgression seem to be contingent on a particular theoretical model that is a better fit for gender theory than language. Though as Abraham Lincoln is reputed to have said, 'People who like this sort of thing will find this the sort of thing they like'!

22 *Slovo* could also be translated as 'utterance' or 'discourse.' Pennycook (2007: 72) quotes a similar passage from Bakhtin (1934–35/1981: 293) in which Bakhtin, as so often, recycles Voloshinov – see Bronckart and Bota (2011); an English translation is forthcoming.

4
THE GRAMMAR OF ELF

> educated English, wherever it is found, almost always has the same grammar
>
> Smith and Rafiqzad (1983: 57)

> the amount of grammar that is needed in order to support the vast majority of daily human activities is substantially less than is often supposed to be the case
>
> Gil (2009: 20)

As already outlined in Chapter 1, eager attempts in the early years of this century to codify ELF as a viable alternative to ENL and a model for language learning seem to have been largely superseded by a broad consensus that ELF is a *function* of language rather than a specific variety or a set of forms. But of course if that function of language produces forms that differ from any variety of native English, they can be analysed and described. Even if no-one is trying to write grammars and dictionaries describing ELF (or, more modestly, 'European ELF,' 'Asian ELF,' etc.), or produce coursebooks that would enable it to be taught, it is easy to identify recurrent and predictable lexicogrammatical features in ELF. On the other hand, were someone to announce a codification of ELF, most users would probably feel unconcerned; as Mauranen (2012: 199) says, 'What clearly looks like being relegated to a secondary role is grammatical accuracy, as interaction does not seem to be much hampered by uncertainties and fluctuations in grammar.' To put it another way, structural features 'tolerate a good deal of turbulence without disrupting communication' (p. 123), and 'ELF speakers show a good deal of linguistic creativity in producing novel expressions that solve the communicative problem at hand, even if they result in ungrammatical forms or non-existent lexis from a Standard English viewpoint' (pp. 199–200). Mauranen even concludes that 'The variability of structure in use and the frequency of non-standard structural features would appear to call into question the significance of structure to successful communication' (p. 130), even in the high-level academic communication which makes up the million-word Helsinki/Tampere English as a Lingua Franca in Academic Settings corpus (ELFA).[1]

'Non-existent' lexis will be considered in the next chapter; this chapter will describe some of the more regular grammatical features (or 'ungrammatical forms') of ELF, and their probable causes, of which three seem to be important. Some regularities involve the simplification (and reconceptualization) of inherently 'difficult' elements of English grammar – those which appear odd or afunctional or idiosyncratic from the perspective of speakers of most other languages. Other features in the grammar of specific ELF users are clearly the result of crosslinguistic interaction with (or interference or transfer from) particular L1s. Still other features result from an orientation to increased explicitness and clarity, which is often necessary in a heterogeneous and unstable lingua franca. All such non-standard and non-native features are in competition in ELF. Many of them probably go unnoticed a lot of the time, but the simpler and more useful ones tend to be picked up and re-used as speakers accommodate to each other's uses.

Standard and non-standard native grammars and L2 learners

Before we come to the discussion of the grammar of ELF, a few remarks about ENL are in order. It is often overlooked that the grammar used – regularly and systematically – by the majority of NESs does not correspond to the grammar set out in most English language teaching coursebooks and grammar manuals. Such books are based on a construct that, for want of a better term, is usually called 'educated standard English,' or StE for short. The same applies to other languages. Kirkpatrick (2010: 154–55) cites a study which reports on tests of the language of L2 Swedish speakers who were taken to be NSs of Swedish by 'real' NSs of Swedish. Extensive tests revealed that 'only a few of the early learners and none of the late learners exhibited actual, linguistic nativelikeness across the board when their performance was examined in detail' (Abrahamsson and Hyltenstam 2009: 293). Yet none of the Swedish NSs who took the same tests scored 100 per cent either, which rather problematizes normative notions of nativelikeness.

Trudgill has long argued that StE is the home dialect of only about 12 per cent of the British population (see Trudgill 1974, 1999, 2002: 71). Everybody else uses some or many non-standard forms. As Widdowson (2003: 37) puts it, 'Most speakers of English, even those who are to the language born, speak non-standard varieties of the language and have themselves to be instructed in the standard at school.' There was a lot of kids in my school in London what spoke different to what the teachers did, and one of them who was well cocky, all four foot nothing of him, actually told a teacher 'We ain't never gonna stop saying all them things you was calling wrong cos it's a lot more easier our way, and anyway, it don't matter.' The teacher went mental but we all thought he'd done brilliant, innit.[2]

The previous two sentences illustrate most of the 'common core of non-standard forms that are used by the majority of people in [England], and which don't appear to be regionally circumscribed' (Britain 2007: 78):[3] There was a lot of kids (*is/was* in plural existential) in my school in London what (*what* for *that* as a relative pronoun) spoke different (adverbs without-*ly*) to what the teachers did (*what* as relative pronoun again), and one of them who was well cocky (adverbs as intensifiers), all four foot nothing of him (absence of plural marking on nouns of measurement), actually told a teacher 'We ain't (*ain't* instead of *isn't* or *aren't*) never (double or multiple negation) gonna stop saying all them things (*them* as a distal plural demonstrative) you was (*was* in the second person, and third person plural) calling wrong cos it's a lot more easier (irregular comparatives) our way, and anyway, it don't matter' (*don't* for third person *doesn't*). The teacher went mental but we all thought he'd done brilliant (adverb without-*ly* again), innit (*innit* as an invariable question tag).

Some of these non-standard forms – namely plural *is* (*There's two of them*), multiple negation, default singulars (*They was*), and absence of plural marking on nouns of measurement – occur so frequently in the world's Englishes that they have been described as *vernacular universals*: grammatical processes that occur in working-class and rural vernaculars, child language, pidgins and creoles, as well as in interlanguage varieties.[4] There is certainly nothing new about them: see, e.g. H.L. Mencken's (1921: 388) parody, 'The Declaration of Independence in American':

> first, me and you is as good as anybody else, and maybe a damn sight better; second, nobody ain't got no right to take away none of our rights; third, every man has got a right to live, to come and go as he pleases, and to have a good time whichever way he likes, so long as he don't interfere with nobody else. That any government that don't give a man them rights ain't worth a damn [etc.]

All of these non-standard forms are widely shared dialect features, and hence not to be confused with intentionally idiosyncratic or transgressive language use by individuals, which can also be found in any form of English, native or otherwise. An important caveat is that this largely applies to the *spoken* language alone; written English (excluding text messages and internet chat rooms) more often conforms to StE norms.

However the model in foreign language teaching is generally the language of the minority of NSs who speak the standard educated version of their language. But to what extent do NNSs actually need to emulate this language, or approximate the knowledge of NSs? Seidlhofer (2011: 50–52) discusses a well-known study by René Coppieters (1987) which reported 'near-native' NNSs of French with 'important professional positions in France' stating they hadn't developed any intuitions about complicated grammatical distinctions such as that between the imperfect and the *passé composé*. Although Randolph Quirk (1990) uses this study to argue for the importance of nativelikeness and native teachers, Seidlhofer very reasonably suggests that 'Coppieters' results indicate very clearly that speakers can get by perfectly well in an L2 and that they can be successful in "important professional positions" without developing native-speaker intuitions about every aspect of the language' (Seidlhofer 2011: 52).

ELF speakers, largely communicating with other NNESs, have even less need than most L2 speakers to master all the complicated grammatical patterns used by NSs – or indeed to be aware of all of their grammatical conceptualizations. As mentioned in Chapter 2, the orthodox SLA position is that foreign language learning should involve conceptual restructuring and the acquisition of new grammatical and lexical categories. For example, Kramsch (2006: 103) states that

> Many students abandon their study of a foreign or heritage language after one or two semesters because they do not understand what is entailed in learning to mean in another language. They think it is just a question of replacing one label with another on the familiar furniture of the universe. They do not expect that the furniture itself will be changed in the process.[5]

At the grammatical level, this 'furniture' might well involve such things as the categories of mass and count nouns, and event conceptualization patterns.

The English categories of mass and count nouns, and the system of singulars and plurals, are manifestly different from those of most other languages, but few learners abandon their study of English because of this. At first (and second, and third) glance, the English mass/count distinction appears to be arbitrary, but Anna Wierzbicka (1985) offers a set of reasons. For example, plural *peas* can be seen as *individual entities* and are clearly bigger than uncountable grains of *rice*. One might prepare a meal with a few *onions*, but only use a small amount of *garlic*. You tend to see and use *chives* in small quantities, whereas you often see vast expanses of *grass*. You can see individual *oats*, but not when they are turned into 'stuffs' such as *porridge*. Entities like *water* are *arbitrarily divisible*. If you divide some water into parts, each resulting part will still be water, but if you chop up a *chair*, the resulting parts will not be chairs; indeed one cannot remove the part without destroying the whole. Dual objects such as *scissors* are countable and logically plural; one part of them on their own is fairly useless. *Furniture* and *clothing* are mass nouns because they involve counting *different kinds* of heterogeneous objects, unlike, say, counting different types of *tree* or *bird*, which are all trees and birds. *Groceries* and *leftovers* are plural because they are the names of heterogeneous collections of objects and/or stuffs, some of which may not be separate things. Some nouns can be both count and mass: you may be able to count *hairs* on your chin, but not the *hair* on your head. You can count small *chocolates* or *stones*, which have different properties from *chocolate* or *stone* in the abstract. And so on.[6] Consequently, Wierzbicka argues, this part of English grammar turns out to be semantically motivated: 'The apparent idiosyncrasies, far from being arbitrary, are revealing of subtle distinctions in the underlying conceptualizations' (p. 334).

From a cognitive linguistic perspective, one would *want* this to be true, and while each of Wierzbicka's explanations – she proposes 16 classes of countables, singularia and pluralia (pp. 337–41) – has a certain plausibility, and may indeed be at the origin of the grammatical behaviour of particular words, it seems very unlikely that individual NESs are aware of, or able to explain, many of these distinctions. Certainly, speakers of many different L1s conceptualize count and non-count nouns differently from NESs, and consequently use English nouns such as *advice* (or rather, *advices*), *equipments*, *evidences*, *feedbacks*, *furnitures*, *informations*, *luggages*, *researches* and *staffs* as pluralizable count nouns. Similar simplification (or reconceptualization) is widespread in African and Asian Englishes (see Brutt-Griffler 2002; Kachru and Smith 2008; Platt *et al.*, 1984; Schmied 1991; Trudgill and Hannah 2008).[7] Thus plurals such as *informations* – used in announcements and leaflets in virtually every airport in the world outside inner circle countries – would appear to be a codifiable (and clearly comprehensible) ELF usage.

Another example of grammatical 'furniture' (or furnitures) that should change if L2 learners are to speak like NSs is event conceptualization patterns. The way events are construed is influenced by the available grammatical categories, which focus attention on certain aspects of a given situation. Grammaticalized linguistic categories such as tense and aspect lead to automatized preferences – language-specific principles of information organization. Some languages obligatorily express aspectual viewpoint – ongoingness (the progressive), perfectivity, imperfectivity – by verbal morphology, while others can only (optionally) convey the same type of information lexically. This leads speakers to segment events in different ways, to pay attention to different things, and to structure their utterances differently; Dan Slobin (1996) calls this 'thinking for speaking.'

A case in point is verbs of motion. English, German and Russian are 'satellite-framed' languages which tend to encode manner in the verb expressing motion, and direction in a 'satellite' such as a preposition, prefix or particle (*run in, sprint in, dash in*), while French and Spanish are 'verb-framed' languages that encode movement in a verb, leaving manner to be optionally marked in a 'satellite' (*entrer en courant, entrar corriendo*) (Talmy 1991). So the English sentence *He swam across the Channel* (with a precise verb) becomes *Il traversa la Manche à la nage* in French, where the verb is vague, but made more explicit by *à la nage*. Getting this wrong – *Il essaie de nager à travers la Manche* – leads to an awkward sounding sentence.[8] Similarly, the French calque *He tries to cross the Channel by swimming* sounds odd to a NES, but is less likely to cause any ripples or breakdowns in ELF communication. It is generally argued that more proficient or advanced 'coordinate' bilinguals tend to shift their cognition towards the L2, by internalizing novel grammatical categories, partly or wholly restructuring their previous L1 categories.[9] In contrast, 'subordinate' bilinguals tend to transfer L1 habits, perhaps attempting word-for-word translations, using what Romuald Gozdawa-Gołębiowski (2008) calls 'contentive' processing (see Chapter 6).[10] This can lead to clumsy-sounding sentences, but once again such linguistic subtleties are less important in a lingua franca. ELF users interacting with other NNESs have less need to approximate the conceptual categories of NESs than immigrants in new linguacultures and people learning languages in order to communicate with their native speakers.

Recurrent grammatical features in ELF

As one would expect, the identifiable regularities in the speech of ELF users which do not coincide with the grammar of ENL, or at least StE, are mainly simplifications of those areas of StE which differ from the majority of natural languages, and which are therefore 'difficult' for L2 learners.[11]

A notable feature in spoken ELF is the *sporadic non-use of the third person singular -s suffix*. Trudgill (2002: 167) describes the (ENL) use of this inflection in an otherwise unmarked verb tense as one of the remaining 'grammatical idiosyncrasies of Standard English,' and a 'typological oddity' (p. 98). Given the accompanying third person pronoun it is communicatively redundant, and just the type of 'afunctional grammatical category' (p. 92) likely to be simplified as a result of language contact.

In a study of the English used in meetings of representatives from a number of European universities (part of VOICE), Angelika Breiteneder (2009) found the use of both inflectionally marked and unmarked third person singular verbs. The percentage of uninflected forms is relatively low, though it becomes more significant if you exclude fixed expressions (or 'chunks') most probably learnt holistically (*this means that, it depends on, it seems that, it makes no sense,* etc.), and the verbatim repetition of what other participants have said previously. Breiteneder also highlights examples of zero marking used with indefinite subjects such as *everybody* and *nobody* which can easily be interpreted as having a plural meaning, even though in StE they combine with singular verb forms. In another study of a spoken corpus, Alessia Cogo and Martin Dewey (2006) found zero marking of the third person singular in 52 per cent of cases, with -s tending to occur in formal settings, often with a NES present.[12]

Since non-use of the third person -s has almost certainly not been *taught* – despite the fact that many applied linguists have long stressed its superfluity (see, e.g. Lewis 1993: 26)[13] – it can be seen as a natural language development, in the expected direction of reduced redundancy and increased regularity, rather than as simply an 'error' and the result of imperfect learning of ENL. Present tense zero marking is also found in East Anglian dialects in England (Trudgill 2002: 97), and about half of all World English varieties (Kortmann *et al.* (eds) 2004), as well as in African American Vernacular English and West African and Caribbean creoles. Seidlhofer (2011: 145) describes this as 'a reductive strategy that follows what might be called the principle of appropriate communicative economy.' However this natural development in ELF is clearly countered by the fact that many (or perhaps most) ELF users do not exist in an ELF-speaking bubble, but are also exposed to ENL in which the vast majority of present tense third person verbs (probably 100 per cent in the written language) continue to have an -s on the end (as indeed do almost 80 per cent in Breiteneder's spoken data).

Cogo and Dewey's claim that ELF speakers limit their non-ENL uses in the presence of a NES makes them sound like children who misbehave when the teacher goes out of the classroom, and as a NES there's no way I can find out *in situ* whether this is true (rather as I can't know for sure that the light in the fridge stays off when I close the door). Alternatively, it 'indicates that speakers in ELF settings will often make use of the resources in their linguistic repertoires in ways that are both efficient and effective, but that they do so with acute awareness of the identities of their interlocutors' (Jenkins *et al.* 2011: 291). However if ELF speakers really do accommodate to NESs in this way, it rather undermines the claim that NESs will need 'an additionally acquired language system' in order to 'communicate successfully in ELF settings where [...] they are no longer the norm providers' (Cogo and Jenkins 2010: 275). (I will return to this point in Chapter 8.)

Another sporadic simplification in ELF is the *regularization of past tense forms*. As outlined in Chapter 3, the regularization of irregular inflectional forms has been occurring in English for hundreds of years, as the language moved from synthetic to analytical structures. The regularization of past tenses is slightly more advanced in American English than British English, but seems to be more advanced still in ELF. There are a number of examples in ELFA (see Chapter 5), including the following:

> and so anyway finland itself was quite unsure if it actually should join the UN er during those years president paasikivi er first of all was against the united nations because he **feeled** that within er the organisation they would be dealt too much with erm great power conflicts and he didn't want finland to get its fingers burned
>
> *(ELFA USEMP01E)*

Although some would argue that getting irregular past tenses wrong is an elementary error, and that the correct forms are normally acquired at an early stage in the learning of English as an L2, ELFA shows clearly that proficient ELF users (such as the one in the excerpt above, who also uses the ENL idiom *get its fingers burned*) occasionally (but not consistently) regularize irregular forms. Even if they are rarely encountered, such regularized forms are readily comprehensible.

The use of *prepositions* in ELF also shows signs of simplification: e.g. Mauranen (2012: 124) suggests that *in* 'seems to be a kind of generalized preposition of time or place,' frequently standing in for *at* as used in ENL. There is also much wider variability in the use of prepositions compared with ENL. ELFA includes accumulate *to*, focus *to*, have an intuitive interest *on*, insisted *for*, obsession *in*, satisfied *at*, etc.; Cogo and Dewey (2012: 57) cite consequences *on*, depends *of*, implications *on*, and to influence *on*, as well as the omission of prepositions, as in *look this picture, listening music* and *it depends the job*. They do, however, concede that 'occurrences of *listen* without *to*' in the VOICE data – six cases out of seventy-eight – are 'relatively low' (p. 54). Similarly, Platt *et al.* (1984) give examples from New Englishes, including put *off* a fire, voice *out* an opinion, result *into*, deprive *from*, cope *up with*, as well as *apply* without *for*, *provide* without *with*, etc.

Cogo and Dewey (2012: 52) suggest that dependent prepositions which (in ENL) collocate with a preceding lexical item have 'little or no semantic value,' which is true unless the preceding lexical item is the first part of a phrasal or prepositional verb, and the preposition distinguishes the verb from many others. But although to some observers, preposition use in ELF seems merely to show a lot of variation, Cogo and Dewey suggest that 'many of the prepositional patterns are undergoing some transition' and that maybe 'distinct patterns of use are emerging' (p. 55). However for a rigid and essentially unmotivated pattern (that differed from ENL) to appear would be somewhat surprising (even if speakers accommodate to each other's uses – see below); a simplification strategy along the lines of 'use whatever proposition seems to fit' would appear to be a much more likely outcome. Kirkpatrick (2010: 175) states that 'insisting on the use of a specific preposition in a specific context,' as used in ENL, is 'an unnecessary waste of curriculum time'; the same would almost certainly be true of teaching supposedly emerging ELF patterns.

One area in which patterns *do* appear to be developing, in ELF as well as in World Englishes, is in the creation of what Nadja Nesselhauf (2009) calls 'new' or 'non-L1' *prepositional verbs* by the addition of prepositions that give more emphasis, as in *address to* (someone), *answer to* (a question), *contact with, criticize about, discuss about, emphasise on, mention about, phone to, reject against, return back, stress on, study about, understand about*, etc. (see also Seidlhofer 2011: 145ff.; Cogo and Dewey 2012: 52ff.; Platt *et al.* 1984: 84). Contrary to the zero third person -*s*, this complicates rather than simplifies the structure, increasing rather than reducing redundancy (from an ENL perspective), although of course the addition of the preposition is designed to make the verb clearer and more explicit (i.e. simpler to understand). Some of these constructions are specifically warned against in grammar books such as the *Cambridge Grammar of English* (Carter and McCarthy 2006), but they appear to facilitate production and reception. The prepositions lend more weight to the verb, as well as giving more processing time. They generally involve regularization by analogy – *discuss about* is on a pattern with *talk, speak, argue* and *chat about; study* and *understand about* are similar to *learn, know* and *read about; ask to* (someone) distinguishes it from, e.g. *ask a question; answer to* is similar to *reply to*, and also distinguishes the verb *answer* from the noun; and so on. There is also an analogy with nominal usage – *an answer to a question / to answer to a question*, etc.

The use of *articles* and *plurals* in ELF often differs from ENL. Both *a* and *the* are often used where ENL doesn't use them, and omitted where ENL does have them. For example, Cogo and Dewey (2012: 98) correctly state that '*the* is often used in ELF for general reference, either with uncountable and abstract nouns, or with plural uncountable nouns.' Yet instead of seeing this as a probable transfer pattern from languages that do not distinguish between countable and uncountable, and generic, concrete and abstract nouns, they describe it in terms of speakers emphasizing the 'keyness' of a noun in an utterance by adding the definite article before it (p. 100). Similarly, they consider the use of zero article as a case of the speaker considering a noun to be relatively unimportant, although most analysts would consider Polish speakers saying, e.g. *from Polish perspective* and *in Polish language* to be simply instances of transfer from a language without articles. Moreover, article use in ELF can be both non-standard and inconsistent: Mauranen (2012: 52) gives examples of speakers using *the* and zero article with the same nouns in the same sentence entirely arbitrarily.

Given all the 'rules' concerning countable and uncountable, and concrete and abstract nouns, as well as the myriad of fixed expressions containing articles, article use in ENL is extremely complicated – e.g. *hunger* but *an insatiable hunger*; *elegance* but *a Parisian elegance*; *nature* but *the nature of the beast*; *last year* but *in the last year*; *as a last resort* but *in the last resort*; etc. Consequently, it is unsurprising to find different but somewhat unpredictable usages of *a*, *the* and zero article in ELF. Platt *et al.* (1984: 55–56) also report an absence of articles in Indian and West and East African Englishes. However Mauranen (2012: 125) puts trust in statistics: given that *a* is more frequent in the 1.8 million word Michigan Corpus of Academic Spoken English (MICASE) than in ELFA[14] – the seventh as opposed to the eleventh most used word – she says that non-standard article use is not necessarily a collection of random errors, but 'may reflect an ongoing reshuffle of article functions.' She speculates, very tentatively, that this 'may mean sliding towards a system where zero replaces *a(n)*' (p. 129). Some ELF speakers also substitute *some* for articles before both singular and plural nouns.

The use of *plurals* in ELF similarly differs from ENL. The frequent use of plurals with nouns that are uncountable in ENL was mentioned above. Nouns are also sometimes used without a plural when there is an explicit number in the sentence, e.g. *200 degree / two type of / We have four parameter / two more condition*, etc. (Björkman 2008b: 38; see also Björkman 2008a), as also happens in many World Englishes (Platt *et al.* 1984: 47). In Asian Englishes (both World Englishes and ELF), there is also a phonetic reason for the frequent absence of the plural *-s*, as using it would often create a word-final consonant cluster, which many speakers are unable to pronounce (Platt *et al.* 1984: 48; Kirkpatrick 2010: 106). *Determiners* and *quantifiers* are also occasionally used without plurals – e.g. *all the detail / There are some difference / several conclusion* (Björkman 2008b: 38) – presumably according to the same logic as above: the quantifier already implies plurality. Mauranen (2012: 125, 154) finds increased use of *some* as a plural, often in place of *few* and *a few*, including in the expression like *I would like to say some words about*. Platt *et al.* (1984: 60) also give examples of articles being dropped and quantifiers used in ways that disregard the count/uncount distinction – *so much sweets, buy few articles, few minutes from beginning, say some few words, I did bit shopping, put little bit pepper*, etc.

Another area in which English differs from most other languages is in its use of progressive and perfect *aspectual forms*. Few languages have an overtly specified, grammaticalized progressive form, and many ELF users, like the speakers of many outer circle varieties, use the progressive rather than the present simple where it is infrequently used in ENL, with stative verbs and verbs with habitual meaning (e.g. *I'm understanding, are belonging to*, etc.). Elina Ranta (2006) suggests that the *be* and the *-ing* ending clearly signify that a verb is being used (as opposed to a formally identical noun), which both gives the speaker more time in production and helps the listener's processing. Mauranen (2012: 199) describes the use of the (peri-phrastic) continuous rather than the simple present as another example of transparency, or of analyticity replacing syntheticity, and Benedikt Szmrecsanyi and Bernd Kortmann (2009) describe it as an 'Angloversal' (hence also found in New Englishes; see Schmied 1991).

A further feature common to ELF and outer circle varieties is the conflation of the present perfect and the past simple with definite past time reference, so that there is no distinction between *I have seen him yesterday* and *I saw him yesterday*. Contrarily, the present simple rather than the present perfect is often used to express continuing time spans, as in *He works here for three years*. There is also a frequent blurring of the ENL semantic distinction between *since* and *for*, with *since* being used for the duration of a time span (*since three years*) as well as to refer to its starting point (*since 2010*). All these could be described as examples of over-generalization and consequent simplification, which render an element of the native grammar redundant – or simply as examples of language change. Certainly native uses of aspectual forms do not seem to be communicatively crucial for many outer and expanding circle speakers. Elizabeth Erling (2002: 11) points out that students are often unaware of using tense and aspect 'incorrectly,' and glumly tell teachers 'I thought I was good at English until I took this course.' She suggests that rather than being examples of ENL having been falsely analysed, these uses 'are actually a symptom of a change in the language which is coming about in non-native contexts but is being held back by the standard English tradition.'

As outlined in the previous chapter, Hunston and Francis (1999) describe typical patterns in (native) English usage, such as phraseologies attached to nouns, and verb complementation patterns. They list common verbs found in particular patterns, although they concede that there is a certain amount of 'leakage' across patterns. ELF data show that many *verb complementation patterns* differ from those of ENL. A significant difference is that ELF users extend (or overgeneralize) the use of the *to*-infinitive as a complement in place of the gerund (or in Hunston and Francis' shorthand, use **V to-inf** instead of **V-ing**). In ENL, there are head nouns, adjectives and verbs that can only be followed by a *to*-infinitive (*I want to do*), others that can only be followed by a gerund (*deny doing*), often preceded by a particular preposition (*accused of doing, responsible for doing*), and a smaller group that take both types of complements, sometimes with a difference in meaning (*forget to do, forget doing*) and sometimes without (*chances to win, chances of winning*). Many ELF speakers use the *to*-infinitive where the vast majority of NESs would not, as in *look forward to make, interested to do, suggest to do* and *worth to do*. For speakers of many languages, use of the (unmarked and uninflected) infinitive can be seen as a case of L1 transfer (cf. Nemser 1991), but disregarding the gerund and its accompanying prepositions can also be seen as a case of simplification, equally found in many African and Asian varieties (see Kachru and Smith, 2008, Chapter 6).[15] Other examples of verbs used in different patterns than in ENL include *explain me* instead of *explain to me* (as Hornby noticed in the 1950s), *allows to do* instead to *allows you to do*, etc. In general, Schneider (2012: 76) suggests that if there is a choice (even if one alter-native is non-standard), speakers of both New Englishes and ELF have a natural tendency to prefer finite to non-finite complementation, and particularly fully analytic and transparent or isomorphic constructions in which each word corresponds to a semantic element – e.g. *I want that he should do that* instead of *I want him to do that.*

We also – by definition – find various (putative) 'vernacular universals' in ELF, including the plural *is* in existential constructions (*there is also many factors*), and *would* and *would have* in hypothetical if-clauses (e.g. *if their price would be the same; if I would have left in one month*).[16] Other posited grammatical features of ELF, listed in early articles by Seidlhofer (2003, 2004, 2005a, 2005b), include the interchangeable use of the relative pronouns *who* and *which*; the use of *isn't it?* as a universal tag question (also common in Indian and Singapore-Malaysian English, as well as being widely used in Wales); and the extended use of certain verbs of high semantic generality, such as *do, have, make, put* and *take.*

Mauranen (2012: 127) also states that in ELF, 'lack of concord and agreement is usual (*each sciences, the main ideas is*),' although 'there is nothing essentially simple in non-standard word order or lack of agreement.' This may be true of lack of agreement, but non-standard word order does sometimes appear to be a simplification, as for example in the inversion of verbs and pronouns in interrogative clauses, making them closer to declarative sentence word order, as in *So what kind of research you would like to do?* Björkman (2008a, 2008b) discusses the use of many of the features outlined above by international students in Sweden, and describes all of them as 'non-disturbing.' However the one thing that did cause 'overt disturbance, i.e. miscommunication' (2008b: 40) in her data was non-standard *question formulation.* Björkman (2012) analyses questions in academic ELF interaction, and finds that non-standard word order (as well as non-use of auxiliary *do* and other deviations from StE) can be problematic in *Wh*-questions, because in acoustically unfavourable conditions, the interrogative adverb/pronoun that begins the utterance can easily be missed, leaving fewer cues that the utterance is a question: e.g. *What other equation I would use? Why it is like this? Which kind of the vortex we should have?* Fortunately, Björkman's recorded data suggests that this negative effect can be, and frequently is, overridden by the use of utterance-final rising intonation in *Wh*-questions (which more often than not have a falling intonation in ENL), as well as in Yes/No questions: 'if the syntax is non-standard, intonation can shoulder the task of conveying the question to the listener on its own' (p. 114). This is another example of increased explicitness in ELF, and one which allows Björkman to quote – entirely reasonably – the ELF mantra that 'native speaker usage cannot be prescribed as the ideal target for ELF settings' (p. 114).[17]

Mauranen (2012: 191–92) also identifies a frequent syntactic pattern in ELF (equally found in spoken ENL, but considered to be non-standard in written language), which is designed to enhance clarity and explicitness, namely highlighting or foregrounding the topic of an utterance by '*fronting*' or (to use a term more suited to written language) 'left dislocation.' This means placing the element to be focused on at the beginning of the utterance, to give it prominence, and following it with a pronoun, as in *These differences they are important,* or *This report we'll do it later.*[18] ELF speakers use this structure a lot, and Platt *et al.* (1984: 119) describe it as 'a very common feature in many of the New Englishes' too. Mauranen says (2012:

192) that because 'topic negotiation' by fronting is a common feature in the spoken grammar of many languages, it is found in many ELF speakers' linguistic repertoires, even though it hasn't been taught. Significantly, this 'rather tends to undermine explanations that ELF speech is essentially just learner language resulting from imperfect learning' (p. 198). She even suggests that explicitation strategies such as fronting might be 'discourse universals' (p. 197).[19] Mauranen also points out (p. 167) that explicitation is frequently found in translation (another site of language contact and intercultural communication), to the extent that it has been described as a 'translation universal' (Mauranen and Kujamäki 2004): translators notoriously add clarifying matter to texts as they translate.

By way of summary, we can quote Seidlhofer (2011: 99), who says that in ELF, 'Clarity can be enhanced by giving prominence to important elements, redundancy added or exploited, explicitness can be increased by making patterns more regular, word classes or semantic relations generally can be made more explicit.' Yet although all these processes and all the features described above can be found in ELF corpora, it is also noticeable that the same speakers sometimes use different (standard and non-standard) forms (such as past tenses) on different occasions, or even in the same interaction. Correctness, grammatical accuracy and consistency do not appear to be overriding concerns in ELF. Mauranen (2012: 217) points out that (at least in the ELFA corpus) speakers *do* frequently carry out minor self-repairs of form, such as those adjusting a morphological detail (e.g. *in a very rational and very methodoligical methodoli- methodoli- sorry methodical way; I have sawn some- seen some*). Indeed she asserts (2006: 138) that 'virtually all ELF speakers engage in rephrasing their own speech to a considerable extent while some native speakers do it relatively little.' However she suggests that these repairs are not so much for the benefit of interlocutors, who might be unconcerned by (or unaware of) approximate verbal forms, but more an indication of 'shaky entrenchment.'[20] In ELF, many 'items and forms are less entrenched than is usually the case in speakers' first languages,' and consequently 'searches for items that are not firmly connected through many neural pathways take slightly longer, and the retrieval of a new alternative follows after a delay, even though one item has already been uttered.'[21]

Taken as a whole, however, the grammatical features outlined above – used some of the time by some ELF speakers[22] – are relatively insignificant compared with the total grammar of the language (just look at the contents page of any grammar-based ELT coursebook), and the number of grammatical features that are common to the major native varieties of English, the nativized varieties in Africa and Asia, and the English used as a lingua franca. Moreover, if grammatical variation in ELF is compared with actual ENL usage, rather than with prescriptive grammar books, it suddenly seems less significant: Kirkpatrick (2010: 114) states that there is less syntactical variation in his South-East Asian data than would be found in non-standard varieties of British English. The variable features of ELF grammar do, however, amply demonstrate that languages can and do change. The lexicogrammatical variation found in ELF as a whole, and in the output of individual ELF users, lends weight to the argument that grammar is forever emergent.

On the other hand there are clearly disadvantages to using language without many regular structures. In ENL (and most other L1s), hearers are always prospecting ahead on the basis of the preceding context, rather than listening carefully to each word (see Sinclair 2004, Chapters 1 and 5; and Sinclair and Mauranen 2006). Thus 'as speech unfolds, hearers have usually already made guesses about what is coming next, and need only confirm that their guesses were right' (Mauranen: 2012: 42). Words mostly come in predictable patterns, and colligations carry meanings; as Hunston and Francis (1999: 21) put it (writing about ENL), 'all senses of all words exist in and are identified by the sequences of morphemes in which they typically occur.' However such prospection is more difficult in ELF, in which patterns are more variable. The corollary of a certain freedom for speakers to vary patterns, lexis and morphology, which 'brings in additional and alternative expressions for already existing ones and alters the categories of regular and irregular forms' (Mauranen 2012: 131), is the impossibility for hearers to make precise predictions of form. However Mauranen suggests that in second language use in general, 'since participants' repertoires are less entrenched than in first language conversations, they might not recognize anomalies for what they are, but engage in fuzzier processing both as speakers and also as hearers.' There is a trade-off between freedom to innovate and predictability of processing. Hence 'the potential communicative problems that may ensue from grammatical ELF features are not so much to do with the non-standardness of structures as the lack of stability in their use' (pp. 136–37).

Hunston and Francis (1999: 269–70), who use the term 'International English' rather than ELF, concede that an International English corpus might show different regularities in patterning than a native speaker corpus, but state that they would be 'very surprised' if 'overall, no regularities in patterning were shown,' as they insist that 'patterning is a necessary feature of language.' Hence they deny that 'a language may be used perfectly adequately without adopting the specific phraseologies that native speakers use' (p. 270). However, ELF usage appears to show that Sinclair's (1991, 2004) argument that 'most words have no meaning in isolation, or at least they are very ambiguous, but have meaning when they occur in a particular phraseology' (Hunston and Francis 1999: 270) is more applicable to a native language than a mutable lingua franca. Hunston and Francis state that in general, 'phraseology is a necessary part of the redundancy of language; we can afford to mis-hear some words in a dialogue, for example, because we can reconstruct their meaning from the pattern they are used in' (pp. 270–71). But many verbs in ELF appear in more than one pattern, including patterns that do not appear in ENL, without seeming to cause misunderstanding. Hunston and Francis insist that if a learner of International English

> does wish to be able to converse with expert speakers of English of a particular variety (which does not have to be a so-called 'native speaker' variety) […] then differences between patterns used by the learner and the patterns used in the target variety will constitute 'errors.'
>
> *(p. 271)*

Fortunately, 'a learner does not need to get all the patterns right, but needs to get some parts right, in order to be understood.'

Yes indeed. But learner language will always contain errors, because learners are learners. ELF users, on the other hand, are actually doing things with English words, and they seem to tolerate more variety, uncertainty and fuzziness than Hunston and Francis allow. But the variation comes up against an opposing force: language users, both native and non-native speakers, naturally tend to accommodate to and converge with their interlocutors.

Cybernetics and accommodation

There are plenty of people who will tell you that 'ELF' – featuring all the grammatical constructions described above – is but another name for interlanguage or learner English or intermediate English, a deficient approximation of StE that it is peppered with errors. Yet even if this is true (from a NES's perspective), it needs to be recognized that for the majority of speakers in ELF interactions, the 'errors' *simply don't matter*. ELF users can be good communicators with only moderate proficiency in English. A lot of recorded evidence shows that many ELF speakers accommodate to each other's uses, and (unlike most language teachers over the past couple of millennia) when they encounter a linguistic anomaly they tend, to use Firth's (1996) well-known terms, to 'let it pass' or 'make it normal.'

The standard references for accommodation theory are the works of Howard Giles and colleagues (including Giles 1973; Giles and Smith 1979; Giles and Coupland 1991; Giles *et al.* 1991), but Roman Jakobson already described a similar process in 1953:

> Everyone, when speaking to a new person, tries, deliberately or involuntarily, to hit upon a common vocabulary: either to please or simply to be understood or, finally, to bring him out, he uses the terms of his addressee. There is no such a thing as private property in language: everything is socialized. Verbal exchange, like any form of intercourse, requires at least two communicators, and idiolect proves to be a somewhat perverse fiction.
>
> *(Jakobson 1953/1971: 559)*[23]

Accommodation theory stresses that when people interact (that is people in general, not just ELF speakers), they frequently adjust their speech (accent, dialect, lexis, grammar, phraseology, etc.), so as to approximate the patterns of other participants. Sometimes this involves borrowing or echoing interlocutors' exact words (see Bakhtin 1934–35/1981: 339; Tannen 1989; Carter 2004). Mauranen (2012: 56) points out that in an L2, 'it is a good strategy to pick up the interlocutor's words or phrases, as they can be assumed to be comprehensible to the speaker who first used them, and repeating them (other-repetition or "echoing") is one way of indicating comprehension.'

If people modify their language so as to identify with and resemble more closely the people they are speaking to (and perhaps in this way affiliate to an 'in-group') we can speak of *convergence*. An extreme case of convergence is code-switching completely to someone else's preferred language. People can also adjust their speech *away from* that of their interlocutors, resulting in deliberate *divergence*, if they wish to signal disapproval or social distance from an 'out-group' (see Tajfel 1978). As Le Page and Tabouret-Keller (1985: 181) put it,

> the individual creates for himself the patterns of his linguistic behaviour so as to resemble those of the group or groups with which from time to time he wishes to be identified, or so as to be unlike those from whom he wishes to be distinguished.

Consequently each utterance embodies an 'act of identity,' although accommodation may also have more immediate instrumental goals than achieving social approval or integration, namely manipulating the hearer into doing, feeling or thinking something, to the speaker's benefit (see Wray 2002: 4, and Chapter 6, below).

Trudgill (2010: 186ff.), however, suggests that we do not even need to evoke social factors such as identity and affiliation to explain accommodation, because it is 'a deeply automatic process […] the result of the fact that all human beings operate linguistically according to a powerful and very general maxim' (p. 189), which Rudi Keller (1994: 100) phrases as 'talk like the others talk.' Trudgill continues:

> Keller's maxim, in turn, is the linguistic aspect of a much more general and seemingly universal (and therefore presumably innate) human tendency to 'behavioural coordination,' 'behavioural congruence,' 'mutual adaptation' or 'interactional synchrony,' as it is variously called in the literature. This is an apparently biologically given drive to behave as one's peers do.[24]

In an L1, even the slightest variations of lexis, morphology, syntax, phonology, prosody, etc. can be significant, as language users are aware of the social significance and/or geographical origin of speech variants and lectal varieties (dialects, accents, sociolects, registers, basilects, mesolects, acrolects, speech styles, and so on). Within certain limits, speakers can shift towards other codes or styles which form part of their habitual repertoire, or which they recognize but rarely use. But in ELF, much of this information is either lacking or disregarded, and speech variation is less likely to carry class or geographical information. Instead, accommodation is more often related to ensuring comprehensibility: ELF users – especially those who do not know each other well, and cannot count on shared knowledge or linguistic habits – adjust their speech in order to make it more intelligible to and appropriate for specific interlocutors. Hence this is more often geographical or proficiency-related accommodation than social accommodation.

As Schneider (2012: 60) puts it, using a fine adjective, ELF usage

> is a cybernetic process which involves the continuous monitoring of the success of one's contributions and, consequently, adaptive behaviour, i.e. linguistic negotiation in a broad sense. Hence, ELF usage involves ongoing linguistic accommodation, a gradual increase of shared communicative modes of performance in a specific setting.

Speakers accommodate to their addressees' level of competence, simplifying language use if necessary, and negotiate communicatively successful forms. As already mentioned in Chapter 2, Firth and Wagner (1997: 293) suggest that 'anomalous forms of talk' may be explained by 'the notion of recipient design': speakers using anomalous forms in response to specific interlocutors or specific circumstances. On the other hand, as Mauranen (2012: 131) says,

> if a particular linguistic feature does not hamper communication, it is less likely to be eradicated from a speaker's repertoire than something that does. In the absence of negative feedback, there is no reason to look for alternative expressions [...] other things being equal, features that do not prevent speakers from successfully achieving conversation are likely to live on in their repertoires.

Consequently convergence will always coincide with variety, uncertainty and indeterminacy.

Of course, as Mauranen (2012: 51) points out, it is easier to detect instances of accommodation when speakers converge on a non standard form; if a speaker switches in a subsequent turn to a standard form used by an interlocutor, this can also be interpreted as a result of embedded correction. However 'standardness' does not appear to be a criterion in speakers' convergence on lexicogrammatical forms. Mauranen argues that when ELF speakers adopt each others' words, 'standard and non-standard forms do not get noticeably differentiated,' and expressions do not pass through any 'standardisation filter.' In fact, 'other factors, such as salience, memorability, and interactional meaningfulness are more likely to play decisive roles' (p. 228).

Moreover, when a form is non-standard to the point of incomprehensibility, Firth (1996: 243) suggests that ELF users often adopt the 'let it pass' principle, i.e. 'when faced with problems in understanding the speaker's utterance' (as long as the problems are 'non-fatal'), the hearer 'lets the unknown or unclear action, word or utterance "pass" on the (common-sense) assumption that it will either become clear or redundant as talk progresses.'[25] Although this 'carries an implication of passivity on the part of the hearer,' Firth argues that

> it is more accurate to say that the hearer is actively *though implicitly* engaged in the task of trying to *make* sense of what is being done and said. On many

occasions, faced with the other party's marked lexical selections and unidiomatic phrasings, the hearer behaves in such a way as to divert attention from the linguistically infelicitous *form* of the other's talk

and chooses to '*make the other's "abnormal" talk appear "normal"*' (p. 245).

One way of doing this is by incorporating the interlocutor's marked wordings or grammatical constructions into one's own succeeding speech turn – a pure example of accommodation.[26]

Thus Firth emphasizes the extensive 'interactional work' undertaken in ELF, and the cooperative mind-set that this requires. Although 'linguistic competences vary and are unstable' (p. 252) in ELF, speakers seem to be have a 'remarkable ability and willingness to tolerate anomalous usage and marked linguistic behaviour,' even if it appears acutely opaque (p. 247). As Canagarajah (2007: 931) puts it,

> To accept deviations as the norm, one must display positive attitudes to variation and be open to unexpectedness. Participants have to be radically other-centered. They have to be imaginative and alert to make on-the-spot decisions in relation to the forms and conventions employed by the other.

This frequently seems to be the case in ELF.

Thus unpredictably non-standard grammar is, and will remain, one of the identifying characteristics of spoken ELF. Some of the non-standardness is indistinguishable from what SLA theorists call learner language, and results from an incomplete (or imperfectly learned, or fuzzy, or only partially entrenched) knowledge of standard English grammar, but ELF theorists prefer to stress that ELF speakers are users not learners. Some of non-standardness is the result of the unconscious analogical overgeneralizations and exploitations of redundancy made by L2 learners (also evidenced in the New Englishes of the outer circle countries). Some of it results from deliberate strategies of regularization, simplification and explicitation which are leading to recognizable, widely-shared 'ELF forms.' Some of it is the result of on-the-spot accommodation to interlocutors' language use. Some of the non-standardness of ELF does irritate hearers who are *not* 'radically other-centered,'[27] but in general ELF – like most forms of language use – seems to be relatively successful and self-regulating. It is also – in its spoken forms – relatively independent of ENL norms; written documents produced by ELF users are more often designed to conform to native English norms than to a notion of ELF according to which there can be no errors but only variants, divergent forms, or 'features' (see, e.g. Björkman 2008b: 36).

Some linguists and language teachers would argue, however, that increased exposure to English, and consequently increased proficiency, should lead to firmer entrenchment and routinization of particular structures and idioms – possibly standard ENL ones – which would make language production that much easier and more effortless. Chapter 6 considers ELF and phraseology, but first Chapter 5 considers lexis in ELF.

Notes

1 ELFA (http://www.helsinki.fi/englanti/elfa/elfacorpus) is made up of 131 hours of recorded lectures, presentations, seminars, thesis defences and conference discussions at the universities of Helsinki and Tampere in Finland.

2 For full effect, these sentences require a Cockney accent, with *v* and *d* and *f* instead of *th*, and glottal stops in *don't matter* and *went mental*. The same teacher once unwisely responded to something the same pupil said with the objection 'That's just not English,' to which the (bowdlerised) reply was 'Well, it's not effing Chinese, is it?' Schools in general tend to be an introduction to sociolinguistics for those who choose to notice.

3 Similarly, Trudgill has long argued that only 2–3 per cent of the British population speak received pronunciation (RP), but his criterion for RP use is very rigid indeed: 'it only takes one non-RP feature for a speaker not to be a speaker of RP' (2002: 174). Moreover, defining someone's language use by their 'home dialect' is problematic: many people speak in different ways in different circumstances, and can be fluently standard or non-standard depending on circumstances.

4 See Chambers (2004) and Filppula *et al.* (2009). Many of these non-standard forms can also be explained in terms of the continuing drift of English from a synthetic to an analytic language, and a stripping away of inflections (see Tagliamonte 2009): e.g. the regularization of verbs (*was* in the second and third persons; *it don't*; *ain't* for all three persons), adverbs without *-ly*, the invariable *innit*, etc. Other forms are *not* simplifications, including *more easier* and multiple negation; Trudgill (2011: 70) points out that these uses, bewailed by prescriptivists, also go against the logic of analytic structure and simplification.

5 Cook (2009: 58–59) trumps Kramsch's furniture: 'Acquiring a second language is not propping a lean-to against an existing house; it is rebuilding the property itself.'

6 Not for nothing does Haiman (1998: 158) describe this 'attempt at a refutation' of the arbitrariness of countable and uncountable nouns as 'heroic.'

7 Nouns such as these are even used in the plural form in English by speakers whose first languages treat their equivalents as uncountable (Platt *et al.*, 1984: 52).

8 After living for many years in a Francophone environment, and having explained the logic of satellite- and verb-framed languages in various linguistics and translation classes, I heard myself saying precisely this when telling people about a protagonist of the French film *Welcome* (2009). It can take time to internalize L2 grammatical categories.

9 See, e.g. Jarvis and Pavlenko (2007); Pavlenko (ed.) (2009); Pavlenko (ed.) (2011).

10 These terms come from Weinreich (1953/1968: 9–10) who distinguished among compound bilingualism (when both languages are learned in the same context) which involves single concepts represented by two words; coordinate bilingualism (when two languages are learned in separate cultural environments) resulting in translation equivalents which may be associated with different concepts; and subordinate bilingualism (often associated with school language learners) which means accessing the conceptual representation of an L2 word via its L1 translation equivalent.

11 For a particularly thorough list of grammatical uses and non-uses one should expect to find in ELF, see James (2000: 35).

12 Breiteneder's (2009) and Cogo and Dewey's (2006) articles highlight the strange ambivalence of ELF research mentioned in Chapter 1: eager attempts to demonstrate the existence of widespread features of ELF co-exist with claims that particular forms are less important than the functions they serve, and that it is mainly slow-witted journalists and language teachers who worry about whether ELF constitutes a separate variety of English (see Seidlhofer 2009b: 40ff.).

13 Mollin (2006b: 148), on the other hand, describes 'omitting the third person *-s*' as 'a beginner's error in learner English that English teachers will try to get rid of very early on, probably even in the very first year of English education.'

14 MICASE is at http://quod.lib.umich.edu/m/micase/. See also Simpson *et al.* (2002).

15 Just as with mass and count nouns, Wierzbicka (1988: 69) has proposed a simple underlying functional explanation for -*ing* clauses and *to*-infinitives: -*ing* clauses imply simultaneity with the matrix clause – sameness of time whenever time is relevant (when the complements combine actions, processes and states), and sameness of subjects in atemporal semantic types such as facts and possibilities. The *to*-infinitive offers a motive or a reason, and can be explained as *I think* or *I want* plus a future *will*.

16 See Ranta (2009) on the prevalence of these constructions. Chambers (2009) points out that making expletive *there* agree with a displaced logical subject following the copula requires looking ahead – speakers must code the verb with a marker that agrees with a constituent that is not yet explicit or in short-term memory – and suggests that this might be a kind of grammatical breaking-point that taxes human cognition to its limits! Yet plural *there's* occurs less often in ELFA than in MICASE. Ranta reports that 29 per cent of hypothetical *if*-clauses in ELFA and 2 per cent in MICASE have *would* or *would have*. However, my impression from regularly reading articles quoting American baseball players and managers is that they use it 100 per cent of the time – *if he would have made that play; if he would have gotten a big hit; if he woulda slid, he woulda been safe*, etc. And them Yankees woulda won the World Series!

17 Once again, here the reality of ELF shows some basic assumptions of SLA theorists to be false. For example Winford (2003) paraphrases Cancino *et al.*'s (1978: 230) confident assumption that 'early learners of L2 English employ the same word order in all *wh*-questions,' as in *Who is coming?* and **What John is doing?* 'Later, they learn rules of inversion which they sometimes overgeneralize to embedded questions as well (**I know what is John doing*) [...] Eventually they learn that inversion only applies to direct rather than embedded *wh*-questions.' The *eventually* here needs to be taken in the 'Euro-ELF sense' of *possibly* ...

18 A related construction is the 'pseudocleft' (Hopper 2004: 172), which defers an upcoming segment of discourse, while 'focusing the listener's attention on the next item,' perhaps making the speaker's ideas more accessible by spreading them out, as in, e.g. *What he's done is spoil the whole thing*.

19 Fronting is one of the rare exceptions in English in which one can move a word to a salient position. Normally, emphasis has to be shown by nuclear stress within an intonation group, rather than by word order or the addition of inflections or particles to the end of words to indicate their importance (Jenkins 2000: 46).

20 Mauranen (2006: 139–40) also gives examples of self-repairs which *are* explicitly designed to secure comprehension, and describes the speaker as showing a high level of language awareness.

21 Shaky entrenchment and lexical searching also result in the *the the the, in in in, in in the, mhm hm er,* and *er er er* being the 9th, 17th, 20th, 24th and 25th most frequent three-word sequences in ELFA, alongside expected sequences like *I don't know, a lot of, I think that, one of the, and so on, you have to, there is a, I think it's, a little bit, and I think, and this is, this kind of, would like to, this is a, you can see, a kind of,* and *I would like* (Mauranen 2012: 266).

22 Prodromou (2008: 221) states that 'In the first 100,000 words of my L2 user-corpus there are virtually no grammatical errors,' but this contrasts with much of the data collected by Seidlhofer, Mauranen, Björkman, etc. Seidlhofer *et al.* (2006: 12) argue that Prodromou's successful users of English (SUEs) 'constitute a rather special, more-than-average "anglocentric" sub-group of the totality of ELF speakers.'

23 This argument from Jakobson is the exact opposite of Johnstone's (1996) claim that every speaker needs to be idiosyncratic to express an individuated self; the truth is probably somewhere in between.

24 Trudgill (2004) argues that behavioural congruence or coordination, and not identity, is what makes dialect mixture and new-dialect formation the almost inevitable consequences of dialect contact. For a sociolinguist to play down social factors is unusual, and Trudgill's position has not gone unchallenged: see Trudgill (2008a) and the ensuing discussion in *Language in Society* 37(2), particularly the responses by Schneider (2008) and Coupland (2008).

25 Firth (1996: 243) does not claim paternity of the 'let it pass' concept, describing it as 'emanating from Schutzian phenomenological sociology.'

26 What the speakers in Firth's data (business telephone calls) do *not* do is rephrase or reformulate 'the other party's errant usage' in their succeeding speech turn in such a way that the rephrasing effectively corrects 'the deviant form' (1996: 246) – which would be described as 'embedded repair' or 'other repair.' He also reports few cases of 'candidate completions' when speakers are searching for a word which is easily guessable, as this too would draw attention to the *form* of the other's talk. Other ELF researchers *do* report embedded repairs and candidate completions; I will return to pragmatic strategies in ELF in Chapter 8.

27 Björkman (2009) reports that each of the non-standard features she listed in a questionnaire was described as 'very irritating' by a small minority of engineering students in Stockholm.

5

LEXIS AND COMPREHENSION

I gotta use words when I talk to you
But if you understand or if you don't
That's nothing to me and nothing to you
We all gotta do what we gotta do

      T.S. Eliot, 'Sweeney Agonistes: Fragment of an Agon'

it seems, then, that ELF vocabulary is in many essential ways similar to ENL vocabulary and also fairly similarly distributed.

      Mauranen (2012: 107–8)

The usefulness of words has frequently been pointed out. It is quite hard to speak without them, and educated NESs know a lot of them. Even before it left its home country, English had a large vocabulary, as lexis from the languages of invaders was regularly added to the word stock without necessarily displacing existing words. And today, virtually all NESs know that there are lexical differences among the English, Scottish, Irish, American, Australian, Indian, etc. varieties. Various researchers have estimated that NESs know 16,000–20,000 word families – families rather than individual lexical items because of English morphology, and the way root forms are inflected to derive words in other classes (see Schmitt 2010: 6).[1] On the other hand, they don't use most of them very often. Paul Nation (1990: 16) states that approximately 87 per cent of words in English texts are among the 2,000 most frequent words in the language (see Michael West's General Service List (GSL) 1953).[2] For academic English, if you add the 570 frequent word families identified in Averil Coxhead's New Academic Word List (AWL) (2000) – words which fall outside the most frequent 2,000 words but which make up roughly 10 per cent of academic texts – you get similar figures: the first 1,000 words of English make up 71.4 per cent of academic texts, and the second 1,000 words of the GSL make up another 4.7 per cent, and the AWL accounts for 10 per cent more, leaving only 13.9 per cent made up of low-frequency words (Coxhead 2000: 222–23).[3]

Although Jenkins (2007: *passim*) is waiting in the wings, ready to reprimand anyone who suggests that competent ELF speakers might in any way resemble native speakers or aspire to their norms, it is reasonable to assume that they might require many of the same words as native speakers: after all, we *are* talking about the same language – English is English. I have already argued that a large number of proficient ELF speakers also need or choose to read texts in StE. However, research reveals that L2 speakers (and so, by definition, ELF speakers) do not need a nativelike vocabulary.

Given that most words are only used very rarely, and that one can understand English while only being familiar with 95–98 per cent of the words actually used in any given discourse, a knowledge of a few thousand words generally suffices. Norbert Schmitt (2010: 7) concludes that 'the current evidence suggests that it requires between 2,000 and 3,000 word families to be conversant in English (if 95 per cent coverage is adequate) or between 6,000 and 7,000 word families if 98 per cent coverage is needed.'[4] Of course 6,000 word families give you many more than 6,000 words. Schmitt (p. 8) summarizes Nation's (2006) figures: the 1,000 most frequent word families average about six members (types per family), decreasing to about three members per family at the 9,000 frequency level, and knowing 6,000 word families entails knowing 34,660 words. To these figures must be added the proper nouns in any given discourse.

It will be noticed that this figure is rather higher than the 1,500 words in Nerrière's (2004) simplified version of English that he calls 'Globish.' An elementary objection to Globish is that it is almost certainly easier to learn a rather larger vocabulary – at least 2,000–3,000 word families – than to have to paraphrase much of what you want to say because you lack the words. For example, if what you wanted to say when pointing at a map (or a card – see Chapter 2) was 'The university dormitory is the ten-storey tower just where the avenue widens,' you couldn't do it in Globish, which lacks all the content words in that sentence. I leave it to the reader to consult Nerrière's wordlist and produce a paraphrase. The same criticism can be leveled at Charles Ogden's 'Basic English' (short for British American Scientific International Commercial, designed to be an 'International Auxiliary Language'), and Quirk's 'Nuclear English.' Basic is supposed to be 'an English in which 850 words do all the work of 20,000' (Ogden 1930/1938: 92), although this involves saying *I am able* instead of *I can, make a request* or *put a question* for *ask*, and *take food* for *eat*. Quirk proposes, among other things, 'banning the use of normal modal verbs altogether' (1982: 25n) because they can be ambiguous, as well as many of the most frequent words because they are too polysemous, and replacing variable question tags with *is/isn't that right?* See Seidlhofer's (2011: Chapter 7) *doubleplusgood* critique of this logic.

English used as a lingua franca (as opposed to an L2 in an English-speaking country) represents a rather special and perhaps unique case of what Mauranen (2012) calls second-order language contact (see Chapter 1, above). Consequently, we can expect it to show the influence of many of the world's languages. Contrary to the logic of Globish, an enormous number of words can be used, exceptionally, occasionally or regularly, by speakers from many different countries. These include one-off borrowings and more established loans from speakers' L1s, and established false Anglicisms from various L1s, as well as on-the-spot approximations of established English words, and one-off creations. This chapter will consider these influences on the vocabulary used in ELF. It will also suggest, from the viewpoint of lexical pragmatics, that the dictionary or connotational meanings of words are not always important: the interpretation of words is fine-tuned in discourse, and their meanings are often narrowed or broadened, and there is no reason to suppose that word or utterance meanings are generally literal.

Lexical simplification

Despite all these figures in the thousands, what is remarkable about all language use (something which went unnoticed until the advent of corpora) is that a very small number of common words make up a huge proportion of both spoken and written language. Mauranen (2012: 90–91) reveals that in the Brown Corpus of (written) American English, a mere 135 words (types) account for 50 per cent of the total words (tokens).[5] The figure for MICASE, a corpus of spoken academic (American) English, is just 58, which shows that spoken English, even about high-level subjects, uses a higher proportion of common words than written English. However, in the ELFA corpus, a mere 44 words account for 50 per cent of the data – less than a third of the Brown figure of 135.

Most of these 44 words are grammatical, closed-class words. To be precise, there are determiners (*the, a, this*), pronouns (*I, you, we, they, it*), a relative pronoun (*that*), syntactic organizers (*there, it's*), conjunctions (*and, so, but, if, or, because*), prepositions (*of, to, in, for, on, with, as, about*), one *wh*-word (*what*), one sequencer (*then*), auxiliaries expressing tense, mood and modality (*have, can, be, is, are, was*), and a negator (*not*).[6] Because ELFA is a spoken corpus – and an L2 one – there are also plentiful hesitation markers and back-channelling noises (*er, yeah, erm, mhm*).[7] There are no nouns or adjectives in the 50 per cent lists, and virtually no lexical verbs: *think* makes it, but only because of its frequent use in *I think*.[8] It is also noticeable that of the top 70 words in ELFA, only four have more than one syllable – *very, about, because* and *okay* – which counters an erroneous belief that long (Latinate) words always predominate in ELF and 'the multitude of expressive monosyllables […] recede into the background' (Snell-Hornby 2000: 38).

Mauranen reveals that 38 of the most frequent 46 words (i.e. 83 per cent) are shared by both ELFA and MICASE, showing that 'The basic building blocks in ELF are the same as in ENL, and their distribution is also very similar' (2012: 82) – or to put it another way, English is English. It is significant that the second most frequent 'word' (or hesitation marker) in ELFA (between *the* and *and*) is *er,* while *erm* is 23rd: ELF is L2 use, and hesitation is common, though it is also common enough in native speech: *um* and *uh* come in 14th and 15th position in MICASE. All in all, these word lists show that 'when it comes to fundamental vocabulary, first and second language use are highly similar,' and 'a small set of very frequent items accounts for both first and second language use' (p. 100).

Yet given that the number of different words making up 50 per cent coverage of the ELFA corpus is 24 per cent lower than the comparable figure for MICASE (44 to 58), 'we must conclude that ELF leads to notable lexical simplification' (p. 92). Similarly Meierkord (2005: 101), investigating 'interactions across Englishes,' states that the lexicon

> contains only a few phrasal verbs or idioms, which are usually held to char-
> acterise BrE or AmE. The type-token ratio as well as the lexical density of
> the conversations indicate that speakers in IaE use a restricted vocabulary, and
> the low amount of derived or compounded words suggests that the voca-
> bulary is also simplified in comparison to that used by native speakers of
> English.[9]

Mauranen suggests, convincingly, that language contact and bilingual processing in general tends to lead to lexical simplification. This is also found in both learner language (see, e.g. Granger (ed.) 1998a; Granger *et al.* (eds) 2002) and translation, in which a tendency to overuse core vocabulary and under-represent rarer words has been posited as a universal feature, or at least a very strong tendency (see Mauranen and Kujamäki 2004).[10] As Mauranen puts it,

> The affinities between ELF lexical simplification, learner language, and
> translated language suggest that bilingual processing biases lexical choices
> towards the most frequent, presumably the most deeply entrenched, voca-
> bulary. That translations show the same tendency means it is not just
> imperfect learning that is at stake.
>
> *(2012: 117)*

Given that the simplification of vocabulary in both learner language and translation often produces discourse that is rather *flat*, it is fortunate that in *ELF* there are also countervailing tendencies.

Lexical approximation

Although lexical simplification in bilingual processing is not always the result of imperfect learning (most translators have *not* learned their native languages imper-fectly), it does appear that imperfect learning, or at least 'less deeply entrenched memory representations' (Mauranen 2012: 37), are regularly involved in the approximate use of less common words in ELF. Mauranen suggests that taking processing shortcuts and resorting to approximate forms of the language – albeit forms which are reasonably close to target forms – is an efficient way of using limited resources economically, because 'the nature of processing is fuzzy in most areas of cognition, including speech perception and production' (p. 41).[11] Hence 'we can posit that at the cognitive level, approximation is involuntary and results from realities of perception, memory, and access' (pp. 41–42). But because 'a complex environment like ELF seems to require stretching the tolerance of fuzziness wider than usual' (p. 42), speakers seem to adapt to inexact words, making approximation a successful communicative strategy. This endorsement of approximation obviously contrasts with the orthodox SLA position, summed up, e.g. by Donald Winford (2003: 220): after giving examples of words produced by advanced German learners (from Nemser 1991), including *cowardish, cruelism, dumbfolded, nervosity, sparcity* and *unguilty*, he states confidently that 'Such "errors" disappear as learners achieve greater familiarity with the T[arget] L[anguage].' This does not seem to be the case in ELF, in which communication can succeed despite approximations.

Thus contrary to the 'usage-based' theory of language according to which frequently encountered linguistic items become entrenched, ELF shows signs of intermittent variation arising from regularization and simplification. For example, in ELFA, alongside many standard uses of irregular past tenses, we also find a number of regularized past tenses (most of them helpfully tagged with <SIC>), including *binded, bringed, digged, drawed, feeled, felled down, fighted, heared, losed, meaned, striked, stucked* and *teached*, and not-quite-regularized past participles including *breaken, choosen, growned, sawn* (for *saw*) and *wonned*.[12] These are used by speakers showing a high level of competence and fluency in English, who sometimes also use the standard form in another speech-turn. Another simplification strategy found in ELF appears to be 'use the negative prefix of your choice': ELFA includes, among others, *disbenefits, discrease, inequal, inofficial, undirectly, unexperienced, unpossible, unrespect, unuseful* and *unsecure*.

Many other non-standard words found in ELF corpora result from word formation processes that are widely attested in both native English and the New Englishes of Africa and Asia, as well as in the creation of false or pseudo-Anglicisms in many languages. These include affixation (prefixes and suffixes), compounding, blending, conversion, modification, and shortening of the base (backformation and truncations) (see Plag 2003). False Anglicisms are coinages that resemble English words, but which would not be recognized or understood by monolingual native speakers of English. Examples from French, German and Italian include new compounds of free morphemes, such as *autostop* (hitchhiking), *recordwoman* (record holder) and *skipass* (liftpass or ski-lift pass), ellipses of compounds (*basket* for basketball, *cocktail* for cocktail party), clippings of parts of words (*happy end*), analogies (*footing*, on the model of rowing, riding, etc., and following the widespread authentic Anglicism football), and semantic shifts or meaning extensions, such as the Italian *mister* for football coach or trainer, and *box* for lock-up garage. They can also be metaphorical shifts, such as the Italian *bomber* for a prolific goalscorer, and synecdochic or meronymic shifts, such as *flipper* for the game of pinball and a pinball machine (see Furiassi 2010; MacKenzie 2012b). Some of these false Anglicisms get transferred to ELF.

These processes can also be seen at work in the non-standard lexis found in ELFA. There are backformations, including *colonisators, introducted, presentate, registrate* and *standardisate*. There are truncations like *automously, categoration, decentralation, phenomen* and *significally*. Suffixation, conversion and modification, or what Mauranen (2012: 126) calls the 'extension of productive derivational principles beyond their conventional boundaries,' can be seen in a large number of words, including the approximate or invented verbs *intersectioning, maximalise, plagiate, resoluting, satisfactionate, securiting* and *successing*; the nouns *addictation, analytism, assaultment, assimilisation, chemics, competensity, controversiality, governmentality, interventing, methodics, militarians* and *paradigma*; and the non-standard adjectives and adverbs *deliminated, devaluarised, disturbant, emperious, femininised, homogenic, intentiously, methodologic, nationalisised, proletariatic, quitely, strategical* and *theoretitised*. As Mauranen says, 'Morphology tends to be potentially overproductive in natural languages. While convention and acquired preference keep it in check in stable language communities, its possibilities are liberally utilised by newcomers such as non-natives' (p. 127).

Although L1 interference (or interaction) is always a possible factor in the use of non-standard words, particularly in Europe where many languages share cognate lexis, L3 (or L4, etc.) interference is also possible. For example, while *phenomen* was said by a speaker of German (which has *Phänomen*), and *homogene* and *prognose* by a speaker of Finnish (which has *homogeeninen* and *prognoosi*), *instable* and *sportive* (athletic) used by German speakers, *synthetise* used by an Italian speaker, and *performant* (efficient, competitive) used by a Romanian speaker, could all be transfers from L3 French.

There are also a few non-standard words in ELFA which fill genuine semantic gaps, including the very useful pronoun *themself*, which is the first deviation from StE in the wordlist ranked by frequency, coming in 3,514th place, with seventeen occurrences (Mauranen 2012: 88), as well as the noun *interpretee* (a person being interpreted), and the verb *visiblelise* (to make something visible to other people, which is not the same as *visualize*, which is to form a mental image), as in 'i liked very much the graphs that you have er er put inside so and they are very they visiblelise very nicely your arguments' (ELFA UDEFD020).

Hearers sometimes use a standard version of a non-standard form in the next speech-turn (an embedded correction), but corpus evidence suggests that ELF users are more inclined to let them pass, or indeed that they go unnoticed by both speakers and hearers. The immediate co-texts of non-standard words like those listed above, with what Mauranen calls their 'simultaneous deviance and recognisability with respect to a standard form,' show that they 'were not repaired by the speakers as if slips of the tongue, and none caused any noticeable reactions in their extended contexts' (2012: 103). None of them seemed to provoke any ripples or breakdowns in communication.

As well as form-based irregularities, ELFA shows many meaning-based irregularities, when speakers use near-synonyms with a semantic affinity to the more standard word, e.g. *negated* for *denied* (in *they demand a power, that is negated to them*); *strength* for *power* and *visioned* for *envisaged* or *seen* (in *it was visioned as a wicked political strength*); and *normal* for *ordinary* (in *for normal persons it's really hard to understand*).

Semantic approximations such as these can only be detected in context. Mauranen points out that 'in the European context,' some of these approximations 'have the additional advantage of being related to a Latin origin, which would make the shared semantic components familiar via other languages that the speakers know' (p. 103).[13]

Grosjean's theory of 'language modes' – states of activation of languages and language processing mechanisms at any given time – and his 'holistic view of bilingualism,' involving the 'coexistence and constant interaction' of a speaker's never totally deactivated languages (2010: 75), were outlined in Chapter 2. Words from a speaker's other language or languages are always liable to appear; as De Bot (2004: 26) puts it, it is 'like holding down ping-pong balls in a bucket filled with water. With your hands you can hold down most of the balls, but occasionally one or two will escape and jump to the surface.'

As well as making bilingual speech production errors (or unconscious transfers or interferences), ELF speakers in the bilingual mode can use willed borrowings or 'insertional' code-switches – deliberately embedding an L1 word or short expression in an utterance otherwise using English (ELF) as the base or matrix language.[14] One reason to borrow words is to find *le mot juste*, or express a concept or a precise nuance that is only lexicalized in one language; *performant* might be an example of this. Another reason could be a genuine lack of vocabulary or a fleeting inability to access a word in the language one is speaking. Jenkins (2011: 930) insists that gaps in linguistic knowledge are a very rare occurrence in ELF, but the majority of plurilinguals happily admit that being unable to activate a given word in a given language at a particular moment is an everyday occurrence. It appears unlikely that ELF speakers are any different from all the other people who regularly use more than one language.

Where Mauranen sees largely involuntary approximations resulting from a lack of firm entrenchment in long-term declarative memory, the ELF researchers in Vienna working on VOICE tend to see acts of creativity. For example, Marie-Luise Pitzl *et al.* (2008) analyse 'coinages' and lexical innovation in a sub-corpus of VOICE in relation to established word formation processes. They describe some of the coinages they find as filling permanent gaps in the lexicon, e.g. *forbiddenness* for 'the state of being forbidden.' They also argue that suffixes can be used not to change the word class of the base form but to *emphasize* the original class, to increase clarity, as in *increasement*, which is clearly a noun, whereas *increase* could be either a noun or a verb. Another example is *supportancy* instead of *support*. Similarly, *characteristical* and *linguistical* emphasize adjectivalness (*characteristic* and *linguistics* are nouns). This is true, although do we not know how many ELF users would find such added emphasis useful or necessary, and how many would merely experience it is a further instance of having to accommodate to unexpected forms.

Prefixes can also be changed – e.g. in the use of *unformal* rather than *informal* – in the aid of regularization and, consequently, clarity, as the *in-* prefix can also mean *in* or *into*. Seidlhofer (2011: 143), who argues that 'conformity to the patterns of conventional idiomatic wording is likely to inhibit rather than facilitate ELF communication,' describes non-standard use of affixation as what Sinclair (1991: 110) calls the 'open-choice principle' (see Chapter 6) being employed at the level of inflectional and derivational morphology rather than that of whole words.

Yet many of the words in VOICE that Pitzl *et al.* classify as 'lexical innovations' and 'coinages,' as they are not found in the reference dictionary they used (*Oxford Advanced Learner's Dictionary,* 7th edn) are attested elsewhere (in the actual rather than the virtual language), as they readily concede (2008: 39). For example, the *Oxford English Dictionary* includes the following words, with the dates of the first recorded uses: *conformal* (1647), *cosmopolitanism* (1828), *devaluated* (1898), *devotedness* (1668), *examinate* (1560), *forbiddenness* (1647), *importancy* (1540), *increasement* (*encreasement*) (1509), *non-transparent* (1849), *pronunciate* (1652), *re-enrol* (1789), *re-send* (1534), and *urbanistic* (1934). Of course the *OED* is a historical dictionary, and some of these words are wholly obsolete in native English, but others are still widely used. *Forbiddenness* does indeed fill a lexical gap, but it first filled it a long time ago. Then again, it may feel to individual speakers as if *forbiddenness* is being coined online and *ad hoc* each time it is used today, although it gets about 18,000 hits on Google (an unreliable statistic), compared with only one in the British National Corpus (BNC) and one in the Corpus of Contemporary American (COCA). But the fact that Pitzl *et al.* list *econometric* and *webmail* as 'coinages' rather suggests that they should have used a larger reference dictionary.

The processes identified by Pitzl *et al.* have also been widely attested in the New Englishes of Africa and Asia, e.g. by Thomas Biermeier (2008), who analysed the International Corpus of English (ICE) which includes a number of new words and compounds, including *crimeproneness* (India), *futurelessness* (Jamaica), and so on. But Biermeier points out that unique items, or what philologists and corpus linguists like to call *hapax legomenae* or *hapaxes* – words that appear only once in a given corpus – could be simple production or performance errors (slips, mispronunciations, or misspellings) as well as neologisms. Yet in accordance with what I call the angelic view of ELF shared by the Vienna researchers, Pitzl *et al.* prefer to describe what other interpreters might consider simple performance errors, or instances of unwilled crosslinguistic interaction, as creativity and *ad hoc* coinages. For example, they analyze the VOICE hapax *re-emplace*, in '*in two years the person who will re-emplace me*' as a coinage 'derived from the base word *place* via attaching two prefixes' (2008: 34), before conceding that 'another interpretation is possible' – the speaker is French and so might simply be borrowing (and slightly adapting) the French *remplacer*.[15] Yes indeed.

All in all, alternative analyses suggest that Pitzl *et al.* have rather fewer examples than they think that are clearly creative, on-the-spot nonce-formations (most of which have also been produced on-the-spot by many other people). Furthermore, although the VOICE data reveal coinages that can indeed be analysed in terms of backformation – e.g. the verbal forms or adjectives *examinates*, *devaluated* and *fragmentated* from the nouns *examination*, *devaluation* and *fragmentation* – is it really necessary to analyze *manufacters*, *contination* and *diversication* in terms of deliberate reduction, rather than as examples of involuntary approximation due to a lack of entrenchment (or as production errors)? Pitzl *et al.* insist that 'most of the lexical innovations' they describe as coinages 'are not erratic, irrational or unmotivated but follow well attested word-formation processes and in this respect represent a continuation of the long-standing history in the natural development of languages' (p. 40). Perhaps so, and languages, as outlined in Chapter 3, are always forever emergent, but these 'innovations' are just as likely to be the unintended consequence of a lack of entrenchment through repetition. Furthermore, given that hearers are always prospecting, making guesses about what is coming next, rather than listening carefully to each word (see Chapter 4), it is quite likely that many hearers fail to notice 'creative coinages,' especially those that involve suffixes. But for the corpus analyst, they do indeed enrich ELF!

Larry Smith, an expert on World Englishes, has long argued that understanding has at least three dimensions, namely intelligibility, comprehensibility and interpretability (see Smith 1988, 1992, 2009). Intelligibility involves the recognition of words or utterances; comprehensibility involves ascertaining the meaning of a word or utterance; and interpretability is the degree to which one is able to perceive the intention (or illocutionary force) behind a word or utterance. Intelligibility can of course involve pronunciation, and although Pitzl *et al.* combine 'pronunciation variations and coinages' in their < pvc > tag, I will not discuss pronunciation until Chapter 7. But as Smith (2009: 19) points out, in the absence of pronunciation difficulties, it is clear that 'we can have high intelligibility with low comprehensibility; and high comprehensibility with little or no interpretability.' Even though ELF may require a greater than usual tolerance of fuzziness, too high a percentage of novel or unfamiliar words can also slow down or derail comprehension. An ELF speaker who does not know all the members of the most frequent word families in English will have to approximate or coin words by guesswork, or by way of affixation and similar processes. While such creations aid expression, they may also require additional processing effort on the part of the hearers.

Such coinages are also likely to present more of a problem to ELF speakers who do not speak other (western) European languages which share the same prefixes and suffixes, such as many Asian speakers, but once again, the situationality factor inherent in ELF interactions is likely to prevail here; most of the ELF data we have (VOICE, ELFA) contain a majority of European speakers. Certainly the extracts from the Asian Corpus of English (ACE) in Kirkpatrick (2007, 2010) show no examples of the creative use of affixes in word coinages, and indeed Kirkpatrick (2010: 93) states that, unlike in various varieties of Asian English, speakers of Asian ELF[16] specifically avoid borrowed words and neologisms, as well as idioms, hybridization and code-mixing, precisely because it is used for crosslinguistic and crosscultural communication.[17] Similarly, Meierkord finds very little evidence of speakers of nativized varieties using lexis from their own variety in what she calls 'interactions across Englishes.' Yet Meierkord (2005: 110) says that notwithstanding her corpus, 'a number of studies indicate that the lexicon of IaE potentially develops stable particularities. This seems to be the case in regular interactions of a stable group of participants.' She states explicitly that 'When participants engage in regular and prolonged contacts, in social networks, communities of practice, or discourse communities, they seem to select from each other's L1s, and also to use individual lexical items with new meanings' (2012: 171).

Variation is intrinsic to ELF, but the logic of repetition and entrenchment that prevails in native language use is not entirely absent. Pitzl *et al.* borrow Björkman's (2008b: 37) term 'non-disturbing' to describe the coining of words in ELF, but there is evidently a trade-off between the advantages they perceive – increased clarity, economy of expression and regularization – and the number of words that hearers have to pay (fractional) extra attention to because of their unfamiliarity. All unfamiliar words and constructions involve an extra processing load, however minimal, even among multilingual and metalinguistically aware ELF speakers.

Words, concepts and meanings

Quite apart from using approximations and coinages, ELF speakers do not necessarily need to use 'ordinary' words in the ways NESs use them to refer to native English concepts. The argument in Chapter 4 about conceptual restructuring and the learning of new grammatical categories also applies, *mutatis mutandis*, to lexical categories. Although Kramsch (2000: 138), e.g. states that 'Learning a new language [...] reconfigures one's whole classification system,' ELF speakers may simply want to express their existing concepts in a lingua franca.

For proficient compound bilinguals, words and their combinations (structures) in different languages carry prior experience of their use in social interactions, and so often have particular sociocultural 'baggage' attached to them. In other words, they might represent (slightly) different world views. This is simply a weak version of the so-called Sapir-Whorf hypothesis about linguistic relativity, such that linguistic categories determine aspects of thought.[18] Compound bi- and multilinguals acquiring or learning a new language adjust or restructure their existing knowledge or 'world view' according to the requirements of the language and the culture attached to it. According to Istvan Kecskes (2010),[19] bi- and multilinguals have a single integrated system of blended or synergic concepts (or a 'common underlying conceptual base') that operates two or more language channels. Thus a blended conceptual domain will not be the same as the concept expressed by a word in a given language.

On the other hand classroom learners, usually subordinate bilinguals, tend to transfer L1 naming habits, and use many L2 words as translation equivalents of L1 words and their conceptual representations. This is because it is clearly easier to learn a linguistic code – lexical items and structures – than the sociocultural information that these items encode for the language's L1 speakers, without direct access to the target culture or any of the experience which results in that speech community's particular world view. Unfortunately word-to-referent mapping, or naming, obviously differs greatly across languages. It cannot be assumed that concrete nouns in different languages are almost exact translation equivalents, let alone abstract nouns and other parts of speech. As Aneta Pavlenko (2011b: 199) puts it,

Even the most common objects may be named differently by different speakers (*inter-speaker variation*) or by the same speaker on different occasions (*intra-speaker variation*). Some objects, actions, events or phenomena may have no name at all and others may elicit an array of competing alternatives, none of which seems particularly fitting. The learning of an L2, then, constitutes a process of re-naming the world, and the degree of destabilization created by this process depends on one's learning context, the languages involved and the theory of language held by the speaker in question. Some perceive the process of re-naming as a linking of new forms to pre-existing categories, others as a drastic change in understanding and experiencing the world, and yet others may situate themselves somewhere in between.

Many L2 learners take many years even to come close to matching native speakers' patterns of word use. This is a major problem from an SLA perspective, but less so from an ELF perspective, at least if ELF speakers' 'theory of language' is that they are expressing *their* concepts, rather than native English concepts, by way of English words. If speakers transfer L1 conceptions and thereby perplex their interlocutors, they may be quizzed or corrected; alternatively their speech partners might just let it pass. For example, there are many crosslinguistic differences among the names for food containers (bottle, jar, container, tube, box, etc.) and drinking vessels (cups, glasses). *Cup* in English and *chashka* (чашка) in Russian are not equivalent, and neither are *glass* and *stakan* (стакан). A porcelain cup is called *chashka* (cup) in Russian, but a paper or plastic cup is called *stakan* (glass) (see Pavlenko 2011b: 219–28). A Russian in Britain or the US who calls a paper cup a glass is likely to be corrected; a Russian speaker in ELF contexts (with their attendant cognitive approximations) perhaps less so. However, a conceptual shift towards L2 categories is generally easier and more successful for object naming and categorization than for expressing the temporal and spatial elements of actions and events discussed in Chapter 4.

Moreover, it is also argued in the wilder reaches of pragmatics and semiotics that interlocutors rarely understand the same words the same ways. Although it usually helps to know what one's interlocutors mean by their words, no two people need understand them the same way. As Jakobson (1959/2004: 139) put it, 'For us, both as linguists and as ordinary word-users, the meaning of any linguistic sign is its translation into some further, alternative sign, especially a sign "in which it is more fully developed," as Peirce […] insistently stated.' This makes a change from the usual trope about things getting *lost* in translation. Charles Sanders Peirce argued that a word, or to be more precise a *sign*, 'addresses somebody, that is, it creates in the mind of that person an equivalent sign, or perhaps a more developed sign. The sign which it creates I call the *interpretant* of the first sign' (1931–58: vol. 2, para. 228). In other words, a sign (word), when used, is almost immediately converted into another sign, perhaps a synonym, or a translation, or an equivalent in another signifying system, or a definition, a paraphrase, and so on. The interpretant gives rise to another sign, *ad infinitum*, so that there is an infinite regression, or what

Umberto Eco, in *A Theory of Semiotics* (1977), joyfully proclaims to be an unlimited semiosis. However Peirce argues that interpretants can become stable, because signs produce intermediate responses and establish, little by little, a habit or regularity of behaviour in the interpreter or user, a tendency 'to behave in a similar way under similar circumstances in the future' (1931–58: vol. 5, para. 487).

An alternative argument is that word meanings are never stable because speakers seldom intend a literal interpretation of the words they use, and comprehension invariably involves inference. For example, Deirdre Wilson and Robyn Carston (2007) argue that words rarely convey their exact lexically encoded meaning. Instead, word meanings are pragmatically adjusted – narrowed or broadened – in context. Broadening can range through approximation and other forms of loosening to hyperbolic and metaphorical extensions.

This is, of course, merely the narrowing of the principles of relevance theory from the utterance or sentence level to that of the individual word. According to relevance theory (Sperber and Wilson 1986/1995), utterances are only interpretive representations of thoughts, and so they have to be inferentially enriched before they can communicate thoughts. Hearers try to understand a communicator's intentions, guided by contextual clues. They make pragmatic inferences, assigning an utterance a propositional form, disambiguating it if the grammar permits more than one semantic representation, and completing it if it is in any way elliptic or semantically incomplete. Hearers also have to identify the referents of all referring expressions, enrich any vague terms until they are semantically explicit, and loosen the meaning of any concepts used non-literally, until they can identify an utterance's propositional attitude or illocutionary force. Wilson and Carston suggest that 'lexical narrowing and broadening (or a combination of the two) are the outcomes of a single interpretive process which fine-tunes the interpretation of almost every word' (2007: 231).[20] 'Almost every word' is itself a splendid hyperbole, as, e.g. reading the page of the article from which this quotation comes (or, alternatively, reading this page) and looking for narrowings and broadenings will show.

Here are some examples of words (in bold) whose meanings need to be narrowed or broadened from VOICE (EDsed31, a seminar about Austrian stereotypes and cultural differences), five of them fairly conventional metaphorical extensions, and one a conventional case of narrowing:

> I belong to the Italian group which has **colonized** Linz University
>> so stereotyping is you put them all in one **pot**
>> I can't give you a **recipe** say okay this is how you deal with Austrians
>> it's not coldness but it is something that's **behind** this that makes them behave the way they do
>>> I'm sure you have some kind of **picture** about Austria and you can also write that down
>>> Austrians would go out and **drink** [alcohol]

However ELF interactions and interactions across Englishes may also require interlocutors to pragmatically adjust (narrow or broaden) the meaning of words used entirely literally, because words from different varieties of English, and translation equivalents from other languages, can have different meanings. An example from a global English context is the West African meaning of the word *cousin*. Hans-Georg Wolf (whose L1 is German) describes meeting a Cameroonian who introduced a woman (in English) as his cousin. Wolf assumed there was a genealogical relationship, but later discovered that 'cousin' only meant a friend from the same village. Wolf and Frank Polzenhagen (2009: 191–92) argue that relevance theory does not account for this case of intercultural misunderstanding, based on different (metaphorical) conceptualizations of community and kinship, because the African was not speaking loosely, but merely using 'cousin' with the standard West African meaning. Instead, they invoke Hans-Georg Gadamer's hermeneutic theory, in which encounters with texts, and works of art and people require us to examine the legitimacy of our 'fore-projections' and 'fore-meanings' – or in short, our 'prejudices' (Gadamer 1960/2004: 269ff.).

Gadamer argues that we have to 'remain open to the meaning of the other person or text' (p. 271). However, his hermeneutic approach works better for texts from other times and places than for fleeting encounters with speakers of different varieties of a shared language. Gadamer suggests that temporal distance 'lets the true meaning of the object emerge fully,' although 'the discovery of a true meaning of a text or a work of art is never finished; it is in fact an infinite process' (p. 298). Temporal distance 'not only lets local and limited prejudices die away, but allows those that bring about genuine understanding to emerge clearly' (p. 298) (see MacKenzie 1986). Approaching a work with an open mind allows us to adjust our 'horizon of expectation,' but without ever abandoning it: true understanding involves, at best, a 'fusion of horizons' (Gadamer 1960/2004: 305). Yet as Wolf and Polzenhagen themselves point out (2009: 204), cultural distance usually has to be negotiated on the spur of the moment, and not in a prolonged encounter with a text in one's armchair. Similarly to Wolf, I learned the African meaning of 'cousin' by way of a Congolese acquaintance who regularly introduced young women (in French) as *ma cousine*, until it became clear that he was not using the European sense of cousinhood. This could be seen as a case of me changing my 'fore-projections' and 'fore-meanings,' but it seems simpler to describe it as a case of inferential lexical broadening in a repeated context.[21]

To summarize, although ELF, like L2 use in general, tends to have (in numerical terms) a more restricted vocabulary than L1 use, ELF speakers also seem to use, and accommodate to, an array of approximations, creative coinages, false Anglicisms, loan translations and multilingual borrowings, as well as – just like NESs in international communication – lexis from different native and nativized varieties. Given the range of influences on ELF, by way of second-order language contact, and the consequent abundance of non-routinized or weakly sedimented forms, ELF speakers appear to have a high tolerance for fuzzy processing and lexical variation. Whether the underlying processes are conscious or unconscious, and examples of creativity or simply a lack of entrenched memory representations, ultimately makes little difference: ELF reveals an intriguing combination of lexical simplification and lexical richness.

Notes

1 Pinker (1994: 150) cites evidence that 'an average American high school graduate' knows 45,000 words, to which he says you can add another 15,000 'proper names, numbers, foreign words, acronyms and many common undecomposable compounds,' which gives you 60,000, or a 'tetrabard,' because Shakespeare used 15,000 different words. Moreover, 'superior students, because they read more, would probably merit a figure twice as high, an octobard.'

2 West's General Service List, designed with the needs of ESL/EFL learners in mind, was developed from a corpus of five million words and contains the most widely useful 2,000 word families in English.

3 Unsurprisingly, more than 82 per cent of the words in the AWL are of Greek or Latin origin (Coxhead 2000: 228–29).

4 Nation (2001) gives higher figures. He states (p. 147) that it takes nearly 4,000 word families to give you roughly 95 per cent of the words of a text; that for 'pleasurable reading' 98–99 per cent text coverage is needed; and that 'to read with minimal disturbance from unknown vocabulary, language users probably need a vocabulary of 15,000 to 20,000 word families' (p. 20).

5 The Brown University Standard Corpus of Present-Day American English contains 500 samples of written texts, totalling approximately one million words, compiled from works written by native speakers of American English published in the United States in 1961.

6 The fact that so many of these words are grammatical words is partly a statistical anomaly: they appear in fixed forms because their morphology doesn't vary (Mauranen 2012: 100). For example, if you add all the forms of *do* in the most frequent 200 words, it comes in 19th place in ELFA and 21st in MICASE.

7 The full list is in Appendix 2 of Mauranen (2012).

8 *Know* is at 51 in the ELFA list, and 22 in MICASE, largely because of the expression *you know*. In his corpus of non-native 'successful users of English' Prodromou (2008) found far less use of short pragmatic markers such as *you see* and *sort of* than in native English, but *see* is at 77 in ELFA and 70 in MICASE, and *sort* is in the 120s in both corpora.

9 See also Meierkord (2012: 10, 171).

10 As mentioned in the previous chapter, ELF and translation, which both cross cultural and linguistic boundaries, also share a tendency to enhance explicitness.

11 Writing, however, generally allows more careful formulation and revision and re-reading.

12 The regularization of irregular inflectional forms such as past tenses was discussed in Chapter 4.

13 Cf. Hulmbauer's argument in Chapter 2.

14 Muysken (2000) distinguishes between 'insertional' and 'alternational' code-switching. Alternational switches are switches into the L1 for an entire utterance or speech turn, especially if a word or concept particularly associated with the L1 'triggers' a switch into that language. For the concept of matrix and embedded languages, see Myers-Scotton (1993). Insertional switches, syntactically and morphologically, though not necessarily phonologically, integrated into the recipient language, can also be described as 'nonce borrowings' (Poplack *et al.* 1988, following Weinreich 1953/1968), or 'speech borrowings' (Grosjean 1995: 263), in contradistinction to established loanwords, widely used in a speech community, or what Grosjean calls 'language borrowing.'

15 *Reemplace* is also one of the forms of the Spanish verb *reemplazar* (to replace or substitute), and as stressed in Chapter 2, many European ELF speakers are multilingual. Other words from VOICE that Pitzl *et al.* confidently analyse as creations, including *misstand* and *supportancy*, are also words in other European languages, in this case Dutch.

16 More precisely, Kirkpatrick's data are from the countries of the Association of Southeast Asian Nations (ASEAN), a political and economic organization whose founding members were Indonesia, Malaysia, the Philippines, Singapore and Thailand, which have since been joined by Brunei, Cambodia, Laos, Myanmar (Burma), and Vietnam.

17 Many Singaporeans notoriously mix bits of Malay, Mandarin or other Chinese dialects, and Tamil into their English (widely known as Singlish) when they are not using it as a lingua franca. Many Filipinos also mix English and Tagalog to the extent that the resulting mixture has been named Taglish.

18 Proponents of this 'hypothesis' actually tend to treat it as an established fact, rather than as a hypothesis to be tested. Although Anglophone linguists generally cite the American lineage of Boas, Sapir and Whorf, and Whorf's use of the term *Weltanschauung*, they were preceded by Humboldt, who used the term *Weltansichten* in discussing languages and world views in 1836. Boas (1940: 289) stated that 'the categories of language [...] impose themselves upon the form of our thoughts'; Sapir (1929/1949: 162) that we are 'very much at the mercy of the particular language that has become the medium of expression for [our] society'; and Whorf (1956: 213, 221) that 'We dissect nature along lines laid down by our native languages,' so we 'must arrive at somewhat different views of the world.'

19 See also Kecskes and Papp (2000), and Chapter 2, above.

20 Wilson (2004) also suggests that the repeated application of such lexical-pragmatic processes can lead to semantic change: what starts as a spontaneous, one-off affair may become regular and frequent enough to stabilize in a community and give a word an extra sense.

21 See also Mesthrie and Bhatt (2008: 112–13) on kinship terms in Africa and African Englishes.

6

FORMULAICITY AND VARIATION IN ELF

Would I had phrases that are not known, utterances that are strange, in new language that has not been used, free from repetition, not an utterance which has grown stale, which men of old have spoken.

Khakheperresenb, c.2000 BCE[1]

the human mind is far less remarkable for its creativity than for the fact that it remembers everything.

Bolinger (1976: 2)

From a cognitive point of view, we would expect ELF speakers to approximate English forms because this would allow them to attain reasonable economy in processing while securing a good chance of achieving comprehension.

Mauranen (2012: 57)

Once upon a time, Barbara Seidlhofer (2011: 135) tells us, at the end of a meal, a Cretan waiter called Yannis served a round of *raki* to herself, her NES friend Peter, and three Norwegians, 'with the words "this is from the house" (maybe trying to use a phrase that Peter has taught him, but not quite "getting it right").' Unfortunately one of the Norwegians didn't recognize the expression and failed to thank Yannis for the free drink. Peter explained that Yannis meant 'ON the house,' which Leila still didn't understand, so Barbara explained that it meant it was a free drink, by which time it was far too late to say thank you.

Seidlhofer describes this episode of failed communication as resulting from what she calls *unilateral idiomaticity*, by which she means 'the use by one speaker of marked idiomatic expressions attested in ENL that may well be unknown and unintelligible to the other participants in ELF interactions' (p. 134). To indulge in unilateral idiomaticity is to show a lack of concern for one's interlocutor, a neglect of the need for accommodation, for sensitively gauging the other person's likely familiarity with expressions of a particular kind – in short, precisely the kind of awareness and skill that accomplished ELF speakers are so good at employing.

(p. 135)

Even if we choose to label Seidlhofer's friend Peter, the wicked, unsuccessful teacher of idioms, whoever he is,[2] the villain of the piece, I prefer Yannis in the role of hero rather than victim. Here is someone who regularly deals with both NES and NNES customers, and who presumably thinks he's simply speaking English rather than ELF. (By Seidlhofer's own definition, he is not an 'accomplished ELF speaker.') Jenkins (2007: 2) says that 'ELF does not stop being ELF if inner or outer circle members happen to be present,' but you could equally say that English does not stop being English if expanding circle speakers are present. Yannis was talking to a group including at least one person he knew to be a NES,[3] so his use of the idiom wasn't entirely 'unilateral,' and besides, many Norwegians speak very proficient English that includes a lot of ENL expressions. Many of them may even know the expression 'on the house,' and also be able to understand the 'ELF variant' 'from the house.'[4] And some ELF researchers, notably Mauranen, argue that approximation and fuzzy processing are central to ELF usage. So should we really criticize Yannis for trespassing on ENL territory (even though his attempted use of an idiom failed)?

Before answering that question, let us work backwards from here. Why do NSs use metaphorical fixed expressions, why might Yannis have got this one wrong, and what is the place of formulaic language in ELF?

NESs and formulaic sequences

For the past twenty years or so, much of the ELT profession has been endeavouring to raise learners' awareness of collocations and formulaic phrases and multiword 'chunks' of language (although millions of teenage language learners continue to clutch their little vocabulary notebooks with neat lines drawn down the middle of the page dividing single-word 'translation equivalents' in two languages). This follows from the corpus-driven demonstration that in English (and in many other languages – at least as used by NSs) there is a phraseological tendency, which is to say that units of meaning are largely phrasal, and speakers choose several words at a time, often relying on memorized (or 'entrenched') formulaic sequences or prefabricated phrases, rather than generating or improvising phrases *ex nihilo* (i.e. from a vocabulary of thousands of lexical items and a stock of internalized grammatical patterns or 'rules'). This account of language, which collapses the distinctions between lexis and syntax, and between grammatical constructions and formulaic sequences, clearly has huge implications for theories of language acquisition, language use, and language teaching, not to mention for theories of human cognition.

However it is debatable as to how far this account of processing and production applies to languages learned by adolescents and adults, whose generally imperfect performance (by NS standards) is at least partly due to their lack of instantly recalled fixed and semi-fixed expressions. It is also debatable how far it applies – or should apply – to ELF, in which speakers are not (or are said not to be) concerned with NS usages and phraseology. Contrary to the logic of frequency and entrenchment discussed in Chapter 3, ELF seems to show a great range of phrasal variation and may require us to reconcile usage-based accounts of cognitive processing with a radically variationist account of language.

In an article explaining the goals of linguistic theory as he saw them, Chomsky (1964: 7–8) wrote that 'it is evident that rote recall is a factor of minute importance in ordinary use of language,' and, quoting a translation of Herman Paul (1886: 97–98), 'that a minimum of the sentences which we utter is learnt by heart as such – that most of them, on the contrary, are composed on the spur of the moment.' However some years later, in a ground-breaking article, Andrew Pawley and Frances Hodgetts Syder (1983) pointed out that although few people are able to encode, either in advance or while speaking, anything longer than a single clause of eight to ten words, we all regularly produce far longer fluent, pause-free, multi-clause utterances in spontaneous speech (at least in our L1s), precisely because we employ a great many institutionalized utterances. It appears that we retain language in chunks, and that much of our mental lexicon is stored in lexical phrases.[5] Pawley and Syder argue that 'memorized clauses and clause-sequences form a high proportion of the fluent stretches of speech heard in everyday conversation […] Coming ready made, [they] need little encoding work,' so the speaker can concentrate on 'constructing a larger piece of discourse by expanding on, or combining ready-made constructions' (p. 208). Memorized sentences and phrases also 'provide models for the creation of many (partly) new sequences which are memorable and in their turn enter the stock of familiar usages' (p. 208).

Regular ways of speaking (and writing and spelling) come in useful because people can only process a limited number of bits or chunks of information simultaneously – six according to Anthony Wallace (1961), or the better-known 'magical number seven, plus or minus two' according to George Miller (1956), although this depends on what the chunks consist of: Miller suggests that working memory can hold around seven digits, six letters, or five words. If ready-made constructions are processed as chunks rather than as collections of individual words, this frees up space in working memory to formulate the next part of a discourse.

The most remarkable thing about this argument, however, is the *size* of the postulated stock of familiar usages: Pawley and Syder suggest that 'the number of sentence-length expressions familiar to the ordinary, mature English speaker probably amounts, at least, to several hundreds of thousands' (1983: 213).[6] Similarly, Igor Mel'čuk (1998: 24), who uses the term 'phraseme,' states that 'in any language – i.e. in its lexicon – phrasemes outnumber words roughly ten to one,' although most phrasemes are collocations (recurrent and habitual combinations of words) rather than full expressions. As already suggested in Chapter 3, this somewhat contradicts Chomsky's frequent insistence on the 'poverty of the stimulus' from which children develop a competence in their native language. On the contrary, we seem to memorize, over many years of exposure to speech, many thousands of expressions which we can produce when necessary. When we find ourselves in similar situations, or retell the same stories (or teach the same linguistics classes), we tend to use the same multi-word chunks.[7]

Prefabricated or lexical phrases include many regular *institutionalized expressions* with specific pragmatic functions, which can be used verbatim as separate utterances in distinct social situations (such as *Call me after work, Can I come in? Can I take a message? Do you live around here? I'd be glad to, I see what you mean, Just a moment please, Nice meeting you*). NESs also use a great many *sentence heads* or *stems* – lexical phrases providing the framework for whole sentences, and containing slots for parameters or arguments (e.g. *Have you heard about X? I'm a great believer in X, I'm sorry to hear about X, I think that X, My point is that X, That reminds me of X, What did you mean by X? What really surprised me was X, What would you say to X?*), as well as lots of *discourse devices* such as logical, temporal and spatial connectors (*as a result of, as soon as, around here*), fluency devices (*and so on, as a matter of fact, I think, you know*), exemplifiers (*for example, in other words*), evaluators (*as far as I know, I'm not absolutely sure but*) and so on.[8] Because these formulaic sequences are stored holistically but *could* also be created and decoded analytically (as products of syntactic rules), a grammar needs to specify them twice.[9] Wray (2002: 261ff.) puts this another way: the mental lexicon is heteromorphic (involving considerable redundancy) – we store entire unanalysed phrases, with meaning and phonology, as well as their constituent parts.[10]

However regular formulaic expressions appear to be outnumbered by semantically *opaque* or *non-compositional idioms*, in which the meaning of the whole phrase is not the sum of its parts, so that interpreting word by word does not yield the phrase's accepted, institutionalized, unitary meaning.[11] Rosamund Moon (1998) analyses English fixed expressions and idioms (FEIs), and of the 6,776 FEIs in her database, approximately 45 per cent are what she calls anomalous or ill-formed collocations, while 33 per cent are metaphors, and only 21 per cent grammatically regular formulas. Anomalous collocations are in some way lexicogrammatically defective or idiosyncratic. Either one of the words has a meaning not found in other collocations or contexts, or is semantically depleted or used in a specialized sense (*at least, in effect, in time, foot the bill, on the house*), or used figuratively (*blue moon, red herring, see red, white lie*), or the expression breaks the conventional grammatical rules of English (*at all, at the ready, by and large, come what may, gimme a break, guess what? hard done by, how come, how do you do? in the know, in case, let alone,*[12] *long time no see, needless to say, no way, of course, of late, of old, point taken, quote unquote, thank you, to date, to hand*). It is because formulaic sequences are stored and processed holistically that they can become fossilized and stranded from the standard rules and combinations of a language, with grammatical irregularity or semantic illogicality or opacity going unnoticed.

Despite using the term 'fixed expressions and idioms,' Moon states that 40 per cent of the items in her database have lexical variations or strongly institutionalized transformations, and 48 per cent have slots to be filled according to context, so that we need to replace the notion of an idiom's canonical form.[13] This obviously causes difficulties for L2 learners. Examples of variable phrases include *bad/rotten apple, ballpark figure/estimate, be/feel sorry for someone, bend/stretch the rules, close/near to the bone, down the chute/drain/pan/plughole/toilet/tubes, miss the boat/bus, say/kiss goodbye to something, set/start the ball rolling, step into/fill someone's shoes, wash/air/do/ launder one's dirty linen/laundry/washing in public,* etc. Similarly, Sinclair (1991: 104) states that 'One is first struck by the fixity and regularity of phrases, then by their flexibility and variability, then by the characteristically creative extensions and adaptations which occur, sometimes more often than the ordinary form.' This seems to be particularly the case with proverbs and sayings, which are commonly truncated or exploited, especially in journalism.[14]

Quite apart from institutionalized lexical phrases, there are also many thousands of strong *collocations* or words that habitually go together (adjective + noun, verb + noun, verb + adverb, adverb + adjective, verb + adjective + noun, etc.), as well as thousands of compound nouns, phrasal and prepositional verbs, and all the colligations discussed in Chapter 3. As Sinclair (2004: 19) says, 'words in English do not normally constitute independent selections [...] the choice of one word conditions the choice of the next, and of the next again,' or as Scott Thornbury (1998: 8) puts it, 'words hunt in packs.' Hoey (2005: 10) goes as far as to argue that natural language is a result of collocation: 'It is part of our knowledge of a lexical item that it is used in certain combinations in certain kinds of text,' and 'the mind has a mental concordance of every word it has encountered' (p. 11). According to this theory, each time we hear or read a word (or combination of words), we subconsciously keep a record of the context and co-text (the surrounding words). As we cumulatively re-encounter a word, we build up a record of its collocations, so that 'every word is mentally primed for collocational use. [...] The same applies to word sequences built out of these words; these too become loaded with the contexts and co-texts in which they occur' (p. 8). This account of primings diminishes the roles of grammar, and accounts for what sounds *natural* in language rather than what is *possible*. Hoey further suggests that 'many users of a language never construct a complete and coherent grammar out of their primings. Instead they may have bits of grammars, small, self-contained mini-systems that do not connect up but represent partial generalisations from the individual primings' (p. 181).[15]

Clearly words are never primed per se, but only for an individual speaker. Everybody's language is unique because all our lexical items are primed differently as a result of different experiences,[16] although there are harmonizing forces such as education, the media, and self-reflexivity. Primings can of course change over time – every time we hear or use a word the experience either reinforces the priming (confirming an association between the word and its co-texts and contexts) or weakens it, if the encounter introduces the word in an unfamiliar co-text or context.

Wray (2002: 130–32, 2008: 17–20) offers an opposing account of language production and processing, such that language is only analysed when necessary, according to a 'Needs Only Analysis model.' Whenever possible, people produce formulaic language, and interpret utterances holistically.[17] Wray describes utterances that can be understood holistically, without any grammatical analysis or the matching of meanings to particular words (even though they might include gaps in which to insert variable items), as 'morpheme equivalent units' (MEUs). Formulaic sequences are MEUs that are used and processed as such by large groups of individuals in a speech community. Only where input does not correspond to known formulaic sequences is it subjected to analysis. Consequently, 'Native speakers often simply fail to see the many irregularities in languages that the rule-based system and the logic of morphological level semantics ought to reveal' (2008: 24).

Thus *pace* Hoey, Wray argues that MEUs 'constitute a layer of wrapping that protects the components from analysis under normal circumstances' (p. 67), so we don't have a 'mental concordance' of the collocates of all the words we know. On the contrary, NSs have very poor intuitions about collocational patterns.[18] The same applies to (NS) language teachers: given that collocational pairs are stored holistically as MEUs, teachers are unlikely 'to think of the most common collocational pairings for isolated words, when providing examples in class' (p. 228).

However, many MEUs *can* also be analysed if desired (even according to the logic of Needs Only Analysis). Andreas Langlotz (2006) shows with great thoroughness how supposedly noncompositional metaphorical idioms can in fact be decomposed, their individual lexical items re-analysed, and their literal meanings exploited, usually for humorous effect, as in *a very red herring, by and not so large, he barely nudged the bucket, one of the blinder alleys, put a pigeon among the cats,* and *the bull of controversy was grasped firmly by the horns.* Supposedly opaque idioms can be used creatively, with adnominal modification, lexical substitution,[19] passivization, pluralization, flexible use of determiners, and so on. Indeed Samuel Glucksberg (1993: 20) states that 'purely noncompositional idioms may not exist at all.' Langlotz suggests that the composition of the literal meaning cannot be totally suppressed in actual processing of metaphorical expressions, and Wray (2008: 28–29) concedes that it is possible that literal readings are activated and discarded, below the level of our consciousness.

Yet whether it involves a subconscious concordance of collocations, or holistically stored unanalysed MEUs, NESs *do* use a lot of formulaic language. Estimates of exactly how much language is formulaic vary greatly, because of differing definitions of formulaicity. Douglas Biber *et al.* (eds) (1999) found that approximately 30 per cent of the words in their conversation corpus, and 21 per cent in their academic prose corpus, were parts of lexical strings or bundles. (Lexical bundles are strings of consecutive words computationally identified in corpora, and so are not always structural units – *one of the, you have to, this is a, you know what, so this is, and then you,* etc.) Britt Erman and Beatrice Warren (2000) come up with a much higher figure, calculating that 58.6 per cent of the spoken English discourse they analysed and 52.3 per cent of written discourse consists of formulaic sequences of various types, while Bengt Altenberg (1998: 102) suggests that 'on a rough estimation over 80 per cent of the words in [a spoken English] corpus form part of a recurrent word combination in one way or another.'[20] In contrast, Kecskes (2007: 198) reports formulaic expressions making up only 7.6 per cent of the total words in recorded conversations of NNESs living in the USA.

Consequently Sinclair (1991: 110) contrasts what he calls the 'open-choice principle' and the 'idiom principle.' The open-choice principle is 'a way of seeing language text as the result of a very large number of complex choices,' so that at each point where a unit – a word or a phrase or a clause – is completed, 'a large range of choice opens up, and the only restraint is grammaticalness.' The idiom principle, on the other hand,

> is that a language user has available to him or her a large number of semi-preconstructed phrases that constitute single choices, even though they might appear to be analysable into segments. To some extent this may reflect the recurrence of similar situations in human affairs; it may illustrate a natural tendency to economy of effort; or it may be motivated in part by the exigencies of real-time conversation.

Sinclair suggests that most texts and discourse are produced and interpreted by the idiom principle. Choices of words in one slot in a sentence tend to dictate which elements will fill the next slot or slots, and prevent the exercise of free choice. Units of meaning are expected to be largely phrasal, so relatively few words are chosen by the open-choice principle. Indeed, 'the whole drift of the historical development of English has been towards the replacement of words by phrases, with word-order acquiring greater significance' (p. 68). Hence Sinclair states that we need to 'elevate the principle of idiom from being a rather minor feature, compared with grammar, to being at least as important as grammar in the explanation of how different meaning arises in a text' (p. 112).

Thus it seems fair to say that NESs use a lot of formulaic language. Not everyone approves of this. For instance, George Orwell (1946/1968: 130) famously complained that writers on politics used 'phrases tacked together like the sections of a pre-fabricated hen-house.' He stated that if you use ready-made phrases, 'you not only do not have to hunt about for words; you also do not have to bother with the rhythms of your sentences, since these phrases are generally so arranged as to be more or less euphonious' (p. 134).[21] Yes indeed, and by reducing their processing load, interlocutors are also able to do other things, such as assess the ideas thrown up in a conversation. But Orwell believed that one needs to be 'constantly on guard' against the 'invasion of the mind by ready-made phrases,' every one of which 'anaesthetises a portion of one's brain' (p. 137). He would perhaps have been cheered by the fact that most L2 speakers use less or different formulaic language than L1 speakers, an issue to which we now turn.

Language learners, three types of processing, and major catastrophes

Once the essentially phraseological nature of English, and the large proportion of formulas and strong collocations used by NESs, had been revealed by corpus research, it didn't take long for the ELT profession to stress the importance of raising learners' awareness of prefabricated multi-word chunks. Michael Lewis (1993, 1997) developed a whole theory of foreign language teaching which he called 'the lexical approach,' based on the notion that the essential units of language are what James Nattinger and Jeanette DeCarrico (1992) called lexical phrases, rather than single words or grammatical structures. Lewis also argues that language consists of grammaticalized lexis rather than lexicalized grammar, and that 'grammar tends to become lexis as the event becomes more probable,'[22] which is to say that there will generally be prefabricated expressions available for use in frequent events and situations, allowing us to handle them effortlessly and fluently.

Thus it is argued that learners should be introduced to institutionalized utterances and lexical phrases at the early stages of learning *without* any grammatical analysis. Such phrases and collocations, which the learners can use immediately, tend to include the most basic words and structures of the language. It is simply not the case that 'advanced' learners use ever more complex sentence structures – on the contrary, they use more formulaic sequences more often. Instead of writing down words and their translations in their infamous little vocabulary books, learners should be encouraged to pay attention to co-text or surrounding words. For example, high content nouns should be taught with collocating verbs and adjectives which form relatively fixed, communicatively useful collocations, and learners should be shown how to 'chunk' language, directing their attention to lexical phrases rather than individual lexical items, which gives more time for processing meaning.

The underlying logic here is that learners first use unanalysed, internalized, holistically processed prefabricated phrases, and only later begin to segment these chunks, which thereby serve as the raw data from which they gradually perceive patterns, morphology and what is traditionally called grammar. Rather than being the product of 'rules,' or the conscious learning of sounds and structures, most language is acquired holistically and then broken down into shorter strings so that it becomes available for re-assembly in potentially new combinations. Unfortunately, this is essentially the model of *first* language acquisition (see, e.g. Peters 1983), and there is quite a lot of evidence that SLA does not work the same way.

The fundamental difference (apart from age and increased maturity) between first and second language acquisition is that most people trying to learn (as opposed to naturalistically acquire) an L2 have achieved literacy in their L1, and are likely to use this as a major aid in acquiring the L2. Thus formulaic material will not play the same role in second language acquisition and use as it did and continues to do in the L1. Adolescent classroom learners seldom have to communicate genuine messages with even the slightest consequences for their physical, intellectual or emotional well-being, so there is no necessity to find the perfect formulaic sequences for a given situation. As a result they are inclined to focus on grammatical form, break down sequences, analyse and rationalize patterns, and store small units. Teaching with more written than listening materials tends to reinforce this approach, as writing makes the separation of individual words very clear. In L1 input, words quite simply *belong* together; in L2 production, they are often disassembled and put back together. As Wray (2002: 206) describes it, 'The result is that the classroom learner homes in on individual words, and throws away all the really important information, namely, what they occurred with.'

Building utterances word-by-word by using 'rules' provides a more manageable outcome and a stronger sense of control over the language than using memorized strings without knowing how they break down or are written. But breaking down and analysing formulaic sequences and collocations (even if they are recognized as such), in order to extract their lexical material, often results in misremembering them and using them incorrectly. (This, at least, is the EFL perspective; unsurprisingly, ELF researchers see things differently.) Various researchers have given examples of misremembered formulaic sequences such as *a friend of her, are to blamed for, being taking care of, make a great job, on the meantime, put more attention to, take advantages of, those mention above, with my own experience,*[23] *a great advancement on, a staple question, dining and wining, funny enough, how could I know?, I couldn't make heads or tails of it, I didn't think about it twice, in a justice manner, in the weekend, on my personal opinion* and *stick to their memory.*[24]

Regarding collocations, Wray suggests that when a NES first comes across the string *major catastrophe* in contextualized input, it will remain unanalysed by default. As a result, the NES will know that this is the idiomatic way to talk about a big disaster. They won't memorize the individual words, and later talk about a *major intestine* or a *major toe,* or indeed about a *large* or a *big catastrophe.* In contrast,

> the adult language learner, on encountering *major disaster*, would break it down into a word meaning 'big' and a word meaning 'disaster' and store the words separately, without any information about the fact that they went together. When the need arose in the future to express the idea again, they would have no memory of *major disaster* as the pairing previously encountered, and any pairing of words with the right meaning would seem equally possible: *major, big, large, important, considerable* and so on, with *catastrophe, disaster, calamity, mishap, tragedy,* and the like. Some sound nativelike, others do not, and the learner would have no way of knowing which were which.
>
> (p. 208)

This means that a non-native learner at a high level who broke all input down into word-sized units could in principle have a larger lexicon of individual words than most NSs. This could lead, for example, to an appreciation of poetry and a capacity to use language imaginatively, but a deficient store of formulaic sequences will always make language production and comprehension feel more effortful than in the native language; there will remain situations where the NS calls on a sequence and the NNS has to construct one, which is both more labour intensive and more risky. The conventional solution to this, also suggested by Wray (p. 210), is 'residing and fully interacting for some time in the L2 environment.' This, however, is not the solution for ELF, a language without native speakers, and Wray (2008: 20) readily concedes that although adult L2 learners often express messages in meaningful but non-nativelike ways, 'Such formulations may serve the individual fairly well – indeed they may be preferred in lingua franca situations […] where there are no native speakers to impose the particularities of their variety.'[25]

Although Wray laments that L2 learners often fail to acquire stable collocations, or to speak in memorized chunks, Mauranen (2012: 108ff.) suggests that evidence that ELF speakers *do* process speech in chunks of language as well as single-word units, comes precisely from the instances when the chunks go wrong, in rephrasings. Although speakers sometimes rephrase single words, trying to be clearer or more accurate – e.g. 'the increase in population size doesn't *seem look* very strong'– they also repeat longer phrases when only one word in it needs to be changed – 'I've been *investigating* this university so *evaluating* this universities'; 'the point I *said* er earlier that I *made* earlier'; 'it's not the *case* it's not the *factor*'; 'if we want to kind of *have* if we want to kind of *set* the stage'. These rephrasings clearly suggest that the processing unit is a chunk rather than a single word, even if the desired chunk, not having been encountered frequently enough, is insufficiently entrenched to be fully accessed at the first time of asking. Echoing – when speakers repeat exact phrases that their interlocutor has just used – is also evidence of the processing of a multi-word chunk. Consequently Mauranen argues that Wray's account of classroom learners does not seem to apply to ELF users. Although ELF contains great phraseological variation, due to 'fuzzy' or 'shaky' or imperfect entrenchment, ELF speakers also process (some) language in chunks and use (some) fixed expressions.

However the examples above, taken from the ELFA corpus, all involve ELF users with a rather high level of English. Although Wray suggests that language users have a choice between holistic and analytic processing, there is a third possibility (for production rather than reception) – simply inserting L2 words into L1 syntactic patterns. Roger Andersen (1990: 62) describes this as the 'relexification principle': 'When you cannot perceive the structural pattern used by the language you are trying to acquire, use your native language structure with lexical items from the second language.' Similarly, Gozdawa-Gołębiowski (2008) describes what he calls the *contentive* mode of sentence processing (with the stress – at least in ENL – on the first syllable), which he says is used by many lower-level learners, who focus on individual content-bearing lexical items, and transfer basic L1 syntax, while disregarding (annoying) grammatical elements such as inflections marking the thematic functions of the main meaning-bearing words.[26] After all, until you've internalized the grammatical system or learned enough constructions and formulas, what else can you do? In his data – English written by B1 level Polish learners – Gozdawa-Gołębiowski finds 'all-pervasive transfer from Polish at the level of morphosyntax and lexicon' (p. 79) and very little formulaic language.

Using this approach can in fact get you quite a long way, as many tourists have discovered, particularly in inflectionally poor languages rather than, say, languages with lots of cases, although English, whose grammar compensates for a lack of inflections by largely depending on word order, is not necessarily the best language for it either.

However the usage-based theory of language requires us to assume that unlike lower-level classroom learners stuck in the contentive and analytic modes, ELF speakers, like all other language users, use ready-made expressions that they have heard other people say, even if this stock is not very reliably entrenched. Yet the Yannis example above indicates that ELF researchers do not subscribe to the EFL or SLA belief that L2 learners and users should imitate the fixed expressions of NESs.

The idiom principle and the territoriality principle

The processing advantages of formulaic sequences have already been outlined: using a ready-made expression both buys the speaker time to plan the next part of an utterance and aids the hearer's comprehension – as long as he or she is familiar with the expression, of course. Many synthetic formulaic phrases in English are longer than their analytic equivalents, but this regulates the flow of speech, adding redundancy (all the unanalysed morphemes or syllables) and reducing the amount of information contained in an utterance, so that it is more readily interpretable. Without elements of lexical, syntactic or phonetic redundancy, hearers would not be able to absorb information at the speed with which it could be emitted in normal speech.[27] In contrast, in an L2, if the hearer is not familiar with a formulaic sequence, and processes it analytically, morpheme by morpheme, rather than holistically as a 'morpheme equivalent unit,' this adds to the processing load. Even though most L2 speakers have a receptive knowledge of many more formulaic sequences than they actively use, they are unlikely to know as many as NSs. This leads to false starts and lexical searches and rephrasings due to a lack of entrenched sequences. Mauranen (2012: 113) suggests that such rephrasings also give all participants more processing time, which is true, but it is still more work for the speaker than using a prefabricated expression.

However Wray (2008: 4) argues that the use of prefabricated phrases has an overriding purpose over and above aiding fluency and reducing processing effort: 'formulaic language is a linguistic solution to a non-linguistic problem – namely our need to promote and project ourselves in relation to others.' We regularly use language to get the hearer to do something, feel something or think something, for the benefit of our physical, emotional or cognitive needs, in short to manipulate the hearer:

> Requests, demands, warnings, orders, and so on, are intended to get someone else to behave in a particular way, often acting as an agent in achieving something that we want for ourselves but cannot do personally. We are

profoundly motivated actively to seek our own physical and emotional comfort (Maslow 1968), and from the earliest age are programmed to enlist the help of others in attaining it.

(Wray 2002: 88)

These needs include being provided with information when required, expressing information fluently, being listened to and taken seriously, and being perceived as a full member of whichever groups we deem desirable. All of these things are more easily achieved if we use language the hearer will immediately recognize and understand. Formulaic material is more likely to be decoded or interpreted the way the speaker intends, as opportunities for alternative interpretations are minimized.[28]

Consequently Wray argues that we express our identity as an individual by using particular deliberately memorized strings and stylistic markers, and our identity as a group member by adopting customary idiomatic turns of phrase and collocations. We use sequences that we have stored because they 'sound right' to us, because we have often heard them in the speech of others. And by using them, we contribute to what others hear most often and therefore store in their own inventories. The desire to sound like others in the speech community leads to a virtuous circle of cause and effect, and formulaic language plays a central role in maintaining the identity of the community.

Yet Wray explains all this in relation to NSs interacting with communities of NSs, and noticing and imitating their prefabricated phrases. NNSs needing to control their environment and manipulate hearers are said to need to pick up the idiomatic turns of phrase of the host speech community. Using idiomatic and nativelike formulas that NSs can decode easily will greatly enhance the success of the speaker's intended interactional purpose (especially if decoding involves extra processing effort because of the speaker's non-nativelike phonology).

However this argument clearly does not apply to ELF, in which non-nativelike phonology is taken for granted, and there is no native-speaking 'host speech community' whose uses one is expected to conform to. And indeed Seidlhofer argues that NNESs should *not* imitate sequences of words that are regularly used by NESs in case this should be seen as trespassing on someone else's territory or fraudulently claiming membership of their speech community.

Seidlhofer (2011: 16) states that 'ENL is full of conventions and markers of in-group membership such as characteristic pronunciations, specialized vocabulary, idiomatic phraseology, and references and allusions to shared experience and the cultural background of particular native-speaker communities,' none of which is *a propos* in any given ELF interaction. Thus abiding by 'irrelevant' ENL norms – for instance by using its idiomatic phraseology and cultural allusions – when speaking with other ELF users is 'likely to be perceived as a failure to adapt to the ELF situation' (p. 18). Seidlhofer takes it for granted that ENL and ELF have different sociocultural conditions and communicative purposes, and hence different regulative conventions. Yet apart from NESs' possible desire to express their identity within a (possibly mythical) close-knit (monolingual) community with whom they share strong ties in a local neighbourhood, the communicative purposes of ENL and ELF can be very similar. It is simply not true that 'the situations and purposes in and for which ELF speakers typically use the language vary greatly from ENL ones' (p. 131). For example, VOICE consists of interviews, press conferences, service encounters, seminar discussions, working group discussions, workshop discussions, meetings, panels, question/answer sessions and conversations, and the ELFA corpus consists of lectures, presentations, seminars, thesis defences and conference discussions. All of these are events that also occur in ENL contexts with very similar purposes.

Seidlhofer (p. 119) states that native patterns

> are the result of some creative pragmatic process in the past, but the assumption seems to be that this process is the prerogative of native speakers and once it has produced its patterns of usage, what non-natives have to do is to reproduce them.

Yet if we accept that the most efficient way to communicate (in terms of both processing effort and intended effect) is to use widely shared collocations and formulaic sequences, there are clearly advantages to using established patterns, regardless of who originally produced them, if they are understood by both NSs and NNSs. This is simply the way that (native) languages and human cognition work, rather than a conspiracy designed to exclude NNSs. Moreover, as argued in Chapter 3, the fact that English was learnt by many NNSs in the past is a major determinant in the shape of the language today. ELF necessarily contains a great many patterns that are also found in ENL (English is English), but this in no way prevents ELF users from establishing their own characteristic expressions as well.

Seidlhofer takes it for granted that with ELF, 'we are dealing not with a clearly established community of users' who share presupposed norms, but with 'users of the language many of whom do not,' and that 'There is no reason why ELF users should be familiar with recurrent idiomatic features of ENL usage' (p. 131). This neglects the fact that many of them will have learned a lot of their English from ENL-based materials at school, and from ENL media. The idea that ELF must necessarily differ greatly from ENL also contradicts Mauranen's (2012: 82) observation that 'The basic building blocks in ELF are the same as in ENL, and their distribution is also very similar.'

Seidlhofer (2011: 129) also invokes what Widdowson (1983, 1990) calls the 'territorial imperative' which, she says, makes us adjust our language 'to secure and protect our own space and sustain and reinforce our separate social identity, either as an individual or as a group'. The territorial imperative involves making what you say acceptable to others in the same 'territory' and enhancing differences vis-à-vis others to keep them out. Consequently, 'The very attempt to replicate native speaker idiomatic usage could be taken as an attempted territorial encroachment, an outsider's invalid claim to community membership' (p. 132).

However the very concept of 'territory' is paradoxical in relation to ELF. If ELF is an additional or auxiliary language available to everybody, and not a 'foreign' language, its territory is global.

It is also a form of *English*, rather than a separate language, and so by necessity it uses a large proportion of words from ENL, even though a few of them will be morphologically modified to exploit the meaning potential inherent in the virtual language. It also uses a large proportion of native grammatical constructions and patterns, even though a few of them will be modified in aid of explicitness, clarity, communicative economy or increased redundancy. Given that a language doesn't just consist of lexical items and grammatical constructions, but also a huge number of established collocations, prefabricated phrases, and established tokens of most given constructions, it would be absurd (or more precisely, impossible) to attempt to speak English of any kind that did not to some extent replicate native speaker idiomatic usage. If idiomaticity simply means 'the ways words go together' (Prodromou 2008: xi), ELF could not be totally different from ENL and remain the same language.

Moreover, the very notion of a native speech community with common experience and a shared cultural background, on whose linguistic territory one could trespass, is becoming increasingly untenable. For example, does England constitute a homogeneous native-speaker community? Or London? Or South London? Or the South London district of Clapham? Can we expect the lawyers' imaginary 'man on the Clapham omnibus' to be a representative of this community? He is much more likely to be a member of a smaller sub-community, possibly a bilingual second-generation immigrant, who communicates daily with a myriad of other sub-communities. After all, over 300 languages are spoken in London schools (Baker and Eversley (eds) 2000), and according to Guus Extra and Durk Gorter (2001: 12–13), 'It has been estimated that in the year 2000 about one third of the population under the age of 35 in urbanized Western Europe had an immigration background.'

The idea of homogeneous (and monolingual) NS communities sharing the same language and idioms and references and allusions is increasingly a fiction. As Alan Durant (2010) has argued, it is becoming harder to appeal to the 'man on the Clapham omnibus' or the 'reasonable man' or the 'ordinary reader' or the 'average consumer' in disputes about meaning or defamation. In ever more diverse multicultural societies, in which NSs have different life experiences and educational backgrounds, one can no longer rely on a motley collection of individuals (such as a jury) to recognize the same cultural references and allusions and innuendoes, or to agree on intrinsic or inescapable inferences or meanings. As Durant puts it, 'British society has become much less homogeneous in religious, cultural and ethnic terms than in any previous period,' and given the expansion of the media and the internet, 'the range of material now published has massively increased the variety of language and sources for allusion or reference in circulation.' People are exposed to a wide range of different voices and cultural references, which 'creates a greater likelihood that any given cultural reference or culturally specific idiom will be viewed differently, from often incompatible points of view' (p. 171).

So if we disregard the spectre of territorial encroachment, the question becomes which aspects of the multifarious idiomaticity of NESs are useful for ELF? Clearly using established collocations saves you the trouble of reinventing the wheel every time you speak, but as Wray points out, L2 learners often fail to register and routinize NS collocations, without this being a major catastrophe, or even a considerable calamity or a large mishap. Certainly the imitation (even if only approximate) and hopefully the routinization and entrenchment of many constructions also used by NESs will allow you to communicate with other speakers of English.

And indeed most ELF speakers tend to use many fixed expressions also found in ENL. Seidlhofer's (2011: 138) claim that ELF speakers 'may' – may! – 'have access to some of the most commonly occurring fixed phrases available to them (*of course, on time, by the way*)' is a resounding understatement. As already stated, most ELF speakers had ENL teaching materials, and many of them are also 'consumers' of ENL media, and as Seidlhofer also says, 'ELF users will naturally make use of actualizations in English they have been exposed to, and instructed in,' even though their actualizations 'often go well beyond what they have been presented with as the English that they should emulate' (p. 120).[29]

For example, the first extract in VOICE (EDcon4), a casual conversation, includes, among many others, the following fixed phrases: *sad but true, that's life, say no more, are you staying for lunch? something like that, to cross one's mind, the scene of the accident, don't give a shit about, depends on the situation, off the record, oh my god*. The first extract in ELFA (CDIS01A), a conference discussion, contains, among many others, the following discourse markers and metaphorical idioms: *are there any questions? that's an interesting question, the first thing I said, it is not my responsibility, I would be interested in other people's views, flesh and bone, the flow of ideas, I don't know about the rest of you, made us all lose sight of, in real life situations, but of course I agree with you, I was just trying to account for, you're quite right I quite agree with you, so what I contest is, my point of view is that there must be, so it's a tricky question, which I know quite well, they don't leave you much space to, if you do it right, over and over again*. This rather suggests that English is English, or that ENL and ELF are not two separate languages, and that, given the phraseological nature of the English language, ELF speakers and NESs are likely to share expressions. I will now consider different types of expressions in turn.

Discourse markers

The use of established collocations and constructions, even if they originate with NESs, can enhance communication in ELF, as can the use of many ready-made formulaic sequences and sentence stems, especially those used in recurrent social situations. This is particularly true of semantically transparent and grammatically regular ones, unless they are known (by ELF speakers) to be associated with one particular Anglophone country or culture. The same applies to a lot of discourse devices, or what Moon (1998) calls 'organizational FEIs' and Sinclair and

Mauranen (2006) call 'organization-oriented elements,' which help speakers manage individual utterances and longer stretches of discourse. These include logical, temporal, and spatial connectors, phrases for sequencing, summarizing, checking comprehension, and so on, and as Sinclair and Mauranen say, 'the vast majority of [their] realisations […] are listable in a finite list with very few variable constituents,' and 'they tend to follow the idiom principle' (p. 148). Although, as Hopper puts it, grammar is forever emergent, discourse devices are often relatively static. Once again, rather than being irrelevant ENL norms many of these are useful, learnable phrases.

Writing specifically about ELF and phrases that help organize interaction, Mauranen (2009: 224) says that we might expect speakers 'to use them, because they are necessary for ensuring successful communication,' and 'to get them mostly right, because they are frequent and a restricted class.'[30] But she also expects them 'to show variation in form that ignores some conventions and preferences of native English speakers, because English is a foreign language to most of those who use it as a lingua franca.' As in several other articles, she gives the example of a frequent expression in the ELFA corpus used to preface an utterance in which the speaker gives his or her opinion (without wishing to appear too aggressive or non-consensual) – *in* (or *on*) *my point of view*, which appears to be a blend conflating two ENL expressions, *in my view* and *from my point of view*.[31] (These two ENL expressions are also found in ELFA, along with *in my opinion*.) The fact that this expression appears repeatedly in ELFA, used by speakers with different language backgrounds, shows that it is indeed an essentially ELF-specific expression, and not merely many cases of NNESs' failed, approximate attempts at using a target expression. There must be a reason for this, and Mauranen plausibly suggests that speakers prefer the greater visibility and expressivity of the longer form, and compares this to Ranta's (2006) finding that the progressive *-ing* form of the verb is used much more often in ELF than in ENL: 'The longer expressions would seem to carry more prominence, more weight' (p. 230).

Some organizational expressions and idioms have direct translation equivalents in many languages, but many others are actually non-transparent, or what Moon describes as anomalous collocations (including *above all, all in all, and so on, as a rule, as follows, as well as, as yet, for example, for instance, in addition, in a nutshell, in a way, in brief, in case, in effect, in general, in fact, in order to, in question, in part, in short, in spite of, in terms of, in the meantime, no longer, not least, once in a while, of course, on the one hand, on the whole, quote unquote, sort of, such a/an, such as, to date* and *what's more*). As argued in Chapter 3, although English has undergone extensive syntactic regularization and simplification of verbal morphology, losing various conjugations, declensions, inflections and case-marking, it still contains a large inventory of opaque metaphors and expressions. The examples just given (all to be found, usually several times, in ELFA), and indeed all of 'the 505 most frequent nontransparent multiword expressions in English' in Ron Martinez and Norbert Schmitt's (2012) 'Phrasal Expressions List' for use by materials writers and teachers, demonstrate that ELF users are bound to use a lot of irregular fixed expressions.

Metaphorical expressions

On the other hand, ENL also has a large number of less frequent metaphorical expressions that are less useful to ELF speakers, which might easily be misunderstood, and whose use could be described as unilateral idiomaticity.

Prodromou (2008: 6) singles out one such British expression for analysis – *Put hairs on your chest, that one* – discussing when and where it could conceivably be used ('at the moment of handing someone a [strong alcoholic] drink or at the beginning of a drinking session'), how it might be elided or varied, how it might be pronounced, and so on. Expressions such as these, especially those used with humorous, ironic or sarcastic intent, and designed to achieve specific pragmatic effects, are highly pronunciation-sensitive (requiring a particular stress, pitch, intonation and tone of voice) and hence accident-prone. Moreover, they depend on both repeated exposure from an early age (perhaps less so for alcohol-related ones), which L2 users, as a rule, do not have, as well as what Prodromou calls a 'deep commonality,' including shared socio-cultural knowledge and ways of speaking. Most ELF interactions, with their different constellations of speakers, and ELF discourse communities are much more likely to have shallow commonality. Therefore such infrequent, culture-bound idioms are stubbornly resistant to acquisition, even by advanced L2 users of English who tend to avoid them.

Where L2 speakers do know canonical colourful idioms, they often have conscious rather than subliminal knowledge (or declarative rather than procedural knowledge) of them, and are unsure as to what extent they can conventionally be varied (see MacKenzie 2000a). Furthermore, when L2 speakers do try to use idioms creatively or playfully, L1 speakers might simply take their wording to be a mistake (see Prodromou 2008: 231–32, 263–64). In sum, Prodromou says that 'as far as idiomaticity is concerned, L1-users are playing at home, with rules that they can bend according to need; L2-users are playing away and if they break the rules they may be penalized' (p. 238). All of this leads to what he calls the 'idiomatic paradox' (p. xi) in L1 and L2-user discourse: the same factors that make idiomaticity so natural and necessary in native speaker discourse – deep commonality, ease of processing, promotion of fluency, etc. – so that corpus linguists describe it as the heart of spoken grammar, are precisely the reasons NNSs find idioms so elusive, and why some ELF researchers call them 'irrelevant' and an obstacle to mutual intelligibility.[32] Hence we can agree with Seidlhofer (2011: 124) that in ELF, 'Total conformity with ENL conventions would in effect be dysfunctional.'

Consequently, NESs tend to have a large repertoire of opaque and metaphorical expressions that are not shared by NNESs. This is one of the reasons Trudgill (2009: 100) says that adult L2 learning invariably leads to pidginization, of which one of the characteristics is reduction: 'there is simply *less of* a language as compared to the form in which it is spoken by native speakers.'

Kecskes (2007: 200), on the other hand, discussing data from NNESs living in the USA, suggests that they may indeed know these formulaic expressions, but avoid using them because they are worried that their interlocutors will not understand them properly. [...] ELF speakers try to come as close to the compositional meaning of expressions as possible because they think that if there is no figurative and/or metaphorical meaning involved their interlocutors will process the English words and expressions the way they meant them.

Kecskes suggests that lacking mutual knowledge, NNSs 'use the linguistic code itself as a common ground,' rather than socio-cultural background knowledge, as this 'differs significantly with each participant' (p. 204). This concentration on the linguistic code 'results in the priority of literal meaning over non-literal, figurative language and formulaic language.' However, like Seidlhofer and Pitzl (see below), Kecskes also suggests that lingua franca speakers frequently coin or create and share their own non-standard ways of expressing themselves effectively.

However this does not mean that ELF speakers never use *any* ENL idioms; all the evidence shows that they do. Furthermore, international communication in English often involves both L1 and L2 (or ENL and ELF) speakers, or what Meierkord calls interactions across Englishes. As Prodromou puts it, 'ELF encounters slip and slide from NNS-NNS to NNS-NS encounters in a matter of seconds, in real or cyber-space' (2008: 30), and

> ELF cannot be insulated from ENL. An L2–L2 conversation can become an L2–L1 exchange from one moment to the next; it can evolve from shallow to deep commonality within the same speech event; a business deal can grow into friendship or marriage.
>
> *(p. 248)*

The Yannis/*from the house* example with which I began this chapter was precisely an exchange involving L1 and L2 speakers. Seidlhofer (2011: 110) says that ELF speakers 'use English to get a job done, to foster interpersonal relations, and express identity, with a focus on communication, intelligibility, and efficiency rather than on correctness and idiomaticity in ENL terms,' but here was an ELF speaker (possibly aided and abetted by the villainous Peter) who seemed to be trying to communicate, foster interpersonal relations, and express identity by using an ENL idiom, albeit incorrectly.

But is a European speaker of English really supposed to mentally tag each and every phrase he knows as either 'something I've heard or read in ENL' or 'something I've heard and used in ELF'? Or learn ENL phrases receptively but never use them, either in case he is taken to be trespassing on NS territory or because a NNES interlocutor may not know an expression? Or consider every time he speaks whether he's talking to NESs or NNESs (or both) and adjust his English accordingly? All of these things would seem to be inordinately difficult to do. Many plurilingual speakers find it hard work keeping similar foreign languages apart (e.g. Catalan and Spanish, Czech and Slovak, Danish and Norwegian, Russian and Ukrainian), not to mention not so similar languages (French and Italian, Italian and Spanish, Russian and Polish). Enforcing the separate development of two versions of *the same* language would seem to be impossible.

Quite apart from waiters who deal with both L1 and L2 English speakers, there are a great many English users in continental Europe who read or watch a lot of ENL media. Proficiency in foreign languages, particularly English, is often higher in countries where television and cinemas regularly show subtitled programmes in foreign languages.[33] Greece is a subtitling (as opposed to dubbing) territory, as are the Netherlands and Flanders. Eline Zenner *et al.* (2010) cite corpus evidence for the use (as opposed to the citation) of over fifty catchphrases from British and American television series and movies in everyday spoken and written *Dutch*, including *And now for something completely different, Frankly my dear I don't give a damn, I'll make him an offer he can't refuse*, and *There's no place like home*. It seems improbable that Dutch and Flemish speakers with an extensive familiarity with Anglo-American culture and media who use these phrases in their L1 will avoid using them when speaking English for fear of linguistic 'trespassing.'

Seidlhofer gives a second example of unilateral idiomaticity (also discussed by Prodromou 2008: 218) – an American interacting with a German and a Chinese speaker who uses the expression *bottom line* for 'lowest price.' She accepts that 'the phrase simply "pops out,"' rather than being used to belittle a NNES, but says

> the idiomatic expression employed in this case seems uncooperative: the use of the non-transparent phrase in an interaction with two non-native English speakers appears inappropriate and inconsiderate in this specific situation, and is in fact unsuccessful in that it requires repair by rephrasing. It is thus a clear example of conformity to a native-speaker norm of usage being communicatively dysfunctional in an ELF interaction.
>
> *(2011: 136)*

Yet once again, the American probably just thought he was speaking English, or maybe international English, rather than taking part in 'an ELF interaction.' Few NESs can be expected to have the linguistic awareness to know whether an expression could be judged to be transparent, opaque or non-compositional (which is a matter of degree), let alone frequent, infrequent, likely or unlikely to be known to NNESs, etc. Non-specialist NESs might think the expression so common that any English-speaking businessperson will have come across it in conversation or the media.[34] Many of them may not even be aware of the meta-phorical nature of expressions like *on the house* or *the bottom line*.[35] In short, words and expressions that people have in their active vocabulary tend to 'pop out.' NNESs may be better than NESs at regulating their language usage, though per-haps not if they think they are simply speaking English rather than ELF. All in all, I find Seidlhofer's judgement of Yannis and of the American speaker as unco-operative and inconsiderate to be overly harsh. Although I have gradually come to accept several of the arguments of ELF researchers, I find this argument a step too far and this is where I definitely part company with Seidlhofer.

Moreover it would be a brave person who states unequivocally that a given idiom is only to be found in (native) English. The splendid 'Widespread Idioms in Europe and Beyond' project (Piirainen 2012) has analysed hundreds of idioms that are found right across Europe (in up to seventy-three languages including, among others, Germanic, Romance, Celtic, Baltic, Slavonic, Indo-Iranian, Finno–Ugric, Turkic, Caucasian and Semitic ones).[36] These idioms have been spread as a result of bilingualism and linguistic and cultural contact over hundreds of years, including the dissemination of proverbs and narratives (fables, legends, fairy tales, etc.) and printed works (including the Bible and Greco-Roman classics), as well as interactions among people who were not afraid to utter what might be seen as 'unilateral' idioms. Quite simply, how many ordinary NESs or ELF speakers can be expected to know that, e.g. *a black day, a storm in a teacup, a tough nut to crack, an open secret, at any price, at full steam, come as a real bombshell, fifth column, give the green light, hit below the belt, light at the end of the tunnel, on the same wavelength, recharge your batteries* and *tip of the iceberg* are all widely found in different languages across Europe, but *the bottom line* is not (given that financial statements are just as widespread as green lights and batteries, and rather more so than icebergs)? Some English idioms also have equivalents outside Europe: e.g. Yano (2009: 253) gives a list of expressions that have identical Japanese counterparts.[37]

Multilingual speakers will be aware that some idioms they know are shared across the languages they use; they may also know or suspect that others are specific to one language, and be unsure about many more because they speak different languages with varying levels of proficiency. But this does not preclude calquing (translating word for word) idioms into foreign languages, hoping they will be understood. Many multilinguals habitually do this (when they are not simply code-switching), without fear of being reprimanded for 'unilateral' behaviour.

Translating or adapting an opaque idiom necessarily requires analysing its form – it ceases to be a holistically-processed 'MEU.' Pitzl (2009) gives examples of this process in VOICE, and describes such translations as creative re-metaphorizations. For example, *we should not wake up any dogs* is nowhere near the canonical English *let sleeping dogs lie*, and probably not an attempt to produce it, so Pitzl describes it as being 'created and employed successfully in the context' (p. 308). But it is also an approximate calque, uttered by a German speaker, of the similar German proverb *schlafende Hunde soll man nicht wecken*, and so would appear to be more an act of translation than of creation *per se*. Pitzl gives another example – *put my hands into the fire for it*, used by a Dutch speaker in an interaction with German speakers. While this sounds creative in English, it is a translation of an idiom used in both Dutch and German, so again no exceptional creativity is involved. This is simply the kind of translation that bi- and multilinguals regularly find themselves doing, often an unintended consequence of crosslinguistic interaction, and of having a partially integrated bi- or multilingual lexicon and phrasicon, or a common underlying proficiency or conceptual base (see Chapter 2). Pitzl also gives examples of speakers announcing that they are translating an idiom – e.g. *it's a saying in Holland that er we don't have savings but under the bed we have a lot of er money in the sock* (p. 315).

Pitzl also states that

> The chances of (sleeping) metaphors inherent in idioms being re-activated
> are presumably much higher in ELF than in ENL, where the con-
> ventionalization and institutionalization of idiomatic expressions can be seen
> to hamper the possibility for re-metaphorization and make the occurrence of
> this process (though not impossible) less likely.
>
> *(pp. 316–17)*

Yet as mentioned above, both Sinclair and Langlotz show how so-called non-
compositional idioms can be (and are) decomposed, re-metaphorized and used
creatively in ENL.

As well as translated idioms, Pitzl (2012: 43–44) gives a few examples of entirely
novel ones (*they're locking the wheels so to speak, I feel that many times I am pulling on
brakes, we should er put on full armour and er take out the old swords and lances*, etc.) and
therefore rightly states that there can be three types of metaphors in ELF: ENL
idioms and variations of them, transplanted idioms from other languages, and
genuine *ad hoc* creations.[38] But all of this is normal, expected bilingual behaviour,
and does not require any glorification of the abilities of ELF users or denigration of
the native speaker.

Using translated idioms from other languages in a predominantly ENL context –
such as putting hairs on your chest in a British pub – or when translating for an
ENL target audience, is not wholly cooperative behaviour; it is indeed what
Seidlhofer calls unilateral idiomaticity. Yet ELF interactions among multilinguals
are perhaps the ideal setting in which to be adventurous with transliterated metaphorical idioms. Metaphors and sayings, especially proverbial ones, *are* often deci-
pherable; indeed the French translation theorist Antoine Berman (1985/2004: 287)
argued that we have 'a proverb consciousness which immediately detects, in a new
proverb, the brother of an authentic one.' Of course this consciousness isn't
infallible: Prodromou (2008: 219) quotes lots of examples of unilateral idiomaticity
that led to misunderstanding. Yet his informants stated that if they felt bewildered
by an idiom they simply asked for clarification, or let it pass.

All in all, it seems hard to disagree with Prodromou's (2008: 251–52) statement
(already quoted in Chapter 2) that

> when idioms do appear [in ELF], they will appear in modified form, taking
> on the shape of the mother tongue of the speaker and the pluralistic nature
> of the speech encounter. [...] ELF speakers will poach on L1 linguistic
> territory when it suits them and when they are able to do so. Their use of
> phraseology will be different from, but on an equal footing with, their L1-user
> counterparts.

However the evidence seems to show that ELF speakers also poach on ENL linguistic 'territory' rather more than Seidlhofer suggests, without fear of being

reprimanded for encroachment. If idioms which take on the shape of the speaker's mother tongue are *not* cases of unilateral idiomaticity, ENL idioms are not necessarily out of bounds either. In fact Seidlhofer's insistence that ENL idioms should be avoided brings to mind the constrained writing exercises of the 'Oulipo' school (short for *Ouvroir de littérature potentielle*) such as 'lipograms' which arbitrarily avoid a particular letter or group of letters (like the rather useful vowel 'e' in Georges Perec's novel *La Disparition*). This can be great fun,[39] but it is obviously much more difficult than using all the resources of the language. Similarly, communication in English will often be facilitated by employing ready-made syntagms used by the language's native speakers. Meanwhile Seidlhofer's converse recommendation to exploit the whole of the 'virtual language,' rather than limiting oneself to the established phraseology of actual ENL, reminds me of another radical approach to formal potential associated with Vienna – the atonal or twelve-tone technique of Schoenberg, Berg and Webern which involves composing music using all twelve semitones of the chromatic scale rather than restricting oneself to the more usual eight (including the repeat at the octave). However twelve-tone music can safely be described as a minority taste, and most people improvising on a piano or other instrument find themselves knocking out something in a recognizable key, because it somehow *sounds better* that way. Similarly, many learners of English might prefer using a lot of the established lexis and phraseology of the actual language (both ENL and ELF) to exploiting the unconstrained potential of the virtual language.

Formulaicity and variation in ELF

One thing that Seidlhofer's *this is from the house* example *does* demonstrate (if we don't accept arguments endorsing a phraseological *apartheid* of ENL and ELF speakers), is that when established ENL phraseology *is* used (up to a point), it is often varied. As argued in the previous chapters, ELF speakers show a high tolerance for variation or fuzziness, and as Dwight Bolinger (1976: 1) suggested, writing about ENL, English has 'an incredibly large number of prefabs, which have the magical property of persisting even when we knock some of them apart and put them back together in unpredictable ways.' Upon encountering knocked apart expressions in ELF, NESs in an analytical rather than a let it pass mood, and teachers who expect L2 speakers to use native idioms verbatim, might think 'Thou com'st in such a questionable shape,' as Hamlet says to his father's ghost. But analytical NESs and prescriptive teachers are only ghostly presences in genuine ELF contexts.[40]

ELF corpora reveal lots of approximate forms of recognisable ENL expressions. Some of these are grammatically (morphosyntactically) non-standard, often using different articles and prepositions from ENL use – e.g. *by the time being, carved in stones, does it make any different, from other point of view, in accordance to, in the right track, it's very much important, on the long-run, pieces by pieces, put the end on it, take closer look to the world, there is quite much problems*. Others use semantic or lexical approximations – e.g. *building stones* (for building blocks), *divide and govern* (for divide and rule), *the hen or the egg* (for chicken and egg), *keep in the head* (for bear in mind), *lift an eyebrow* (for raise), *a side-product* (for by-product), *small and middle business* (for small and medium-sized businesses), *a streak of good luck* (for stroke), *turn a blank eye* (for blind), etc.[41] As Mauranen (2012: 144) puts it, 'speakers use sequences which approximate conventionalised, phraseological units, but in ways that do not quite match the target,' but – importantly – although 'ELF speakers tend to get them slightly wrong,' they 'also get them approximately right'! In a frequent (if approximate) multi-word unit, the non-standard elements 'get embedded in the larger schematic unit, which is sufficiently conventionalised to be recognisable as a unit in a given function.'[42]

Seidlhofer (2011: 134) explains idiomatic variation in ELF by stating that the idiom principle must 'allow for non-conformity with any existing idiomatic expressions where this is necessary or appropriate, that is to say where shared knowledge of the exact wording cannot be taken for granted.' Yet she also says that

> if the idiom principle is a natural feature facilitating language use, it cannot be in abeyance. […] It must also involve the dynamic on-line application of the principle, and we would expect this to result in changes in wording, and the use of local idiomatic coinages devised to meet an immediate communicative need. And this is indeed what we do find in the use of English as a lingua franca.
>
> *(p. 131)*

However 'changes in wording' only fit the idiom principle, as defined by Sinclair, if these changes result in fixed or semi-fixed expressions which become established in a speech community. If 'local idiomatic coinages' means making up phrases, creatively putting one word after another, so that 'a large range of choice opens up, and the only restraint is grammaticalness' (Sinclair 1991: 110), this is not so much the on-line application of the idiom principle as the use of the open-choice principle. Seidlhofer says this too: the 'virtual language' is the resource that allows ELF speakers 'to assemble on-line idiomatic expressions by exploiting the open-choice principle' (2011: 134), which is to say that in ELF, the idiom principle *is* in abeyance to a considerable extent.

Getting phraseological units approximately right is considered insufficient by orthodox accounts of ELT (or EFL). The standard complaint about the written language of proficient learners of English – i.e. those who have mastered the grammar – is that they use non-standard phraseology. For example, Sylviane Granger (1998b: 152) says they use the open-choice rather than the idiom principle, which results in 'atypical word-combinations' – 'learners' phraseological skills are severely limited: they use too few nativelike prefabs and too many foreign-sounding ones' (p. 158). (Then again, they *are* foreign, and most of them are learning English as a Foreign Language!) Peter Howarth (1998) argues that NNES students overuse restricted collocations (e.g. *do attempts, do a measurement, get contact with, make a reaction*, etc.), thereby failing to meet the stylistic expectations of the academic community, and deflecting the reader's attention from content to form. According to Howarth,

> learners need to understand that restricted collocations make up a significant part of a typical native speaker's production in both speech and writing. Conforming to the native stylistic norms for a particular register entails not only making appropriate grammatical and lexical choices but also selecting conventional collocations to an appropriate extent. Such combinations are not optional stylistic adornments on the surface of a text; they are essential for effective communication, and their use by non-native writers is a clear sign that these learners have made an essential adjustment to the academic culture they are entering.
>
> *(p. 186)*

The ELF perspective is obviously different. As Mauranen (2012: 235) puts it, 'The wide variety of purposes that English is put to in the academic world, for instance in international student and staff mobility, research groups, and research centres, is in effect ELF.' Hence the varied (and not always ENL-like) forms of ELF should be accepted for what they are, and the model in academic environments should be 'the "educated speaker of English" without strings to nativeness' (p. 238). In such an environment, conventional ENL collocations are not necessarily 'essential for effective communication' but are indeed 'optional stylistic adornments.'

Mauranen also finds some expressions which seem specific to ELF, including *I would like to say some words about*, already mentioned in Chapter 4, and *in my point of view*, discussed above. She also finds more occurrences of *as the matter of fact* than *as a matter of fact* in the ELFA corpus. She suggests (2009: 230) that these expressions are examples of '"approximation," the tendency of ELF speakers to latch on to salient features of a phraseological unit, which they use in its established sense, but without exactly reproducing the standard form.' Approximations of established phrases (from both ENL and ELF) 'contain enough familiar material for the hearer to go on to ensure comprehension,' thereby giving some freedom to the speaker: 'by virtue of the conventional and fixed parts which ensure recognition, phraseological units allow a measure of freedom for innovation or approximation in details without risking comprehensibility.' Linguistic forms which users find to be communicatively successful are likely to stabilize and spread and become entrenched (to some extent), at least in relatively stable contact environments. Mauranen (2012: 160) therefore concludes that these are examples of 'incipient patterns' and that 'ELF speech is thus converging on new preferences,' which is a reasonable enough conclusion, even though (as the matter of fact, in my point of view) the examples of incipient patterns are somewhat limited.

Even if it is not true that the less speakers deviate from StE, the greater are their chances of communicating successfully, it is true that the more entrenched constructions and expressions they have, the less analytic processing work they will have to do and the less energy they will have to expend in composing their utterances. Although ELF-like pragmatic strategies such as explicitation, clarification, rephrasing, etc. are useful and/or necessary with less proficient ELF users, it can hardly be considered a disadvantage to possess a large repertoire of fixed and semi-fixed expressions which save you the trouble of composing phrases from scratch (or reinventing the wheel) every time you speak. These entrenched constructions do not, of course, all have to be those of ENL – as shown in Chapter 4, different uses of prepositions, countable plurals, extended use of the continuous aspect, non-native verb complementation patterns, etc. are perfectly acceptable – but if they come prefabricated they save the speaker a lot of processing effort. The same clearly applies to phraseological units or fixed and semi-fixed expressions.

Notes

1 Khakheperresenb was an Egyptian scribe; translated from a fragment of a pupil's writing tablet now in the British Museum (Bate 1970: 3–4).
2 Coincidentally, Trudgill (2008b) has written an interesting book about Crete.
3 Seidlhofer has revealed that back in the day Randolph Quirk briefly took her for a NES, although soon afterwards she discovered on holiday that Cretans didn't understand her British English, and the rest is history. See Interview, *Spiegel Online*, 1 April 2008 (not an April Fool), http://www.spiegel.de/schulspiegel/wissen/0,1518,544335,00.html.
4 Can someone do a survey? Or maybe the problem is cultural – you never get free drinks in Norway?
5 The terms prefabs, prefabricated phrases, lexical phrases, phrasemes, institutionalized utterances, formulaic sequences, etc. are more or less synonymous (at least for present purposes). There is little terminological agreement in this area; Wray (2002: 9) lists over 40 competing terms.
6 This figure seems remarkably high, but by way of example Pawley and Syder give a list of forty-six common English expressions including just one word, *think*, and I found over twenty more by consulting a few good bilingual dictionaries: see MacKenzie (2000b: 76–77).
7 Theorists of simultaneous interpreting stress that interpreters concentrate on the *sense* of what is being said, not individual words (they *interpret* rather than translate), and that units of sense are 'deverbalized' in being transferred into another language; the actual words used rapidly disappear from short-term memory (see Lederer 2003). Yet while this appears to be true of interpreting, in ordinary circumstances we seem to have an uncanny ability to remember a huge amount of verbatim language; see Gurevich *et al.* (2010).
8 See the classification of types of lexical phrases in Nattinger and DeCarrico (1992: 37ff.).
9 Ever since Chafe (1968) described idiomaticity as an 'anomaly in the Chomskyan paradigm,' it has been conventional to describe idioms as part of the grammar of a language; indeed construction grammar begins with irregular items and extends its analysis to regular ones.
10 Wray (2002: 3) begins with the attested fact that a lot of people couldn't tell you what *Rice Krispies* are made of, notwithstanding their rather ricy and crisp appearance, because the brand name is stored as a holistic unit in the lexicon, separately from *rice* and *crisp*. Whereas *Golden Grahams* …
11 Numerous linguists have proposed overlapping definitions of idioms and idiomaticity, including Smith (1925), Hockett (1958), Weinreich (1969), Makkai (1972), Bolinger (1976) and Fernando (1996), but this definition will suffice for present purposes.

12 Fillmore *et al.* (1988) drew on an extended analysis of the idiom *let alone* to argue for a construction grammar that takes account of the syntax, semantics *and* pragmatics of idiomatic expressions or phraseological units.

13 Clearly *identical* word-strings will occur less frequently in languages with many inflexions.

14 For example, the saying *You shouldn't count your chickens (before they're hatched)* is rarely used in its basic form; Sinclair (2004: 196n) says 'Of the 16 instances of *chicken* and *count* in a corpus of 200 million words, only one instance of the presumed canonical form is to be found.' A quick internet search throws up sentences like *Not quite time to count the chickens*; *I don't want to indulge in premature chicken counting, but* … ; *I don't want to be accused of unhatched chicken-counting* … ; *Of course, this is all chicken counting since I haven't signed a contract yet*, and so on.

15 In fact Hoey goes further than this in knocking grammar down to size: 'What we call grammatical categories are best regarded as post-hoc generalisations from the individual instances of lexical primings' (p. 156); 'What we count as grammar is the accumulation and interweaving of the primings of the most common sounds, syllables and words of the language' (p. 159).

16 Hoey (p. 8) suggests that lexical priming is a bridge between what Chomsky (1986) calls E-language (externalized language) and I-language (internalized language), the language found in speakers' brains.

17 It is because we process holistically that slips of the tongue, semantic incongruities, performance errors and typos often go unnoticed (except by language teachers …).

18 Hunston (2002: 20–21) goes further, suggesting that intuition is also a poor guide to frequency, prosody and phraseology. See also Alderson (2007).

19 Oscar Wilde does this throughout *The Importance of Being Earnest*, with lines like 'Divorces are made in heaven' and 'It is simply washing one's clean linen in public.' See MacKenzie (2000a) on improvisation, creativity, and formulaic language.

20 Altenberg was using the half-million word London-Lund Corpus of Spoken English. His figure presumably includes grammatical units of more than one word (such as *be going to*, *have to*, etc.). Kecskes (2003: 4) argues that there is a formulaic or functional continuum, with grammatical units at one end, semantic units or fixed formulas in the middle, and situation-bound utterances and pragmatic expressions or idioms at the other.

21 See MacKenzie (2000b).

22 This particular formulation is from Mark Powell, quoted in Lewis (1997: 41). Lewis was by no means alone in theorizing grammaticalized lexis; by the 1990s even Chomsky had recognized the primacy of lexis. *The Minimalist Program* (1995) is (loosely speaking) lexically rather than syntactically driven – selected lexical items are inserted or arranged into structures.

23 From written work by advanced ESL students in the USA, in Yorio (1989: 62–63), quoted in Wray (2002: 199).

24 From Prodromou's (2008: 221–22) corpus of SUEs or successful users of English.

25 Wray (2009: 236) refers explicitly to ELF research, which 'rais[es] the status of the L2 pattern beyond that of "imperfect L1 pattern."'

26 This is in a sense the obverse of what Muysken (2000: 186) calls 'congruent lexicalization,' a form of code-switching between typologically related languages with a similar grammatical structure, where any part of a sentence can be filled by lexical elements from either language.

27 With the help of logarithms and the theory of entropy, Weaver (1949) estimated that the English language is no less than 50 per cent redundant.

28 Wray's perhaps excessively self-focused account of language provides a useful counterpoint to ELF researchers' emphasis on accommodation. E.g. Mauranen (2012: 219–20) says that 'Making one's talk clear and explicit is in itself a way of adapting to interlocutors, a form of recipient design, and can be seen as accommodating to interlocutors in a wide sense of accommodation.' Yes indeed, but the point of that accommodation might well be to get the interlocutor to do something for us.

29 Seidlhofer and Widdowson (2009: 105) use a different verb: ELF users will be influenced by the varieties 'they have been constrained to learn in the context of classrooms,' which makes English teaching sound like a process of intimidation.

30 Organizational expressions can also be used with different frequencies in ELF and ENL: e.g. *I mean* is used proportionally several times more by speakers in the ELFA corpus than by NESs in the MICASE corpus.

31 Barlow and Kemmer (2000: xvi–xvii) describe blends as a common way of making semi-fixed, semi-creative structures, and suggest that this process requires us to rethink the distinction between productive syntax vs. fixed expressions.

32 Prodromou (2008: 42) gives a nice catalogue of negative adjectives and nouns that various linguists have applied to idiomaticity, including anarchic, capricious, dangerous, elusive, Janus-faced, Protean, slippery and treacherous; a jungle, a minefield, a nuisance, a scourge and a stumbling block; dangers, traps and pitfalls.

33 In Europe, subtitling countries include Belgium (Flanders), Croatia, the Czech Republic, Denmark, Greece, Greek Cyprus, Finland, the Netherlands, Norway, Slovenia and Sweden. Foreign language proficiency is often lower in countries where foreign programmes are dubbed, including France, Italy and Spain – and also, of course, in Britain, where virtually all foreign programmes are in American English. (Germany, a dubbing country, is something of an exception.) For this reason, Van Parijs (2011: 107), who boldly asserts that 'language learning is at least as much the task of our media as it is of our schools', calls for a ban on dubbing.

34 I included this expression in most of my business English books (namely MacKenzie 1995, 1997, 2006, 2010, 2012c), but only in the (almost) literal sense – the last line on a profit and loss account or income statement (at least until accountants invented 'below the line' items), showing the net profit or net income (or net loss) – and not in the idiomatic lowest price sense, precisely because this is an ENL idiom rather than a piece of financial terminology.

35 British people with *particularly* poor language awareness and a total inability to moderate their use of opaque idioms get hired to interview foreign footballers on British television.

36 See also http://www.widespread-idioms.uni-trier.de.

37 There *are* native English expressions that come with a lot of country-specific cultural baggage, and which are not part of a shared European culture (*the white man's burden, manifest destiny, one nation under God,* etc.), but *on the house,* or an approximation for it, and *the bottom line* are not examples of these.

38 I have not had access to Pitzl's longer doctoral dissertation on this subject.

39 For example, Harry Matthews has rewritten 'To be or not to be: that is the question' without the letter *a* – 'To be or not to be: this is the question'; without the letter *i* – 'To be or not to be: that's the problem,' and without the letter *e* – 'Almost nothing, or nothing: but which?' (Bénabou and Fournel (eds) 2009: 21–22)!

40 I owe this line in this context to Sixta Quasdorf, one of the researchers at the University of Basel responsible for HyperHamlet, a splendid database of (mis)quotations from and allusions to Hamlet: http://www.hyperhamlet.unibas.ch.

41 From Mauranen (2012, *passim*), Prodromou (2008: 221–22), and Pitzl (2012: 42).

42 This should be of considerable interest to people who try to teach conventionalized phraseological units, and even more so to those of us who put them in ELT coursebooks as models for acquisition. This is an argument I tried to make in my presentation at the 2002 ESSE conference ('Language teaching and the uses of so-called English as a lingua franca'), but judging by Jenkins' (2007: 41) paraphrase, I obviously didn't express it very clearly. The reason for the 'so-called' in the title is revealed in MacKenzie (2009: 233).

7

ELF AND SELF: IDENTITY AND ACCENT

As human beings we are able to change our behaviour. The idea that we act as free agents is fundamental to our self-conception. Every word we say reinforces this conviction, for whenever we speak we make choices.

Coulmas (2005: 1)

it is of course recognized as inevitable that virtually all ELF users with a first language other than English will speak the language with some trace (more or less pronounced, so to speak) of an L1 accent. From an ELF perspective, this accent is perfectly acceptable (and even desirable as an expression of identity) as long as it does not cause serious intelligibility problems.

Seidlhofer (2011: 128)

A true evaluation of one's English language comprehensibility should be based on the judgement of both native and non-native speakers. Native English speakers should be judged for comprehensibility by non-native speakers too.

Smith and Bisazza (1983: 59)

One of the more persistent arguments of ELF researchers is that speakers of English as an international language – provided that they ensure intelligibility, for example by respecting the 'Lingua Franca Core for pronunciation' – should otherwise express their (national and linguistic) identity by speaking with their natural L1 accent, rather than seeking to imitate a NES accent. In this chapter I will discuss the concept of identity, and suggest that this account of L1-based identity and pronunciation is inadequate in these times of 'high' or 'late' modernity or post-modernity. If more than half of the world's population is bi- or multilingual, why should speakers seek to define themselves (linguistically) by their L1 alone, or by the deliberate use of an L1 accent in English? This notion reflects a rather old-fashioned and static (and surprisingly monolingual, or at best monolingual-plus-ELF) concept of identity. Jenkins (2007: 25) takes it as given that in any L2 there is an 'intelligibility–identity conflict,' and that many NNESs have an 'apparent desire [...] to project their L1 identity in their L2 English' (p. 23). Yet a lot of people in the contemporary world consider their plurilingualism – or to adapt Pierre Bourdieu's (1991) terminology, their plurilinguistic capital – to be a defining part of their identity.

Identity, Kokoschka and Modigliani

In *Nations and Nationalism*, Ernest Gellner (1983: 139) famously contrasted two imagined maps of the world, one pre-industrial, and the other modern, built on the principle of nationalism. The first map resembles a painting by Kokoschka:

> The riot of diverse points of colour is such that no clear pattern can be discerned in any detail, though the picture as a whole does have one. A great diversity and plurality and complexity characterises all distinct parts of the whole: the minute social groups, which are the atoms of which the picture is composed, have complex and ambiguous and multiple relations to many cultures; some through speech, others through their dominant faith, another still through a variant faith or set of practices, a fourth through administrative loyalty, and so forth.

The political system in the pre-industrial world is just as complex as the sphere of culture. In contrast, the ethnographic and political map of an area of the modern world

> resembles not Kokoschka but, say, Modigliani There is very little shading, neat flat surfaces are clearly separated from each other, it is generally plain where one begins and another ends, and there is little if any ambiguity or overlap. We see that an overwhelming part of political authority has been concentrated in the hands of one kind of institution, a reasonably large and well-centralised state.

This is because the economy of a modern society, controlled by the state, depends on mobility and a level of communication between individuals which requires them to be socialized into the same high culture.

Today, however, the idea of the essentially homogeneous and probably monolingual modern nation state already seems to be something of an anachronism. Borders and cultures have become more porous, and a huge number of people speak English as an additional language. Clearly separated neat flat surfaces à la Modigliani are again giving way to ambiguity or overlap. As James Clifford (1988: 13–14) put it, writing five years after Gellner:

> This century has seen a drastic expansion of mobility, including tourism, migrant labor, immigration, urban sprawl. [...] In cities on six continents,

foreign populations have come to stay – mixing in but often in partial, specific fashions. The 'exotic' is uncannily close. [...] Difference is encountered
in the adjoining neighborhood, the familiar turns up at the ends of the earth.

Even so, most of us still have fairly strong conceptions of national cultural characteristics. Abstracting away from foreign populations who have come to stay,
essentialist accounts of intercultural communication give pride of place to the
influence of national cultures. For example, Geert Hofstede (1980: 16) states that
there is a collective (learned) level of 'human mental programming,' in between
the universal level (determined by biology and physiology), and the individual level
(the realm of psychology). The collective level consists of patterns of thinking,
feeling and acting, and values (or mental programmes) that everyone in a particular
cultural context acquires in childhood socialization and carries through life.[1]
Mental programmes are resilient to change and often contain strong national
components that are passed on from generation to generation.[2] Some linguists also
stress the importance of national identities, e.g. John Edwards (2009: 9) states that
'ethnonational solidarities' must be 'at the heart of any treatment of language and
group identity,' as 'the subjective, intangible, non-rational and symbolic pillars of
group affiliation are by far the strongest and most enduring.'

Yet occupational mobility for many people these days is international rather than
intra-national. People move around. Some of them work for the kind of transnational corporations Kenichi Ohmae celebrated in his book *The Borderless World*
(1990), and identify with their employer more than their home country. (These are
the kind of people who tend to call countries *markets*, even when talking about
their vacations.) Similarly, Thomas Friedman (2007) asserts that this century is the
period of 'Globalization 3,' which involves the globalization of individuals, following 'Globalization 1' (1492–c.1800), which involved countries, and Globalization 2, which involved companies. According to Friedman, in Globalization 3,
'every person now must, and can, ask: Where do *I* as an individual fit into the
global competition and opportunities of the day, and how can *I*, on my own,
collaborate with others globally?' (p. 11).

Robert Reich lamented in *The Work of Nations* (1991: 252) that mobile
knowledge workers, whom he called 'symbolic analysts' – people who manipulate
words and data in management, banking, finance, research, technology, engineering, legal services, media, telecoms, computing, higher education, etc. – 'have been
seceding from the rest of the nation,' and have a sense of global citizenship rather
than a commitment to their nation.[3] Consequently the shared components of a
national culture have to compete with individually chosen ones. Individuals per-
sonify ever smaller fractions of the whole culture, and selfish impulses vie with
collective ones. National cultures are no longer homogeneously distributed among
citizens, but increasingly hybrid. Most nations are now far too diverse to constitute
what Benedict Anderson (1983/1991) called inclusive 'imagined communities' of
people most of whom never meet but still feel that they have something in
common and a shared identity. Thus Ulf Hannerz (1996: 78), taking up Gellner's

metaphor, suggests that today, 'Kokoschka is back, and it seems that he is taking over rather more of the canvas.' State and culture no longer coincide; complexity, ambiguity and multiple relationships have returned. But the new age of greater multilingualism and more fluid identities is clearly not a return to the middle ages or premodern times, because it is also characterized by communications technology and globalization (see Graddol 2006: 21).

Globalization has led to both great mobility and global media that compete with most national cultures. This is not an entirely recent phenomenon: Marshall McLuhan (1962: 31) posited the existence of the 'global village' over fifty years ago. A great many sociologists and linguists have proposed overlapping accounts of identity in the contemporary globalized world. Virtually all of them describe it as malleable, motile, mutable, and so on – the same kind of adjectives that are regularly used to describe ELF.

Le Page and Tabouret-Keller (1985: 14) describe linguistic behaviour as 'a series of *acts of identity* in which people reveal both their personal identity and their search for social roles.' Speakers who want to express solidarity or to avoid mis-communication with others accommodate to their ways of using language. This simultaneously strengthens in-group linguistic affiliations and weakens links with out-groups, allowing the construction of a partial social identity based on the groups to which people belong (cf. the discussion of accommodation in Chapter 4). However, in today's world face-to-face engagement in local speech communities or social groups is massively supplemented by mediated experience, in both printed and electronic forms. In *Modernity and Self-Identity*, Anthony Giddens (1991: 2) describes how the media 'prise social relations free from the hold of specific locales, recombining them across wide time-space distances,' and allow, or rather require, individuals to forge their self-identities. The self has to be reflexively made:

> The reflexive project of the self, which consists in the sustaining of coherent, yet continuously revised, biographical narratives, takes place in the context of multiple choice as filtered through abstract systems. In modern social life, the notion of lifestyle takes on a particular significance. The more tradition loses its hold, and the more daily life is reconstituted in terms of the dialectical interplay of the local and the global, the more individuals are forced to negotiate lifestyle choices among a diversity of options.
>
> *(p. 5)*[4]

Of course, choice can be reduced by issues of class and gender and ethnic inequality. And by declining to have a television or use the internet or take any notice of popular culture.

While Giddens describes the current period as one of 'high' or 'late' modernity, many other theorists prefer to talk about *postmodernity*. For example Zygmunt Bauman (1992: 192ff.) describes the postmodern condition as one of pluralism, variety, contingency and ambivalence, but like Giddens he sees the necessity for self-constitution or self-assembly. Given the quantity of extremely varied and momentary interactions in contemporary life, people are no longer socialized into the norms of a social group, but instead assemble or construct themselves (or as the preferable, widely attested ELF usage would have it, *themself*), by trial and error, in a series of emergent episodes. Importantly, this process or activity or work-in-progress of self-constitution involves disassembling as well as assembling, shedding as well as adopting, forgetting as well as learning.[5]

The majority of people in both developed and developing countries have access to various media, often in English as well as their local language. And they don't just passively consume media products, but creatively and constructively appropriate what they want from them; as Arjun Appadurai (1996: 4) puts it, 'electronic mediation and mass migration [...] seem to impel (and sometime compel) the work of the imagination.' Similarly, Pennycook (2010b: 592) argues that it is 'important to understand the roles of pleasure and desire, and the possibilities that popular culture may hold out for the new cultural and linguistic relations and for new possible modes of identity.'[6]

Some people see globalization as the Trojan Horse of American cultural imperialism and corporate economic and military agendas which will ineluctably lead to the homogenization of world culture. For example, Norman Fairclough (2006: 7–8) distinguishes between the 'flows' of globalization and what he calls 'globalism': the manipulation of these flows by the USA and its allies through the imposition of neo-liberal market economics. Similarly, Phillipson (2008: 260) describes the so-called 'transnational youth culture' as in fact being 'essentially American, promoting a Hollywood consumerist ideology' (see also Phillipson 1992). Other observers, however, see mediated self-assembly as leading to a great deal of diversity, and often to an increase of individualism at the expense of any kind of collective solidarity. As Hannerz (1992: 34) puts it:

> Because there is such a proliferation of messages from everywhere in the media, postmodern culture is characterized by a multiplicity of perspectives and voices. It is a thing of shreds and patches. Juxtaposition becomes the prevalent experience as you zap your way around the television dial, and wander aimlessly through the shopping mall. When you have heard and seen everything and registered the contradictions, irony and scepticism make up a more likely stance than commitment and piety.[7]

Yet Hannerz concedes that accounts of consumer-oriented postmodern identity – you are defined by what you 'do' (or consume) rather than what you 'are' – can go too far, and disputes the idea that 'identities become nothing but assemblages from whatever imagery is for the moment marketed through the media' (p. 35).

Other commentators are less worried about individualism; e.g. Appadurai (1996: 8) suggests that mediated self-constitution can also create communities of sentiment: groups that begin to imagine and feel things together, or to use Raymond Williams' (1965: 64) term, to share a 'structure of feeling.'[8]

Clearly there are also many people who *do* still identify with their local or national culture, and believe that they should have the right to live their life surrounded by like-minded (and similarly coloured) people with an absolute right to their cultural heritage and cultural identity. Moreover, expatriates (who, unlike exiles, have chosen to change countries) and postmodern cosmopolitans who move around and have what might be called elective affinities with the aesthetically agreeable bits of other cultures, depend on other people conserving their local cultures, without which their (essentially narcissistic) cosmopolitan lifestyle could not exist.[9]

All in all, the majority of the 'reflexive selves' of the late modern or postmodern world – or at least those of the outer and expanding circles – are likely to have a lifestyle – and an identity – that involves the use of more than one language.

Is there an identity–communication continuum?

It goes without saying that the great majority of cosmopolitan 'symbolic analysts,' and many other migrants, have English as one of their languages. Despite the arguments of most ELF researchers, many multilinguals clearly *do* feel that they have some kind of obligation to learn languages 'properly,' by which they generally mean as the natives speak them. After all, most people learn most languages to communicate with their NSs. SLA theory may be odds with ELF, but – notwithstanding Cook's strictures about measuring L2 users by L1 native speaker standards – few people espouse the 'imperfect learning' of French, Spanish, Arabic, Russian or Chinese as a pedagogical goal. It seems improbable that most of the millions of European schoolchildren learning two foreign languages have differing attitudes to them – wanting to 'get the accent right' and have their errors corrected in one of them, but not wanting correction or a nativelike pronunciation in English – although I know of no research into this.

Certainly the majority of the thousands of university students I have taught in five faculties thought that they should be learning nativelike English. My current students in a Faculty of Translation and Interpreting are planning to become language professionals and so are obviously unrepresentative. Many of the humanities students I taught were destined to become language teachers, and didn't see English as being any different from other modern languages, despite its status as a lingua franca. Many of the university business students dreamed of working in international marketing or finance, preferably in London or New York (but mostly ended up in auditing companies), and wanted nativelike English. Most of the natural and social scientists knew that they would need to speak and write in English, and assumed that meant a nativelike model. In short nearly all of them have or had made a large investment in the acquisition of 'linguistic capital' which is an important part of their identity. A useful contrast was provided by a short spell teaching part-time in-service business people, some (but by no means all) of whom had an aggressively pragmatic approach to English – all you have to do is make yourself understood. Accuracy according to NES norms was of no interest to this minority, though unfortunately the institution's language examining procedures were not on their side.

Perhaps university students in a multilingual country like Switzerland are unrepresentative language users and ELF speakers, and many are what Michael Clyne (2003) calls linguaphiles. Moreover, most books and articles on multilingualism are written by linguists who mention their friends and acquaintances, and almost certainly over-represent people in intercultural relationships, language teachers, language graduates, etc. What about people who learn English for purely instrumental, professional purposes? To what extent do they identify with an auxiliary language such as ELF?

In 'English as a lingua franca: A threat to multilingualism?' – a dangerously titled article, found in various bibliographies without the question mark – House (2003: 559) argues that ELF is a 'language for communication,' and that as such, 'it can be distinguished from those other parts of the individual's repertoire which serve as "languages for identification."' This distinction is generally attributed to Werner Hüllen (1992), who described international English as the former, because he conceived of a language of identification as one which is acquired or learned in order to integrate (and hence to identify with) its *native* speech community. Similarly, House contends that 'it is local languages, and particularly an individual's L1(s), which are likely to be the main determinants of identity, which means holding a stake in the collective linguistic-cultural capital that defines an L1 group and its members' (2003: 560). Furthermore, 'Because ELF is not a national language, but a mere tool bereft of collective cultural capital, it is a language usable neither for identity marking, nor for a positive ("integrative") disposition towards an L2 group' (p. 560). She also suggests that a paradoxical corollary of the spread of ELF may be an insistence on using one's local language for emotional binding to one's own culture, history and tradition. Thus a countercurrent to ELF might be, e.g. the revival of Bavarian folk music (p. 561).

Kirkpatrick (2007) suggests that signalling identity and expressing culture may be at odds with ordinary communication, and even require a different variety or register: advertising your identity 'might well mean using a variety that other people may not understand' (pp. 11–12). He thus posits an 'identity–communication continuum' going from broad or informal, or what Platt and Weber (1980) call 'basilectal' varieties which express identity, to educated, formal or 'acrolectal' varieties or registers which are suitable for communication with people from other speech communities. (Somewhere in between are general or 'mesolectal' varieties.) Kirkpatrick (2010: 71) mentions 'the ability of many educated multilingual users of English to use different varieties of English along a continuum between the informal and colloquial basilect and the more formal acrolect.' Yet although some outer circle Englishes (e.g. in India and Singapore) have recognizable basilectal registers, rich in idioms and full of mixed-code forms, most expanding circle varieties do not, which would seem to imply that expanding circle speakers can only express their identity by switching to the informal registers of their primary L1 dialect.

But all of this disregards the possibility that being part of an international community, and using a formal, educated register of an L1, an L2, or a lingua franca, could have anything to do with one's identity. Is speaking at a linguistics conference any less an expression of my identity than perhaps starting to sound a bit basilectally Cockney after a post-conference drink or three?

There seems to be little reason to argue that the expression of identity is restricted to part of a linguistic continuum. On the contrary, I would suggest that many professionals – e.g. a lot of scientists, academics, businesspeople, politicians, athletes, etc. – identify with their careers and their international colleagues as much as or even much more than their hobbies (even Bavarian folk music) and the people back home who speak the same way as they do. As the contemporary slogan has it, it's about routes not roots. Professional relationships can exist at most points of a continuum between what James and Lesley Milroy (1985) call strong and weak ties. For many people, this requires having a strong, existential invest-ment in L2 *English*, which they acquire for both instrumental *and* integrative rea-sons, and use professionally as an additional international language.[10] For a scientist, for example, English is not 'bereft of collective cultural capital' but full of it – it is the language most scientists use to communicate professionally, and science is a major part of their culture. They communicate in English, with the scientific community, about *science*, not about any local native Anglophone culture. There is obviously nothing essentially Anglophone about science, and the majority of sci-entists can also express the same things in their L1s, unless these have suffered 'domain loss.' Besides, most English scientific vocabulary comes from Greek and Latin anyway, with the exception of astronomy (with its black holes, red shifts and white dwarfs) and particle physics (with its up, down, strange, charm, bottom and top flavours).

Clearly this kind of professional identification with an (L1 and) L2-using group is different from identification with a group of L1 speakers. It does *not* allow hearers instantly to locate speakers on social and regional dimensions, or to grasp the social significance of phonetic or lexical or phraseological variants, as is gen-erally the case with an L1. But nonetheless, such professional communication is a major component or marker of many professional people's identity, and they may consequently have a positive (and integrative) disposition towards an international community rather than a local L2 group. Jenkins (2007: 53) writes 'The assumption that learning an L2 (the subject here being English rather than any L2) should by definition alter the learner's identity and change them as a person sits uncomfor-tably with the notion of ELF,' but if learning ELF allows one to participate in (and identify with) an international professional community which uses English as an essentially national-culture-free medium of communication, rather than be some-one who identifies with a given Anglophone culture, this is surely a different matter.

Moreover, the dichotomy of an integrative, identity-expressing mother tongue and instrumental ELF cannot accommodate the code-switching that is frequently found in ELF interactions in professional multilingual communities; as Cogo (2009: 269) puts it, 'There is no evidence showing that when participants use their L1s they express their identity, whereas when they use ELF they are talking with some sort of transactional purposes.'

If you regularly work with an international professional community, you will use language (quite probably ELF) to do rather more than 'communicate' (if that just means transmitting information). Various linguists have proposed classifications of the functions of language, including Karl Bühler (1934/1990), Roman Jakobson (1960), and Michael Halliday (1978). Bühler identified three functions: the *representational* function, centred on the context, concerning the relation between the sign and the world; the *expressive* function, centred on the speaker, concerning the relation between the speaker and the sign; and the *appeal* or *appellative* function, centred on the addressee, concerning the relation between the addressee and the sign.[11] Bühler argued that the three functions are always present, but in a hierarchy; which function is dominant depends on the nature of the utterance or discourse. Thus it would be extremely naïve to believe that speakers of a vehicular language such as ELF *only* use the representational function, without attempting to be expressive, or appealing to their addressees.

Jakobson later proposed six cardinal functions, of which the *referential, emotive* and *conative* correspond to Bühler's three functions.[12] Jakobson also adds the *phatic* function, which helps to establish or maintain contact between two speakers (*Hello, can you hear me?* on the telephone, or *Hi / Hi* when you pass a colleague in a corridor); the *poetic* function, in which the message conveys more than just the content and the form is important (rhetorical tropes and figures, alliteration, rhyme, wordplay, etc.); and the *metalinguistic* function, which refers to language itself (*Sorry, what did you say? What does ... mean?* etc.). There is clearly no reason why ELF speakers, who some theorists define in terms of their innovative tendencies, should not play with language and use the poetic function. Moreover, there are probably more reasons to use the metalinguistic function in an L2 than an L1, and certainly no reason to use the phatic function less than when speaking an L1.

More recently, Halliday has proposed an alternative model, including the *ideational* function, which allows speakers to represent their experience of the world; the *interpersonal* function, which allows speakers to intrude in the speech act, by giving opinions and making judgements, and to establish and maintain relationships with their hearers; and the *textual* function, internal to language itself, linking the utterance to the situation, and creating a text or a discourse by structuring sentences and establishing the relations among them (by cohesion, conjunction, reference, substitution and ellipsis, the use of pronouns, repetition, and so on). In other words, for Halliday, the representational/referential function described by Bühler and Jakobson is also ideational or experiential, as we can only represent *our* vision of the world, and the expressive function is necessarily interpersonal, as we express ourselves to interlocutors. We habitually share evaluations and experiences and not just information. Halliday adds the textual function, which allows us to present interpersonal and ideational information in the form of a text or discourse in a given context.

If you work in a profession that requires the use of English, you will inexorably find yourself using the representational or referential function to give information, the appellative or conative function to try to get people to do things, and the expressive or emotive function to express your thoughts and beliefs. Or in Halliday's terms, you will inescapably use the ideational function to represent your own particular experience or conceptualizations of the world, and the interpersonal function to give opinions, make judgements, and engage with other people, because these functions are semantically embodied in the forms of the language.[13] It is hard to see how someone could regularly communicate their experience and/or act on other people in any language without thereby reflecting or revealing aspects of their identity.

In other words, there are a great many people who have invested a lot of time and effort in learning languages, and who consider their multilingual abilities to be an important part of their identity. As Prodromou (2008: 13) puts it, 'lingua-cultural identities seem to be increasingly multiple rather than single and unitary' and 'individuals cross ethnic and linguistic boundaries, borrowing stylistic and cultural resources' as needed, all the while expressing 'their multiple identities and membership of multiple discourse communities.' Most of the languages in a multilingual speaker's repertoire will, by necessity, have been learned primarily in order to communicate with NSs of those languages (they can't all be lingua francas), and the ability not to sound too much like a foreigner is part of the challenge. English is different, but many (though clearly not all) NNESs transfer the same logic of pronunciation to this language: they wish to communicate with both native and non-native speakers of English without betraying a strong, or even a perceptible, L1 accent. As Mufwene (2012: 368) puts it, although outer circle speakers may worry about local norms of English, 'I bet speakers of the Expanding Circle worry instead about being understood by the outsiders with whom they communicate, especially those who speak it natively or are expected to speak it fluently.' Jenkins, on the other hand, believes that they should be worrying about expressing their identity by retaining an L1-influenced accent.

The 'Lingua Franca Core'

Jenkins (2000: 159ff., 2002: 96ff., 2007: 22ff., etc.) proposes a 'Lingua Franca Core' (LFC) for pronunciation, divided into essential (core) items which are necessary for intelligibility, and so need to be taught, and non-essential (non-core) items which do not. The LFC is 'grounded in RP [received pronunciation] and GA [General American]' (2000: 131), but focuses only on features that are said to be crucial for intelligibility among NNESs (i.e. *not* among NNESs and NESs). Fortuitous side-effects of the LFC are that it will 'drastically reduce the pronunciation teaching load' (p. 145), and that it leaves room for the expression of identity. As Jenkins puts it:

> This approach, combining the use of core features and accommodation, along with locally pronounced non-core features and a receptive under-standing of the ways they are produced by NSs of English would, I believe, resolve the intelligibility-identity conflict by enabling NNSs to express both

their L1 identity and membership of the international ELF community, while remaining intelligible to their ELF interlocutors, and still able to understand ENL accents.

(2007: 24–25)

The LFC identifies four areas in which it is necessary to eliminate error (yes – error) if a speaker's pronunciation is to be intelligible in ELF communication: individual consonants, consonant clusters, vowels, and nuclear stress placement. I will discuss these in turn.

Jenkins suggests that intelligibility in international English requires the use of all the consonants of RP or GA except the th-sounds – the voiceless and voiced interdental fricatives /θ/ and /ð/ – and dark or velarized /ɫ/. There can be differences in vowel qualities, although /ɜ:/ or the NURSE vowel needs to be a good approximation of NS pronunciation. Contrasts between long and short vowels (e.g. the KIT and FLEECE vowels) must be maintained.[14] One might ask whether ELF speakers really need all these sounds, or if this inventory is unnecessarily close to RP and GA. Trudgill (2005a: 213–14) points out that some NESs use only nineteen or twenty of the twenty-four consonants of RP (i.e. their speech lacks consonants other than the famous interdental fricatives). So do we need to teach NNESs more than this? The same question arises for vowels: although RP has twenty-one vowels, many varieties of native English have merged some of them, e.g. FORCE and NORTH in the US and most of Britain, STRUT and FOOT in the north of England, TRAP and BATH in most American dialects, and also CLOTH, THOUGHT, LOT and PALM for many Americans. Meanwhile the Scots manage quite happily with twelve vowels, West African English only has ten, and both East African English and Philipino English a mere eight (or five if you exclude the diphthongs). But if we accept that English learners are going to be exposed to many varieties of English (and not just ELF speakers using the LFC and a few accommodating NESs), having a much reduced phoneme inventory would not necessarily help them.

As Trudgill puts it,

> Smaller phonological systems may make things easier for the non-native learner as producer: there is less learning to carry out and less articulatory effort involved. However, crucially, they also make life much more difficult for the non-native learner as *listener* by reducing the amount of phonetic information available for processing.

(p. 222)

NNS listeners usually require more phonological information than natives, not less. As outlined in Chapter 4, L1 speakers use words in predictable collocations and colligations, which allows them both to mis-hear the occasional word and to prospect ahead instead of paying attention to each word. This does not always apply to L2 speakers. Christiane Dalton and Barbara Seidlhofer (1994: 26) state that L2 learners 'have often not been able to develop intuitions and expectations about word frequencies, the likelihood that a word will occur in a situation, or even what counts as a "standard situation."' The same could apply to ELF users, given that patterns in ELF are more variable than in ENL. Dalton and Seidlhofer say that NNSs compensate for this 'by being more analytical,' and that 'They rely – often exclusively – on acoustic information alone' (p. 26).

This would suggest that the more acoustic or phonological information they have the better. If you can't hear a particular phonemic contrast (whether of vowels or consonants), you have less chance of identifying individual words. As Andrea Weber and Anne Cutler (2004: 2) say,

> a good part of the notorious difficulty of listening to speech in a non-native language could arise because of unwanted activation of spurious competitor words [...] Even though the non-native listener knows fewer words of the language than the native listener, the total competitor population may be larger, because inaccurate phonetic processing allows spurious phonemic matches.

Furthermore, as Trudgill (2005a: 221) says, research shows that 'If speakers cannot *produce* a phonemic contrast it reduces their chance of *hearing* it also.' Robert McAllister (1997) calls this a 'perceptual foreign accent.'

However I would not contest Jenkins' argument that the dark ł and th-sounds are unnecessary for production by ELF speakers. Cogo and Jenkins (2010: 276) state that many ELF users, from a range of L1s, vocalise /ł/ so that the sound at the end of *pull* is pronounced as a /w/, or substitute it with clear 'l', which in RP is only used when it is followed by a vowel sound.[15] Yet the vocalised /ł/ is also common in London and South-East England, New York, and elsewhere, so that *milk* is pronounced /mɪwk/. In a London accent this also leads to vowel mergers before the 'l,' so minimal pairs such as *pull* and *pool, doll* and *dole,* and *fill* and *feel* disappear (Trudgill 1986: 46). John Wells (1982: 259) predicted over thirty years ago that l vocalization 'will become entirely standard in English over the course of the next century,' so it clearly is and will be part of ELF.

Similarly with the substitution of other sounds for 'th.' Trudgill (1986: 57) describes the voiced and unvoiced th-sounds as 'unusual in the world's languages, acquired late by children, and subject to loss and change in many varieties of English. They are phonologically marked, and good candidates for variable merger and eventual loss.' Indeed Mesthrie and Bhatt (2008: 128) state that '*all* New Englishes varieties treat /θ/ and /ð/ as something other than an interdental frica-tive,' namely /t, s or f/ and /d, z or v/. They also disappear in Irish and West Indian Englishes, as well as in the speech of many New Yorkers (not only down on da East Side at Toidie Toid and Toid), and Londoners (I fink I said dat in Chapter Free, but I'll say it anuvver time 'ere). Few ELF speakers consistently pronounce interdental fricatives, and Jolanta Szpyra-Kozlowska (2005: 154) points out that people who can employ them to imitate lisping don't carry this over to their pronunciation of English. So as Jenkins (2000: 160) rightly says of substitutions such as these, 'There is really no justification for doggedly persisting in referring to an item as "an error" if the vast majority of the world's L2 English speakers produce and understand it.'

Robin Walker (2010: 30), in a teacher's manual based on the LFC, states that it 'does not suggest that /θ/ and /ð/ should be "replaced,"' or that 'speakers should be discouraged from using them if they are part of the speaker's mother tongue pronunciation' (e.g. Arabic, Spanish, Greek); merely that 'they are not necessary for intelligibility in ELF.' The idea that they should be replaced would thus appear to be one of the many misrepresentations, misinterpretations or misunderstandings of the LFC that Jenkins (2007) bewails, but Jenkins (2000: 228) does state that 'speakers of both these L1 varieties [RP and GA] will have to accept that it may already be better, depending on their EIL interlocutor, to use substitutions of /θ/ and /ð/.' However according to the argument that NNS listeners usually require more phonological information than natives, Trudgill (2005b: 95) argues that 'the act of deliberately turning, say, *through* and *true* into homophones when one does not need to seems perverse.'

Some speakers of British English feel that this is also the case with the way North Americans pronounce intervocalic /t/ as a flapped [r] – did you say a *writer* or a *rider?*, and the way they elide the /t/ from intervocalic /nt/ – did you say *winner* or *winter?* – but we learn to live with it. Americans do not accommodate to British speakers in this respect, and NESs accept the existence of different accents. Jenkins, however, insists on the use of intervocalic /t/ and no /t/ deletion in /nt/ in ELF. She also states that the LFC is rhotic, which is to say that the post-vocalic r (in *car*, *card*, etc.) should be pronounced (as it is in most North American accents, and Scottish and Irish English, but generally not in English English, or Australian and New Zealand accents, not to mention outer circle varieties like Indian English), or that the grapheme [r] should be pronounced whenever it is spelt. As with intervocalic /t/, NESs of rhotic and non-rhotic varieties tend not to accommodate each other.

However it is not unreasonable to recommend that *NNESs* pronounce the intervocalic /t/ and every grapheme [r], in aid of intelligibility. The same applies to aspirating /p/, /t/ and /k/, so that *pear*, *tin* and *coat* do not sound like *bear*, *din* and *goat* (Walker 2010: 30), and to pronouncing (i.e. not simplifying) word-initial consonant clusters. As mentioned in Chapter 4, word-final consonant clusters, including those with the plural -s, are difficult for many Asian speakers of English to pronounce, but are often less crucial to intelligibility than the beginnings of words.

The LFC insists on contrasts between long and short vowels, or minimal pairs. In other words, a French or Italian speaker who fails to distinguish between *bid* and *bead*, a Spanish or Greek speaker who pronounces *bad* and *bud* the same way, or a German, Polish or Russian speaker who makes *bad* sound like *bed*, is committing a pronunciation error (despite the fact that there are a large number of other vowel mergers in various native accents and dialects). But other than minimal pairs, the LFC allows local L2 qualities rather than ENL-like pronunciation of nineteen of the twenty RP vowel and diphthongs, the exception being /ɜ:/ or the NURSE vowel. Jenkins' insistence on the RP-like pronunciation of this vowel is odd, given that the LFC is also supposed to be rhotic, and the vowel in NURSE is usually said to be absent from rhotic accents, along with /ɪə/, /eə/, /ʊə/ and /ɔ:/ (NEAR, SQUARE, CURE and FORCE) (see Trudgill 2005b: 90).

The most common sound in RP and GA is the schwa (/ə/), largely because of its use in weak forms,[16] but Jenkins (2000: 148) says the use of weak forms with shortened and reduced vowels should be avoided. She does at least concede that 'Many EIL learners will also need to understand L1 speakers of English in international contexts,' and that 'These learners will still need to work on weak forms (in their traditional sense) *receptively* in the classroom.'

Given that only a small minority of British people use RP,[17] and that the vowels used in ENL sometimes vary if you travel as little as ten or twenty miles, and the fact that virtually all NNSs of any language have a 'foreign accent,' allowing variation in vowel sounds like a wholly reasonable suggestion. For example, a Francophone who pronounces the first vowel in *fluctuate* rather like a French /y/ vowel doesn't sound so very different from someone using the northern English pronunciation of the word, with a /ʊ/ (the FOOT vowel).[18] On the other hand, many other variant pronunciations do stray into minimal pair territory. Trudgill (2005b: 90–92) points out that Greek speakers of English typically only use five vowels, and that even with long and short versions of these, and diphthongs as necessary, they merge a lot of sounds, thereby turning minimal pairs into homonyms.[19] Thus he suggests that the LFC does not sufficiently cover the English vowel system. He also argues, turning the screw, that Jenkins' proposal

> is totally equivalent to many forms of native-speaker Irish English, which also has strongly retroflected /r/, as well as to Standard Jamaican English. The only difference is that she is happy to permit many, though not all, non-native phonetic realisations. This, of course, is precisely what happens in EFL anyway [...]. So what she seems to be saying is 'aim at Irish English but don't try so hard as before with the phonetics.'
>
> *(p. 92)*

He further evokes what he calls 'the shortfall principle' – in the teaching of phonetics, the goal is hardly ever attained, and learners fall short of the target. So if we relax the phonetic target for EIL, allowing some L2 transfers, 'it has to be at least a possibility that EIL intelligibility will be reduced' (p. 92). The shortfall principle could also be extended to the teaching of lexicogrammar: the explicit acceptance of fuzziness and variation is not an inducement to try to learn everything with which you are presented.

The final element of the LFC concerns word stress. ENL has – or as Jenkins (2007: 149) prefers, 'is said to have' – a stress-timed rhythm, with an alternation of strong and weak syllables, as well as extra prominence accorded to nuclear stress. Although word stress is an important part of intelligibility for NESs, Jenkins does not consider ENL stress patterns crucial, or indeed learnable, for ELF speakers. The vast majority of speakers of World Englishes use syllable-based varieties, in which all syllables occupy similar time intervals, as do most expanding circle speakers. Hence stress-timed rhythm is not a target in the LFC. Yet it seems excessive to try to teach speakers whose L1s *are* stress-timed *not* to imitate native English stress patterns if these come naturally. This applies, for example, to speakers of Arabic, Russian, Portuguese, German, Dutch and most of the Scandinavian languages, a potential pool of about 775 million people to add to the 'small minority' of 375 million NESs who also speak with a stress-timed (or non-syllable-timed) rhythm.

More recently, however, Jenkins (2005b: 147) has quoted research stating that 'three unrelated NNS Englishes,' namely Spanish, Nigerian and Singapore Chinese dialects, tend to place stress on the syllable containing the longest vowel, e.g. *adver'tise* and *edu'cate* (Peng and Ann 2001), and speculated that this might represent 'the emergence of an ELF word-stress rule,' also applying to other L2 Englishes, in which case the Lingua Franca Core 'will need to be adjusted.' So in a radical – and illogical – conceptual shift, rather than being unnecessary, and better left to consenting NESs, word stress suddenly becomes rule-bound, but according to predominantly outer circle rules rather than inner circle ones. Yet as Berns (2008: 333) puts it,

> identification of core features of non-native speech in an effort to control language performance and guarantee the success of this performance – even if the result is the overthrow of the tyrannical native speaker – is simply meeting the new boss who's same [*sic*] as the old boss, or [replacing] the hegemony of the old with the hegemony of the new.[20]

Whether or not there is or will be an ELF word stress rule, Jenkins (2000: 153) rightly states that nuclear stress, particularly contrastive stress, is crucial for intelligibility: 'Nuclear stress, whether unmarked (on the last content word in the word group) or contrastive (somewhere else), is the most important key to the speaker's intended meaning.'[21] This is probably something that needs to be taught.

All in all, for Jenkins (2000: 159) these examples (consonants, vowel qualities, word stress, etc.) demonstrate that

> the assumption that a 'native speaker' is the most intelligible, and therefore that conformity to 'native-speaker norms' will result in greatest intelligibility, is itself flawed. L1 speakers are only intelligible to L2 speakers if they provided the teaching model and, for the vast majority of the world's speakers of English, this is simply not so. Ultimately it is probably true to say that L1 speakers of English are only more intelligible than L2 speakers to other L1 speakers.

Jenkins (2007: 237) gleefully reports a news item about Korean Airlines choosing a French supplier for its flight simulators, because its non-native English was more comprehensible than the ENL of its British competitor. Trudgill (2005b), on the other hand, reports Tessa Bent and Ann Bradlow's (2003) research showing that NESs are generally no less intelligible to Korean (and Chinese) speakers of English than 'relatively high proficiency' Korean speakers. The English of Korean native speakers was only more intelligible to low-proficiency Korean speakers of English.

But this is not the whole story. Bent and Bradlow explain the fact that high-proficiency Korean speakers of English are as intelligible to other Koreans as NESs in terms of a 'matched interlanguage speech intelligibility benefit' (p. 1606). They say that 'non-native language learners from a given native language have a broad base of shared linguistic and phonetic knowledge that facilitates speech communication in the non-native language' (p. 1602). In other words, the speaker and hearer's similar use of vowels, consonants, stress patterns, intonation, etc. will allow the hearer to interpret them 'as the talker intended them to be interpreted, even though they may deviate markedly from the target language norm' (p. 1607). This is not especially relevant for ELF, as speakers of the same L1 on their own have no need to speak English to each other. However Bent and Bradlow also found that

> when the non-native listeners and high-proficiency non-native talkers did not share a native language, the non-native listeners found the non-native talkers equally as or more intelligible than the native talker. This general finding suggests that the interlanguage benefit can extend to the situation of a talker–listener native language mismatch, demonstrating a *mismatched interlanguage speech intelligibility benefit*.
>
> (p. 1606)

In other words, NSs of *different* languages find each other's use of a shared L2, in this case English, equally as or more intelligible than a NES, because of shared features like a lack of fast speech or reduction phenomena. This might explain the success of the flight simulator using NNESs, and clearly does have implications for ELF, the use or imitation of native models, and pronunciation teaching.

All in all, Jenkins and those who disagree with her seem to be engaged in what the French call a *dialogue de sourds* (dialogue of the deaf), which is perhaps not the best way to resolve phonetic issues. Yet even if Jenkins were wholly correct about which pronunciation features are essential to intelligibility in ELF, an obvious problem is that learners do not actually learn everything you try to teach them. There is no simple correlation between input and intake. Seidlhofer (2011) comments on this, borrowing terms she doesn't agree with, such as arrested language and learner language:

> What is achieved, and put to use in ELF, is clearly not the English that has been *taught*, but the English that has been *learnt*. […] there is so much arrested language about – tens, even hundreds of millions of people use it, far more than use English of a supposedly complete and non-arrested kind. […] The non-conformities of EFL learner language are stubbornly resistant to

correction, as every teacher knows. […] learners have a tendency to home in on what is most conceptually salient or communicatively usable.

(pp. 186–87)

Here, Seidlhofer is thinking about the lexicogrammatical features of English and not the phonological ones, but accents are also stubbornly resistant to correction, and a phonemic distinction that learners cannot actually hear (such as /ɪ/ and /iː/ for Italians, /v/ for /w/ for Germans and many Indians, Pakistanis and Sri Lankans, /b/ and /v/ for Spanish speakers, /r/ and /l/ for the Japanese and some African Englishes, /f/ and /p/ for many Korean, Philipino, Malay, Vietnamese and Laotian speakers, etc.) is unlikely to be perceived as 'conceptually salient or communicatively usable.' Moreover, learners do not only fail to acquire things because they seem to be surplus to requirements. There are also things they fail to learn because they are just too difficult. For example, it would be good if Anglophone learners of German instantly seized what indirect objects were and how the dative case works; if it was immediately obvious to Anglophone learners of French what a subjunctive was; if Anglophone learners of Spanish rapidly understood the conceptualization of characteristics and states underlying the two copulae *ser* and *estar*, if Anglophone learners of all three of these languages had an intuitive understanding of who should be addressed with V-forms and who with T-forms, and so on. But they do not. If we apply the logic of difficulty to pronunciation, we must accept that defining a feature as 'core' will not ensure that learners master it.

Consequently *teaching* all the consonant sounds except /θ/ and /ð/ is no guarantee that ELF learners will acquire them. David Deterding (2012) gives examples of misunderstandings from the Asian Corpus of English, including *club* heard as *crowd*, *like the* heard as *rather*, *lunchtime* heard as *runtime*, *return* heard as *leave*, and *Black Swan* heard as *Rex one*, all because of (among other things) problems with /l/ and /r/; *their accent* heard as *the option* because of a confusion of /k/ and /p/; *vagrant* heard as *fragrant* (/v/ and /f/), *north* heard as *law of* (/n/ and /l/), and so on.[22] These examples may be from ELF 'users not learners,' as the mantra goes, but by Jenkins' own logic they still need to learn how to recognize some consonant sounds belonging to the LFC. It is clearly not sufficient to insist that, say, Koreans and Tagalog speakers learn how to distinguish between /f/ and /p/, and pronounce English words accordingly, because many of them do not. An air traffic controller who hears a pilot saying '*MAYDAY, Par-east pive-pour-pive. We have a pire warning on the main gear. Request emergency landing at Port Lauderdale*' with every /f/ pronounced as a /p/, does *not* reply 'Far-east 545, please use the Lingua Franca Core for pronunciation to make yourself more intelligible.' On the contrary, both pilots and air traffic controllers need receptive training in as many pronunciation varieties of English as possible.[23]

While I don't dispute Jenkins' argument that neither native th-sounds nor the dark ł are necessary, insisting on the necessity of all the other consonant sounds is problematic. For example, Jenkins' logic implies that German speakers should not pronounce /w/ as /v/ when speaking English, as millions of them regularly do.

Yet if other European ELF speakers are able to comprehend and/or accommodate to a variety of sounds substituting for [th] – sometimes /t/ and /d/, sometime /s/ and /z/, or even /f/ and /v/ – they can probably accommodate to /w/ pronounced as /v/, if zey vant to. Furthermore, millions of speakers of Indian and Pakistani English equally pronounce /w/ as /v/. Are they to be told that they need to modify their ESL (or possibly native) accent when speaking ELF?[24]

Jenkins (2005b: 147) argues that

> Learners need acquire only the core items and have these in their pronunciation repertoires available for use as and when required. The non-core items, on the other hand, now assume the status of features of the respective (L2) regional accent: German-English, Japanese-English, Spanish-English and the like, thus allowing L2 English speakers the same sociolinguistic rights as those enjoyed by L1 speakers.

Yet non-core items only allow most L2 English speakers a small proportion of the features of their natural accent. To put it bluntly, a French accent in English that doesn't omit initial /h/, or have unaspirated /p, t and k/ that occasionally sound like /b, d and g/, is not really a French accent worthy of the name. The same can be said for a German accent in English that doesn't use /v/ for /w/ or replace /b, d, g, dʒ, v, z, ʒ/ in final position with /p, t, k, tʃ, f, s, ʃ/; a Spanish accent in English that doesn't occasionally confuse /b/ and /v/ or use /s/ for /z/ or use unaspirated /p, t, k/; an Arabic accent in English that doesn't occasionally use /f/ for /v/ or /b/ for /p/; a Cantonese accent in English that doesn't occasionally confuse /l/, /n/ and /r/, and replace /z, ʃ, ʒ/ with /s/, and replace /v/ with /w/ in initial position and /f/ in final position, and replace /b, d, g/ in final position with /p, t, k/; a Hindi accent in English that doesn't occasionally use /p/ for /f/ and use /v/ or an intermediate sound between /v/ and /w/ for /w/; and so on. This list excludes vowel variation, but it contains most consonants, so it seems wholly disingenuous to argue that with the Lingua Franca Core, 'so much of an ELF speaker's accent is legitimately free to transfer pronunciation features from the L1' that 'the speaker is able to retain closer links with his or her L1 identity' (Jenkins 2005b: 152).[25] It does not, and many speakers still succeed in being intelligible by being either more nativelike or less nativelike than the LFC will allow.

Moreover, there is more to communication than intelligibility. As already outlined in Chapter 5, Smith (1988) distinguishes among mere intelligibility, comprehensibility (ascertaining the linguistic meaning of an utterance), and interpretability (ascertaining the speaker's intended meaning). In various studies, Smith has found that speakers find it much easier to achieve intelligibility than either comprehensibility or interpretability.[26] Jenkins (2006b: 36) states explicitly that 'speakers need to be confident that their accents will not prevent them from understanding each other's utterances (even if they then go on to misinterpret each other in the pragmatic sense).'[27] Berns (2008: 328) points out that World Englishes researchers place more emphasis on meaning and interpretability in cross-cultural communication than on liberating NNESs from NES pronunciation models; she quotes Smith (1983b: 8), who states that 'the responsibility for effective communication is shared by both the speaker and the listener,' whatever 'circle' they come from and whatever accent they have. More generally, Berns asserts that 'the view that a common linguistic (formal) core of an international variety of English can be codified, standardized, and then taught' conflicts with the Kachruvian paradigm, which is based on an awareness of multiplicity and creativity rather than a search for norms. In short, 'the ELF movement's identification with World Englishes – whether self-proclaimed or conferred – is tenuous at best' (p. 333).

Attitudes to accents

According to the logic that ENL models are not the most intelligible (or, of course, the most readily learnable), Cook (2002: 337), Jenkins (2007: 25) and Kirkpatrick (2007: 184ff.) all argue in favour of (bi- or multilingual) local teachers who use an 'endonormative' model that they have themselves learnt as a second language – i.e. English as commonly spoken (and pronounced) in their country – and who consequently have an awareness of the difficulties their learners are facing. The accents of such local teachers will incorporate both the core features and the local version of the non-core items.[28] Kirkpatrick argues that using 'exonormative' inner circle models in non-inner circle countries undermines local teachers' own model of English, and requires them to teach a model that they themselves do not speak (which cannot be good for self-confidence – see Medgyes 1994) and which most of their learners will not master – which, again, cannot be good for confidence. Graddol (2006: 114) adds that monolingual NES teachers may be seen as bringing with them cultural baggage in which the learners have no interest, having accents that seem too remote from the people that learners expect to communicate with, and lacking the skills required by bilingual speakers, including the ability to translate and interpret.

I happen to agree with Jenkins' and Kirkpatrick's arguments about endonormative teaching models, *where that is what learners want* – in fact, as I have already implied, I would allow more phonological variation than the LFC does – although I think learners should also be exposed to a range of other native, nativized, and non-native accents besides those of their teachers (see Chapter 11). However, many non-native teachers and ELF speakers themselves seem to think they should learn ENL (both lexicogrammar and phonology) and use it in ELF contexts. Jenkins (2007: 43) laments that 'this is an attitude that was voiced repeatedly by the proficient non-native English speakers' whom she interviewed. A large majority of 326 teachers in twelve countries who responded to a questionnaire about accents ranked UK and US accents as being 'the best.' They were 'unable to conceive of NNS accents as being better than or even as good as NS English accents' (p. 164) for international communication, or even of the concept of ELF. Yet this picture of 'linguistic insecurity' or even 'self-hatred' might also be a consequence of the questionnaire design: why *would* a Brazilian, Chinese, German, Greek, Finnish,

Indian, Japanese, Polish, Spanish or Swedish speaker of English nominate their own accent as 'the best' for *international* communication? Asking 'Do you think everyone should speak with their own accent?' would perhaps be a leading question, but it might also have produced less misleading results.

Jenkins (2007: 199) quotes Aneta Pavlenko and Adrian Blackledge's criticism of sociopsychological theories (e.g. Tajfel 1974, 1981; Giles and Byrne 1982) based on group or ethnolinguistic identities with a supposed one-to-one correlation between language and identity. This approach has 'a monolingual and monocultural bias, which conceives of individuals as members of homogeneous, uniform, and bounded ethnolinguistic communities and obscures hybrid identities and complex linguistic repertoires of bi- and multilinguals living in a contemporary global world' (Pavlenko and Blackledge 2004: 5). Clearly ELF speakers cannot be monolingual, but Jenkins' insistence that ELF speakers should actively retain their own L1 accent (in non-core features) in ELF retains the 'one-to-one correlation between language and identity' criticized by Pavlenko and Blackledge, with the slight adjustment that L1-based identity spills over into an auxiliary language. There is no reason for a multilingual not to want to sound as close as possible to (a chosen group of) NSs of the languages he or she speaks. After all, most people who speak several languages use most of them to converse with NSs. This is not 'ENL ideology' but one particular multilingual ideology. Jenkins (2005b: 152) approvingly quotes Henry Daniels (1997: 82), who likens the link between one's natural L1 accent and the mother tongue to 'a sort of umbilical cord which ties us to our mother,' and argues that 'whenever we speak an L2 we cut that cord, perhaps unconsciously afraid of not being able to find it and tie it up again when we revert to L1.' However, 'a possible way of avoiding the cut is to continue using the sounds, the rhythms and the intonation of our mother tongue while pretending to speak L2.' Once again, this betrays an essentially monolingual concept of identity, if all that one's psyche can handle is *pretending* to speak an L2. In reality, much of humanity manages to cut that cord and become bi- or plurilingual without 'pretending.'

Ivor Timmis (2002) asked EFL learners if they would rather pass for a NES or retain the accent of their country, and received 400 responses from fourteen countries. Approximately two-thirds of the students from expanding circle countries chose the native-speaker answer, although only one-third of students from India, Pakistan and South Africa did so. Timmis concludes from this, in relation to the LFC, 'While it is clearly inappropriate to foist native speaker norms on students who neither want nor need them, it is scarcely more appropriate to offer students a target which manifestly does not meet their aspirations' (p. 242). However, as Michael Remiszewski (2005: 299) points out, Timmis' interviews and questionnaire did not ask learners whether they would be prepared 'to sacrifice all the time, energy, money and other resources necessary' to achieve sounding like a native speaker. Meanwhile Adrian Holliday (2005: 9), in a book which is an extended attack on 'native-speakerism,' quotes a Taiwanese teacher who rejects Jenkins' strictures on how she should or should not pronounce English, saying that she prefers to speak for herself, from the 'periphery,' rather than be told what to think from Britain.[29]

Jenkins (2007: 202) contemplates the possibility of ELF speakers 'being aware of what a NS of English would do at a given point, but choosing to do something else, perhaps in order to signal a shared identity with a particular NNS interlocutor.' Yet she will apparently not entertain the possibility of an ELF speaker choosing to accommodate to and signal a shared identity with a member of that 'small minority' of 375 million NESs. However this appears to be what a great many English speakers in North-West Europe do;[30] indeed Rias Van den Doel (2008) describes such people as having learnt Native English as a Lingua Franca (NELF). He states that NELF can be a model (or a reference point), even if it is not a wholly achievable target, and a rational choice for those who wish to communicate with native and non-native speakers alike. Of course, ELF speakers may wish to accommodate to NESs for purely instrumental as well as integrative motivations, and Van den Doel argues that the LFC doesn't cater for speakers who wish to have both NELF and ELF at their disposal, and use the former in contexts where it is to their advantage.[31] Here one might also mention Mufwene (2012: 368), quoted at length in Chapter 1, who cannot even conceive of someone 'who learns another group's language not caring at all about being understood (and being accepted) by the native-speaking community.'

Jenkins does *not* employ the concept of NELF, but she *does* claim (2007: 21–22) that

> As far as ELF researchers are concerned, it is entirely for learners to decide what kind of English they want to learn, be it EFL (in effect ENL) for communication with NSs, an ESL (outer circle) variety, or an ELF variety for international communication,

with the usual underlying supposition that an EFL variety would leave the learner unable to communicate with ESL or ELF speakers. But she also quotes (2006b: 154), with evident approval, Cook's (1991: 196) statement that learners or L2 speakers who want to follow NS models are comparable in their victimhood to people who want to 'change the color of their skin, the straightness of their hair, or the shape of their eyes to conform to other groups.' She insists (2007: 22) that 'ELF researchers merely suggest that learners should be put in a position to make an *informed* choice by means of having their awareness raised of the sociolinguistic, sociopsychological, and socio-political issues involved.'[32] Yet this statement about raised awareness carries within it the usual problem of 'false consciousness' arguments: the condescending assumption that people need to be told what is in their best interest. The telling is generally done by left-wing political commentators, but in this case it is by applied linguists.[33]

Yet it appears that there are, and will be for the foreseeable future, multilingual English learners and speakers who want to acquire and use what Van den Doel calls NELF, and who believe, like Mufwene (2012: 368), that ignoring inner circle standards means 'narrowing one's range of competitiveness.' Their identity as plurilingual subjects does not depend on retaining an L1 accent in their other languages (although of course they may do this unintentionally). *Pace* Cook, this is *not* the same as wanting to change the colour of one's skin or straighten one's hair. There are also English learners (though no one knows what percentage this is) who are uninterested in native norms and who despair at the linguistic behaviour of monolingual NESs in international communication, and who may indeed consider their L1-influenced accent to be an identity marker. Some or many of these will, by choice or otherwise, have more of an L1-influenced accent than Jenkins' LFC would allow, just as in the bad old days of EFL. But with any luck (or if language teachers pay heed to ELF research), they may also have acquired pragmatic strategies that enable them to overcome any pronunciation deficit. But all in all, the relationship between accent and identity appears to me to have rather more permutations than Jennifer Jenkins will allow.

Notes

1 See also Hofstede (1991). Many other intercultural theorists have sought to explain the national components of 'mental programming' (or more simply, of 'cultures'), including Hall (1959, 1966, 1976), Trompenaars (1993), Lewis (2003) and Wierzbicka (2003, 2006). Hall's (1976) notion of 'high-context' cultures (in which communication can leave a lot of things unsaid, because people share similar experiences and expectations from which inferences can be drawn) and 'low-context' cultures (made up of people with a wider variety of backgrounds, which requires communication to be much more explicit) is relevant to intercultural ELF, which is much more likely to be 'low-context' communication. Multinational companies and tourists seem to like such 'essentialist' accounts of culture, while sociologists and cultural theorists tend to prefer 'non-essentialist' theories in terms of diversity, hybridity, fusion, liminality, postmodernism, transculturation, and so on.

2 Berns (2007) cites Hofstede's model of country-based 'mental programmes' in opposing the notion that the diffusion of the English language around the world will lead to a loss of cultural identity and the adoption of US world views, values and cultural traditions (or, in shorthand, worldwide cultural 'McDonaldization'). A more likely outcome is that contact with and use of English will lead to an additional or hybrid identity.

3 As Hannerz (1996: 88) puts it ('a bit provocatively'): 'what can your nation do for you that a good credit card cannot do?' On the other hand, many of the NES mobile symbolic analysts described by Ohmae and Reich remain more or less monolingual. As Graddol (2006: 19–20) says, 'The growth of multilingualism in Europe' and 'the spread of the English language' are leading to 'the unravelling of modernity,' but paradoxically this can be threatening to 'native speakers [of English] whose identity was created by modernity and is now under challenge.'

4 In case this needs spelling out, this account of motivated, conscious, multiple lifestyle choice is the opposite of the poststructuralist account of the decentred self that effectively ceases to exist, replaced by fragments of language and discourse (Giddens 1991: 170).

5 Similar ideas were outlined in Chapter 4 in the discussion of performativity.

6 Because I have already devoted quite a lot of space to disagreeing with Pennycook, I would like to stress here that I *much* prefer his approach to popular culture to Phillipson's (1992, 2008, 2009) take on the Americanization and standardization of the planet, and to the grim Frankfurt School diatribes against the mass culture industry (e.g. Horkheimer and Adorno 1944/2002) that some of us used to read in the 1970s while listening to rock music. He just has a habit of pushing *all* his arguments and insights too far!

7 Richard Rorty offers a highbrow version of becoming ironic and sceptical: instead of watching television (or zapping) and wandering through shopping malls, you read books

from other times and places, try out new ideas, invent new metaphors, and redescribe things (and hence come to terms with the world by inventing your own terms), and generally become a postmodernist bourgeois liberal ironist. See Rorty (1989, 1991).

8 According to the terms used by Held *et al.* (1999: 2), Ohmae is a *hyperglobalizer* who believes that 'peoples everywhere are increasingly subject to the disciplines of the global marketplace,' as is Phillipson, though of course he decries this development; Hofstede is a *sceptic* who believes that 'national governments [or at least national cultures] remain very powerful'; while Le Page and Tabouret-Keller, Giddens, Appadurai, Bauman and Pennycook (for whom language is always a local practice) are *transformationalists* who believe that 'states and societies across the globe are experiencing a process of profound change as they try to adapt to a more interconnected but highly uncertain world.' Dewey (2007) describes ELF as being central to the transformationalist model, and as separating English from its native speakers; for a sceptical take on this, see Martin Kayman (2009), who argues that '"English as a Lingua Franca" may not be as "frank and free," that is to say, as independent of English culture, nor, therefore, as candid and transparent, as it seeks or appears to be' (p. 101).

9 Hannerz (1992: 247), quoting Paul Theroux (1986: 133), describes tourism as 'home plus' – apart from some exotic local attractions, everything else should be the same as (or as comfortable as) home – and distinguishes it from cosmopolitanism. Urry (1995: 167) describes 'aesthetic cosmopolitanism,' which involves an openness to other cultures.

10 For the distinction between instrumental and integrative motivation see Gardner and Lambert (1972).

11 In German, the *Darstellungsfunktion*, the *Ausdrucksfunktion*, and the *Appellfunktion*.

12 The centrality of the expressive or emotive function is a further argument against Charles Ogden and I.A. Richards' 'Basic English' (see Chapter 5): Ogden (1930/1938: 101) believed that Basic users would need to express ideas and wished to eliminate words 'unnecessarily coloured by some form of *feeling*.'

13 'All languages are organized around two main kinds of meaning, the "ideational" or reflective, and the "interpersonal" or active. These components [...] are the manifestations in the linguistic system of the two very general purposes which underlie all uses of language: (i) to understand the environment (ideational), and (ii) to act on the others in it (interpersonal)' (Halliday 1994: xiii).

14 NURSE, KIT, FLEECE, etc. come from Wells' (1982: 127–67) lexical sets, named after a representative word in which the vowel occurs in RP and GA, as well as a range of other British and American accents. This provides a way of comparing different English accents without describing them as deviations from a standard.

15 Trudgill (2005b: 92n) suggests that this is a rather parochial issue: 'Jenkins makes too much of the RP-type clear /l/-dark /l/ allophony, as GA does not have it, and neither do Scottish or Irish English – and it is also minimal in many forms of Southern Hemisphere English.'

16 The schwa is used in the weak forms of, among other words, *a, am, an, and, as, are, at, but, can, do, does, for, from, had, has, have, just, of, some, than, that, the, them, to, us, was, were, you* and *your*. This list includes the seven most common words in MICASE (see Chapter 4), and 27 of the 100 most common words, with *does, than* and *us* coming in the next 100.

17 According to Trudgill (2002: 171–72) the figure is about 3 per cent – a figure that Jenkins (2007: 29) accuses him of making up. 3 per cent certainly qualifies better as a 'small minority' than the number of NESs in global English use, for which Jenkins uses the same expression.

18 A speaker in the listening material in MacKenzie (1997), a business English coursebook, does precisely this. But after the publisher sent out pre-publication units to teachers for feedback, a native German teacher in a German university phoned my editor and berated him at length about this, because he'd had to waste half a class 'unteaching' these appalling errors (another one being *trustworthy* stressed on the second syllable) after doing us the favour of trialling the material. I don't think he got as far as the units with German, Indian and Chinese accents.

19 He specifically mentions *fact* and *fucked*.

20 It is unfortunate that Berns' most quotable line went unproofread. *Sic transit gloria Margie!* See also Ferguson (2009: 129): 'in codifying an ELF variety one may be constructing an alternative set of norms that has the same potential to exclude, even demoralise, non-standard ELF users in ways not dissimilar to how L1 standard English has at times functioned to exclude and marginalise.'

21 An extreme example is a sentence transliterated from Yiddish in Rosten (2001: xvi) giving rise to a range of insults and innuendos depending on nuclear stress placement: *Two tickets for her concert I should buy?*

22 See The Corpus of Misunderstandings from the Asian Corpus of English, http://www. ubd.edu.bn/academic/faculty/FASS/research/CMACE/home/index.html.

23 See Intemann (2005); Seiler (2009); Alderson (2009). Intemann (p. 74) gives the example of an annoyed pilot reacting to incomprehensible pronunciation by saying 'Taipei ground, confirm your last transmission was in English?' (instead of the approved Airspeak 'Taipei ground, say again'). The International Civil Aviation Organization (ICAO) has developed a set of language proficiency requirements (LPRs) setting minimum standards for language proficiency for pilots and air traffic controllers. Level 4 on the six-point scale is the minimum level required for licensure; its pronunciation descriptor is 'Assumes a dialect and/or accent intelligible to the aeronautical community; Pronunciation, stress, rhythm, and intonation are influenced by the first language or regional variation but only sometimes interfere with ease of understanding' (see Alderson 2009: 172). However, Alderson raises serious doubts as to the quality of several of the aviation language tests and assessments currently available, and the mechanisms for overseeing the implementation of the policy. Alderson also points out that cross-cultural variables can cause miscommunication in aviation settings: with multicultural cockpit crews, factors like silence, repair, turn-taking, and overlapping talk can also be interpreted very differently. See also Gladwell (2008), which is frightening but has a happy ending.

24 Although Jenkins (2006b: 33–35) explicitly describes the substitution of /v/ for /w/ as an error, she has since (2009: 13) moderated this argument: if interlocutors prefer to use /v/ rather than /w/, 'then there would be no advantage, intelligibility-wise, for each of them to replace their mutually preferred use,' but 'it would be important for them to have /w/ in their phonetic repertoires so that it was available for use with ELF interlocutors for whom /v/ might cause intelligibility problems.'

25 Regarding vowels, Mesthrie and Bhatt (2008: 121ff.) and Kirkpatrick (2010: 76) show that vowel length is not distinctive in many African and Asian varieties of English – i.e. long and short vowels are merged, so that minimal pairs are not realized, whatever the recommendations of the LFC.

26 See Smith and Bisazza (1983); Smith and Rafiqzad (1983); Smith and Nelson (1985); and Smith (1992).

27 This sentence from Jenkins casts a suspicious light on the claim made in virtually every paper by Cogo, Jenkins, Mauranen, Seidlhofer, *et al.* that misunderstandings are very rare in ELF interactions: does understanding not include correct interpretation?

28 The contrary argument, if it is needed, can be found in Sobkowiak (2005: 142): Jenkins' 'optimum' teacher with traces of a regional accent is simply an 'under-achiever.' Kirkpatrick (2007: 187) forestalls the objection that a NES model is necessary for learners planning to attend a university in an inner circle country: these universities employ academics from a number of different countries, and have local students with a broad, informal variety of English as well as international students with a range of varieties. Britain and the US (though not Australia) have a wide range of regional dialects, as well as mixed multicultural populations, with concomitant speech variety.

29 This is a fair point; Jenkins seems to see no irony in writing things like 'mutual intelligibility [...] is something to be negotiated and developed by ELF speakers themselves rather than imposed from "above" by NSs or their NNS admirers' (2006b: 36).

30 Specifically this seems to apply to the Netherlands, Scandinavia and parts of Germany, countries with typologically similar languages to English as well as extensive cultural links.
31 Van den Doel (2010) also argues against the LFC on the grounds that it causes intelligibility problems for NESs.
32 To be fair, Jenkins (2007: 26, quoting 2002: 101) does also say 'it will be important not to patronise those learners who, having heard the arguments, still wish to work towards the goal of a native speaker accent, by telling them they have no need to do so.'
33 Clearly knowledge about (or at least theories of) language and education can and do percolate into general awareness and cause people to change the way they act – which is an example of what Giddens (1984) calls the 'double hermeneutic' of social scientific knowledge – but that doesn't mean that the majority of people want or need to be told what to do or think by applied linguists.

8

ENOUGH ALREADY! ANGELIC ACCOUNTS OF ELF

Always look on the bright side of life.

Monty Python, *Life of Brian*

Gott weiß ich will kein Engel sein.

Rammstein, 'Engel'

Most ELF researchers will have you believe that when communication takes place in English as a lingua franca, ideally in the total absence of those pesky NESs, collaboration is total, misunderstandings are vanishingly rare, and harmony prevails. ELF speakers are reified – ELF speakers (a billion of them?) do this, ELF speakers do that, and so on. The *this* and the *that* are invariably things like accommodating to each other with acute sensitivity while collaborating in jointly negotiated enterprises and communities of practice. The 'solidarity of non-native ELF speakers' (House 2006: 94) is revealed by the way they 'establish rapport' and 'shared affective space' and converge on 'shared meaning' (Seidlhofer 2009a: 195), using a shared repertoire of negotiable resources (p. 211), employing humour and goodwill to ensure a collaborative atmosphere (Kirkpatrick 2010: 138) and 'a high level of mutual understanding and cooperation' (p. 127). As Firth (2009: 149) puts it, most of this work suggests that ELF interactions 'are typically characterized by a high degree of interactional robustness, cooperation, consensus-seeking behavior and affiliation, and that explicit and overt miscommunications are rare, despite variance in language form and proficiency.' Yet Firth goes on to point out that 'the database from which existing studies have been conducted is narrow, being mainly focused either on students' casual conversations or business encounters – in almost all cases within a Western European setting.' Consequently, 'The extant findings [...] are likely to reflect this relatively narrow empirical database.'

There is never the slightest suggestion that ELF speakers, like users of any other language, might range from the enviably articulate, co-operative and successful to the alarmingly inarticulate, unpleasant and inept. Despite the occasional reference to code-switching, there is hardly any acknowledgement that ELF users' English might be in any way wanting, not allowing them to express everything they wish to say, even though most bilingualism researchers stress that few bi- or multi-linguals speak all their languages equally well, or use them for all domains of life, and so might easily have lexical gaps in many fields. Deviations from ENL or StE are almost invariably described in terms of creativity and innovation, rather than the dreaded words 'errors' or 'learner language' (a rare exception to this rule being Kirkpatrick 2007, 2010). Indeed Cogo and Dewey (2012: 78) state explicitly that 'Deciding what constitutes an error is […] not a particularly ELF-compatible way of thinking about language' and 'probably the wrong kind of question to ask in the context of ELF.'

This chapter will first give examples of what I consider to be unnecessarily 'angelic' interpretations of ELF, before outlining various attested cooperative prac-tices in ELF interactions. It will then go on to offer a more sceptical account of both language in general, and of ELF and all who sail in her. If ELF really is used 'in all manner of settings and for a fully extensive range of functions […] just like any ENL or nativized version of the language' (Cogo and Dewey 2012: 16), there will inevitably be manifold occasions when interlocutors are not being maximally cooperative.

Angelic interpretations

I have already alluded to what I call angelic interpretations of ELF in the foregoing chapters: many ELF researchers redescribe *everything* that SLA or ESL or EFL theorists would call errors or limitations as signs of 'creativity' and/or savvy, contextually appropriate innovations.[1] Meierkord (2005: 93), who studies actual 'interactions across Englishes' rather than imagined communities of ELF speakers, states that

> the lexicon of speakers of Englishes in the outer or expanding circle needs to be approached as being constrained by the amount of lexemes which have been acquired by the individual speakers. Characteristically, a learner's lex-icon contains gaps, the sizes of which vary according to the stage of second language acquisition which the learner has reached.

As mentioned in Chapter 5, Mauranen (2012: 37) also acknowledges the existence of partial lexical gaps, and describes involuntary approximations of words (*successing, assimilisation, undoubtly, categoration*) in terms of fuzzy processing or 'less deeply entrenched memory representations.' Yet Pitzl *et al.* (2008) see only creative 'innovations' – *examinates, devaluated, fragmentated, manufacters, contination, diversication* and the rest. Both Mauranen (2012: 103) and Hülmbauer (2009: 340) describe semantic approximations – the use of near-synonyms with a semantic affinity to the more standard ENL word (e.g. *negated* for *denied, visioned* for *seen, normal* for *ordin-ary, card* for *map*) – as being communicatively advantageous (especially in Europe, if the words used have a Latin origin which might be shared in other languages the speakers know) rather than merely the imposition of additional processing effort on hearers.

Along the same lines, Pitzl *et al.* (2008) and Pitzl (2009, 2012) prefer to describe apparently transferred or translated words (e.g. *re-emplace*, probably from the French *remplacer*) as creations or innovations. Similarly (as outlined in Chapter 6), transliterating idioms from one language to another (e.g. *we should not wake up any dogs*, probably from the German proverb *schlafende Hunde soll man nicht wecken*) is described in terms of creativity, rather than as just the kind of translation that plurilingual speakers regularly find themselves doing. However, while ELF speakers are free to transfer idioms, a NES using an ENL idiom in an ELF context would be guilty of 'unilateral idiomaticity'; as Jenkins (2006a: 161) puts it, 'any participating mother tongue speakers will have to follow the agenda set by ELF speakers.'

Code-switching too is always given the benefit of the doubt. Firth (2009: 156) describes a Tunisian who asks a Dane hopefully *Tu parles pas français, toi?* not as trying to switch to French because he's finding it difficult to express something in English, but rather as providing 'a vivid example of "multicompetence" (Cook 2002) in action,' marshalling (in this case fruitlessly) his 'multilingual resources.' Similarly, Firth and Wagner (1997) offer an angelic reinterpretation of a one-word code-switch into Danish, previously analysed in Claus Færch and Gabriele Kasper (1983) – *historie* for *story*, seemingly interpreted by the hearer as *history*.[2]

As with lexis, most of the recurrent grammatical features of ELF allow more than one explanation, but the angelic view always chooses the one that makes ELF users sound like uncannily efficient communicators. For example, whereas Platt *et al.* (1984: 73) suggest that the 'extended use of *-ing*' in outer circle or World English varieties could be the result of L1 interference, or merely a case of learners overextending the rules of appropriate use of the progressive, perhaps as a result of the 'overteaching' of the *-ing* form at school, ELF researchers (e.g. Ranta 2006; Cogo and Dewey 2012) invariably see it as motivated by questions of clarity and ease of production and reception.

Similarly (as mentioned in Chapter 4), Cogo and Dewey (2012: 98) show that '*the* is often used in ELF for general reference, either with uncountable and abstract nouns, or with plural uncountable nouns,' as in *the children just play the video game*, and *how to survive in the nature or in the society*. One way of explaining this is that the speakers simply haven't internalized the rather unusual logic of countable and uncountable, and concrete and abstract nouns in English grammar. Hence speakers of languages like French and Spanish in which abstract nouns take articles might well transfer that logic to English, while speakers of Slavic or East Asian languages that have no articles might simplify the English system so that a noun is a noun and can take either a definite or an indefinite article. These things happen, and were traditionally described as transfer or incomplete learning or fossilization or whatever. But apparently ELF speakers cannot conceivably be thought of as failing to master something or making errors or transferring the logic of their L1, or indeed simply having the reflex of using the definite article for uncountable and abstract nouns as well as countable and concrete ones. Hence uses such as *the nature* or *the pollution* or *the abortion* must be seen as deliberate rather than accidental, and given a positive interpretation and explained by way of 'the "keyness" of the word in question,' and indeed as 'an emerging development in the functional properties of the article' (Cogo and Dewey 2012: 100). Meanwhile zero article rather than the indefinite article before a noun must always be the result of the quick-thinking speaker deeming the noun in question to be relatively unimportant, and not because of crosslinguistic interaction with an article-free L1. Always look on bright side of the life.

It is all too rarely acknowledged in ELF research that what can be described, when seen from one angle, as the active, skilful, innovative, creative and resourceful adapting, blending, manipulating, reshaping and co-constructing of lexicogrammatical and pragmatic forms and speakers' linguistic resources to produce localized repertoires can also be reasonably analysed in terms of a lack of proficiency, incomplete learning, fossilization or learner language. An exception to this is Kirkpatrick (2007: 177), who complains that research into new varieties of English and ELF often includes speakers who are not proficient and who therefore produce unnecessarily complicated forms which are clearly learner errors. Researchers needs to know for sure that 'a distinctive feature which does not occur in standard British or American English is a feature of a new variety of English' (2010: 71) rather than simply a mistake.[3]

Mauranen (2012: 129) states explicitly that 'The similarity of [...] recurrent lexicogrammatical ELF features to what are regarded as typical learner errors is clear,' for the obvious reason that both L2 learners and L2 speakers

> use a linguistic repertoire where items tend to be less deeply entrenched than in an L1 repertoire. L2 processing may also involve online choices from competing systems. Such cognitive aspects of dealing with an L2 should cover much of the common ground between learners and users.

Thus 'shaky entrenchment' and transfer in ELF can give rise to forms that are identical to those traditionally described as errors in SLA.

Pragmatic strategies

One reason why it is unnecessary to angelize ELF speakers by redescribing all involuntary approximations as signs of unbridled creativity is that there is already a lot to admire in a lot of ELF interactions. The way in which ELF speakers tend to accommodate to each other's uses was already mentioned in Chapter 4. As was Keller's argument that everybody else does so too, because behavioural congruence is a biologically given drive (which means that ELF speakers would accommodate linguistically even if they were not frantically establishing goodwill, rapport, shared affective space, and so on).

Many researchers have described pragmatic strategies used in ELF. Kirkpatrick (2010: 127ff.) gives a concise account, describing data from South-East Asian speakers, illustrating and giving names to a range of cooperative and convergent interactional strategies, including *listening to the message* (i.e. deliberately disregarding non-standard forms, or letting them pass); *requesting repetition and clarification* when it is clear that a word is too important to let pass; *spelling out a word* if pronunciation seems to be a problem; *making things explicit*, including changes of topic; *repeating a phrase (both self- and other-repetition)*; *speaker paraphrase or self-rephrasing* (adjusting form rather than meaning); *participant prompting*; *participant paraphrase*; and *lexical anticipation and lexical suggestion* (offering a word if the speaker hesitates or appears to stumble over a long word). Kirkpatrick's data seem to be broader than the telephone calls analysed by Firth (1996), who did not find participant paraphrase or lexical anticipation, or maybe these processes are more likely in face-to-face interaction. It would appear that paraphrasing and prompting and anticipating and suggesting are not considered to be face-threatening acts by Asian ELF speakers, as it seems safe to assume that in most of Asia preserving the face of participants is as important a pragmatic goal as ensuring that communication takes place.

Analysing academic discussions, Mauranen (2006) reports frequent speaker repetitions, paraphrases, comprehension checks, and spontaneous additional explanations, explicitations or clarifications, and proactive self-repairs (prospecting ahead), as well as retroactive (backward-looking) interactive repairs and requests for clarification on the part of interlocutors. She also finds several instances of lexical anticipation and suggestion and sentence completion, or '*co-construction* of expressions and seemingly unsolicited clarifications and repetitions, which appeared to arise from a perception of the speaker in need of help' (p. 149). She did not find any interactive grammatical correction (which accords with Firth's 'make it normal' principle), but neither did she find any indication of Firth's 'let it pass' strategy – unless one attributes this strategy to those participants in multiparty discussions who 'remain silent and leave the active participation to others' (p. 147). Björkman (2008b: 40), also in a university context, *does* find instances of other-repair and, commendably straying from the angelic party line, suggests that 'the reason is likely to be irritation, i.e. the non-standard form irritated the other speakers involved.'

Given that many L2 users, including ELF speakers, have smaller repertoires of entrenched collocations and formulaic sequences than NSs, and do not speak quickly and without pausing, Julia Hüttner (2009) proposes an appealing dialogic conceptualization of fluency involving the co-construction of discourse. An essential component of this is adjusting one's language to contextual conditions, and using interactive strategies such as taking up (repeating and paraphrasing) previous utterances to keep conversation running smoothly: 'Viewed like this, a fluent speaker might be more like a skilled jazz musician in a jam session than a solo virtuoso performer' (p. 282).

As already mentioned in Chapter 7, Mauranen (2012: 113) also argues persuasively that processing difficulties provoking pauses, hesitations, repetitions, false starts, restarts and rephrasings – all of which are likely to be more frequent in an L2 than an L1 – tend to come with silver linings: they give everybody more processing time, and lexical searching aloud alerts hearers to the possibility that the speaker might need help, which may lead to collaborative completions. In other words, 'dysfluencies' and speakers' limited processing capacity can actually enhance clarity and explicitness, help prevent communication breakdowns, and lead to interactional cooperation and the co-construction of comprehensibility.

Mauranen cites John Field (2003: 36), who suggests that speakers who hesitate and insert a lot of pauses also assist the non-native listener by marking more word beginnings and endings. False starts similarly give respite from high-attention processing. Mauranen equally finds virtues in repetitions. Although other-*corrections* are quite rare in the ELFA data (let it pass, make it normal), other-repetitions, or 'echoing' are quite common. Repeating something that has just been said can be seen as a speaker playing for time to organize his or her own discourse, but it also has an important role in the co-construction of dialogue. Mauranen (2012: 222) suggests that repeating a word or phrase is a strategy for showing alignment with the speaker, and a way of giving prominence to (and enhancing or maintaining the clarity of) a concept or idea.[4]

Mauranen also highlights the frequent use of discourse reflexivity or meta-discourse – language about language, expressions which organize either the speaker's present contribution or the ongoing interaction. These go beyond the customary discourse markers indicating the different parts of a presentation (as in the standard 'say what you're going to say, say it, then say that you've said it' structure) – e.g. *so I will give you the introduction*; *er okay before we go to the next topic* – and include things like stating what the next speech act will be – e.g. *what I would like to ask you*; *we haven't discussed about*; *I just like to make a brief comment of this*. The ELF speakers Mauranen has analysed seem to make great efforts to make discourse structure and intended meanings explicit.

All in all, Mauranen argues that 'ELF speakers engage in various interactive strategies to achieve mutual comprehensibility; they seem to be prepared for the possibility of misunderstanding and take steps to pre-empt that, which in effect results in misunderstandings being rare' (p. 7). She states that 'ELF speakers typically find themselves in situations where discourse norms are not clear or given. Group norms are negotiated within ELF groups by participants, none of whom can claim the status of a linguistic model' (p. 7). (Some NESs in ELF interactions may feel that they possess the correct linguistic model; others, more attuned to international communication in English, will not.)

On the other hand, speakers who interact over a longer period are likely, as Mauranen puts it, to constitute discourse communities (Swales 1990) which 'regulate their language towards group norms' (p. 20). Another concept that many ELF researchers draw on, following House (2003) and various sociolinguists (e.g. Eckert 2000), is what Wenger (1998) calls *communities of practice*: groups of people who associate with one another in the sustained pursuit of joint enterprises and develop shared ways of doing things. This creates mutual experiences and learning trajectories, resulting in a repertoire of collective communicative resources. Wenger describes individuals' *active* participation in the practices of social communities and the formation of identities in relation to those communities; membership requires more than just the imitation or internalization of norms, and the acquisition of habits and skills. This description clearly fits the academic communities recorded in the ELFA corpus, and some of the groups of people recorded in VOICE. Indeed, as Seidlhofer (2007: 315) states, 'Any professionals worth their salt are expected to feel at home in international networks.'

Kirkpatrick's (2010) account of pragmatic strategies in ELF goes beyond linguistic gambits that aid comprehension, as he gives examples (p. 116ff.) of speakers transferring their local cultural values and pragmatic norms into their use of English. Similarly, House (2006: 88) states that

> When English is used in interactions between, say, Germans and Spanish speakers, underlying differences in interactional norms, in standards of politeness, directness, values, feelings of cultural and historical tradition remain exactly what they were – these norms are not shared, nor need they be.[5]

Hence, to adapt Mauranen's term, ELF is the site of second-order cultural contact. Yet in successful intercultural communication, local cultural values and pragmatic norms need to be, at the very least, attenuated.[6] House (1999: 84) proposes 'The Culture Irrelevance Hypothesis,' such that

> In ELF talk it is not interactants' affiliation with their native linguacultural norms and values that comes to the fore, rather interactants act primarily as individuals and there is no strong attachment to L1 groups. [...] In ELF interaction, national and native language and culture adherence is eclipsed

Yet clearly some linguacultural behavioural patterns still survive. For example, House has frequently analysed data showing that German speakers tend not to bother with 'small talk' but interact in ways that are direct, informationally explicit, and self- (rather than other-) and content-focused, with far fewer conversational routines and interpersonal markers than (native, and most non-native) English speakers. She suggests that all ELF speakers (not just Germans) can benefit from explicit instruction in discourse strategies or gambits, such as specific speech acts for initiating and changing topics, referring back, clarifying, pointing forward, and so on.[7] Seidlhofer (2004: 218), on the other hand, claims that 'Interference from L1 interactional norms is very rare – a kind of suspension of expectations regarding norms seems to be in operation,' while Meierkord's (2002: 118–19) corpus evidence shows that while interference from communicative norms of the 'home' culture is evident in some speakers, in other speakers this is overridden by other contextual factors.[8]

Yet *pace* House, many Asian speakers are unlikely to find their cultural and pragmatic norms irrelevant. Most Asian cultures place great importance on modesty and discretion, and avoiding explicit criticism. There is often a respect for seniority, which feeds into conversation strategies.[9] Whereas many NESs are happy to speak as equals and interrupt each other in meetings, Asian speakers of English are less likely to interrupt and more likely to allow hierarchy, gender and relative seniority to determine the order in which people speak.[10] Similarly, Farzad Sharifian (2011) gives examples of Persian speakers of English using L1 cultural conceptualizations or practices when speaking English – giving frequent compliments while deflecting compliments directed towards them, expressing great modesty, expressing gratitude, making offers but repeatedly rejecting offers received, hesitating to make requests or to complain, frequently apologising, etc. – with the result that speakers from other cultures often consider them to be excessively deferential.

Cultural practices such as these can easily lead to misunderstandings in communication taking place in ELF. For example, the Teheran taxi driver who twice tells a European visitor that it has been such an honour to carry him that he does not wish to be paid expects the visitor to deflect the compliment and insist a third time, upon which he will be told the price of the journey. In Smith's terms (see Chapter 5), the driver's utterances may be entirely intelligible and comprehensible, but not immediately interpretable. Examples like this one clearly show that Paul Grice's (1975/1989: 26–27) well-known Cooperative Principle with its four maxims of conversation is based on 'Anglo' rather than universal cultural assumptions. A taxi driver (temporarily) insisting that he does not wish to be paid (according to a code of politeness known as ta'ârof) would appear to be flouting all four of Grice's maxims: *Quality* – do not say what you believe to be false; do not say that for which you lack evidence; *Quantity* – make your contribution as informative as is required for the current purposes of exchange; do not make your contribution more informative than is required; *Relation* – be relevant; and *Manner* – be perspicuous; specifically: avoid obscurity; avoid ambiguity; be brief; be orderly.

But of course successful communicators in ELF or EIL accept and accommodate to their interlocutors' culture-based communicative practices. Thus Sharifian (2011: 98) suggests that proficiency in EIL is a matter of adopting effective communicative strategies:

> 'more proficient' speakers are those who have been exposed to, and show familiarity with, various systems of cultural conceptualisations, who are capable of participating with flexibility in EIL communication, and therefore effectively articulating their cultural conceptualisations to their interlocutors when the need arises.

For example, Sharifian states that even if Iranians develop a phonological system that is close to American or British English, they might well continue to draw on cultural conceptualizations from their 'native' culture, as well as (some of) those associated with the culture of the taught native variety, or of course 'blend together aspects of the two sets of cultural conceptualisations to which they have access' (p. 99). Thus interlocutors may sometimes assume they are using the same or similar words to mean the same thing when this assumption is unwarranted, and so they must 'consciously adopt communicative strategies that allow for the explicitation and clarification of the underlying conceptualisations' (p. 100). Sharifian describes these skills as *metacultural competence*.

Given the lack of a shared background, and likely differences in English proficiency, ELF speakers often need to use cooperative and convergent dialogical strategies, and corpus evidence shows manifold examples of them doing just this. Yet ELF interactions can also be rendered difficult by the divergent cultural backgrounds and expectations of participants. They would also be rendered more difficult if ELF speakers occasionally behaved like the rest of humanity, i.e. rather less consensually, as indeed they probably do.

Anger, joy, affection, surprise, hate, etc. and ELF corpora

Although it is easy to find all the processes of accommodation described above in published ELF corpus data, it needs to be borne in mind that such corpora may not be representative of the full range of language use. Cogo's corpus (Cogo 2009; Cogo and Dewey 2012) consists of small-talk between a group of friends (also her friends); Seidlhofer (2011: 49) points out that the 110 hours of recordings in VOICE 'are predominantly of a consensual kind where it is in the participants' interest to cooperate and where they do so willingly in the co-construction of agreed meanings,' and much the same can be said of the ELFA corpus: lectures, conference discussions, seminars and thesis presentations in Finnish universities do not seem to be particularly antagonistic or adversarial affairs. Seidlhofer (2004: 218) also states that 'misunderstandings are not frequent in ELF interactions,' and that 'when they do occur' they often 'tend to be resolved by topic change.' Yet this is easier to do in a casual conversation than in a service encounter or a business negotiation. It is unwise to let it pass or nod vaguely or change topics if you don't understand utterances such as 'We can offer you a €150 upgrade to a suite,' or 'So we'll add our standard ten-year exclusive service contract,' or 'Then we all agree that it's your department that needs to tighten its belt the most.' Similarly, Björkman (2009: 244) points out that the topic avoidance that Meierkord (2000) reports in small talk is not possible in high stakes situations like solving a technical problem and reporting the results.

Although Seidlhofer (2009b: 239) scorns Quirk's (1985: 6) suggestion that NNESs only need to use the language for a 'relatively narrow range of purposes,' and asserts that they use English in 'highly complex and sophisticated interactions' (p. 242), this sophistication does not seem to extend to such things as telling lies or being disingenuous. In ELF, all is for the best in the best of all possible worlds. Leibniz, thou shouldst be living at this hour, though ELF hath no need of thee.[11]

This is all a far cry from Voltaire's dictum that men 'use speech only to conceal their thoughts'.[12] The 'shared affective space' that ELF researchers perceive runs counter to John Haiman's (1998: 5) contention that it is 'axiomatic that any interested speaker who exercises personal volition will be dishonest or at least biased.' George Steiner (1998: 47) asserts that 'Obviously, we speak to communicate. But also to conceal, to leave unspoken,' and suggests that 'It may be that the agonistic functions of speech [...] outweigh the functions of genuine communication' (p. 33). Yet the angelic account of ELF attributes exclusively noble intentions to ELF users. We learn early on in *The Hitchhiker's Guide to the Galaxy* that 'they don't have sarcasm on Betelgeuse' (Adams 1979: 15), but that's nothing: in ELF researchers' data nobody ever seems to express indifference or hostility or contempt, no-one obfuscates or dissembles or deceives or speaks in code or gobbledegook, and no-one sneers or postures or shows off. Not even university teachers – so how could you conceivably have a faculty meeting or a hiring committee or write a book review in ELF?![13]

ELF researchers like to describe communities of ELF speakers, as found in ELFA and most of VOICE, but Knapp (2009) suggests that ELF is more commonly used, e.g. by tourists, as an L2-influenced 'linguistic emergency solution' and as a 'restricted transactional code,' often employing fixed expressions drawn from ENL (*Can you call me a taxi? – Yes, madam; How much is it? – Three seventy-five*, etc.). Furthermore, interactions in tourism are not always successful. I can find examples of this just by commuting to work. In the railway station ticket offices cum travel agents in places like Geneva and Montreux in Switzerland, you can listen to ELF interactions between occasionally exasperated Swiss rail employees and visitors from all over the world all day long, and some of them include unresolved misunderstandings, and consequently altered travel plans. And at the tram stop outside Geneva station, many visitors, especially Asians, usually trying to get to various international organizations, assume they can ask *anyone* directions in English, and regularly approach people who fail to understand what they are being asked. Although, e.g. Mauranen's and Björkman's corpus data all come from bi- or multilingual academics and students, ELF is also part of what Jan Blommaert (2010: 8) describes as the fragmented and incomplete or 'truncated' language repertoires of 'new migrants' in many cities. The visiting Asians at the tram stop have an uncanny knack of addressing either new migrants or, shall we say, people with relatively few years of full-time education, even if there are also bi- or multilingual academics and students standing around.

While most tourist encounters are non-conflictual (or there would be less tourism), it is also quite easy to seek out non-consensual ELF interactions in any 'international' city. Where I live I need only go into town and eavesdrop on encounters between the police and (suspected) West African drug dealers; unsurprisingly, the latter tend not to be maximally communicative or to establish a shared affective space or to converge on shared meaning with their inquisitors.[14] Interactions such as these are no less genuine instances of ELF discourse than those to be found in published corpora, which cover a limited range of situations; in fact they may even be *more* genuine, as the participants have not been told beforehand that they are being recorded. Yet they differ from published corpora. For example, Cogo and Dewey (2012) report that the speakers in their data use rapport-building interactional strategies such as signalling understanding with encouraging feedback and back-channelling and collaborative sentence completions (not unlike most NESs in similar situations, in fact). But this may also have something to do with the fact that they are all language teaching colleagues and friends and postgraduate students, altogether the kind of people who are more likely to converse like this than to punch you in the face. To return to my police and (suspected) drug dealers example, alternative sentence completion strategies *do* involve non-verbal ones. This may be a rather extreme example, but it suffices to show that many ELF interactions do *not* take place within a discourse community or a community of practice whose members are eager to show alignment or solidarity or signal affiliation or evoke approval.

Quite apart from issues of language proficiency, which are always relevant in the use of an L2, and inherently conflictual situations, there can be issues of communicative competence. Nikolas Coupland *et al.* (1991: 11ff.) analyse miscommunication on six levels. Their first two levels consist of trivial imperfections (potential ambiguities, incomplete messages, slips of the tongue, interruptions, etc.) which participants tend to overlook. The higher levels of miscommunication involve social identities and group memberships and societal value systems, the sort of factors that can potentially be negotiated by skilled intercultural communicators. In between are communication problems linked to individuals, who may have poor communication skills, personality problems, bad temper and similar inadequacies that prevent them from achieving instrumental and interpersonal goals in communication. Despite all the accommodation skills revealed in various ELF corpora, it seems somewhat unlikely that there are no such individuals who use English as a lingua franca.

A contrary argument is that there are speakers with very good communication skills who use them for self-serving ends. Everybody knows that business negotiations occur in which one or more parties are not being wholly truthful or cooperative and that deceit is often the order of the day. As Adam Smith (1776/1976: 152) famously put it, 'People of the same trade seldom meet together, even for merriment and diversion, but the conversation ends in a conspiracy against the public, or in some contrivance to raise prices.' For all the rhetoric from free market economists about buyers and sellers, employers and employees, landlords and tenants, etc. freely entering into contractual agreements, so that governmental regulation is unnecessary, it is obvious that where people's interests diverge, they speak (and write), as Steiner puts it, to conceal and leave unspoken as well as to communicate. Successful salespeople, just as much as convergent ELF speakers, accommodate to potential buyers' linguistic uses, but any perceived 'shared affective space' is conjured up solely with the goal of making a sale.[15]

Thus it would appear that the data used in most ELF studies do not reflect anything like the full range of human linguistic behaviour. Trudgill (2011: 67) describes modern native English as a creoloid which has undergone admixture and simplification but no functional reduction. If ELF is not to be classified as functionally reduced, it must be used to do rather more than it does in the major published corpora. For example, Larry Smith (1983a: 4), describing what he called 'English as an international auxiliary language,' said that he expected speakers to 'show anger, joy, affection, surprise, hate, etc. in the same way as they always have, but the language used is international auxiliary English.' (This contrasts with Joshua Fishman (1992: 24), who describes English in international communication as being 'without love, without sighs, without tears and almost without affect of any kind.') Smith's argument is a long way from the anger- and hate-free ELF corpora. More recently, Smith (2009: 24) has also asserted that 'Understanding is not common in human interaction. Misunderstanding is the norm. It may be caused by a lack of intelligibility, comprehensibility, or interpretability, or a combination of these. It may be caused by a lack of desire to understand.'

It is not difficult to find comparable assertions from other linguists. Ronald Carter (2004: 76) suggests that 'Lies, white lies, hyperbole, understatement, degrees of deceit and deliberate misinformation may be as much a part of dealing with others as straightforward factual and cooperative communication.' Eco (1977: 7) cheerfully states that 'semiotics is in principle the discipline studying everything which can be used in order to lie.' Haiman (1998: 191) concedes that language provides the means for the most sincere and intimate expression of thought and feeling, and that this may well be what almost all language is about the majority of the time, but suspects that in 'the remaining speck, the vast potential of language for affectation, prevarication, empty formality, and concealment [...] we may find the essence of language.'[16]

Concealment in language is everywhere. People (particularly official spokes-people) use euphemisms and coded expressions that are fundamentally dishonest, such as *friendly fire*, *collateral damage*, *rightsizing*, *non-performing assets*, *advance downward adjustments*, and *negative patient care outcome*. Coded expressions include *getting the government off people's backs* (eliminating welfare), *saving our cities* (giving tax breaks to the rich), *equal opportunities for all* (ending affirmative action), and so on. University teachers write semi-coded references – e.g. *X is a conscientious student and a regular member of the class* does *not* mean 'definitely give this student a place on your MA programme.' Haiman also suggests that sarcasm (along with irony) is so common that the 'sarcastive' could be a mood like the subjunctive (p. 28). Furthermore, sarcasm often relies on distinct suprasegmental features (stress, melody, pitch) that allow us to recognize it even in languages we don't understand (p. 30). None of this is to say that language *doesn't work*;[17] on the contrary it works all too well, but people's communicative purposes are not always cooperation, the establishment of rapport and a shared affective space.[18]

Variable proficiency

It needs to be recognized that whether they wish to converge on shared meaning or to dissemble or lie or express hostility, there remains the possibility that ELF speakers' English proficiency will not match their intentions. ELF researchers habitually describe ELF speakers as 'users not learners,' but there are clearly users whose English does not enable them to do everything circumstances might require. Kachru (1992: 2) stated that although 'a significant segment of the world's population' uses English 'as their *other* tongue,' such use 'varies from broken English to almost native (or ambilingual) competence.' There may be 'more people learning English in China than there are people in the United States,' as Bill Bryson (1990: 177) wrote a generation ago, but it is unlikely that they can all do all the things that most Americans can do with English. Many of them may feel, when called upon to use their English, that they still have much to learn. Unfortunately many ELF researchers overlook the broken English end of the proficiency scale. In fact Jenkins (2011: 928) seems to criticize Firth's (1996) pioneering article because it dared to analyse 'speakers with low proficiency levels,' rather than promulgate the dogma that ELF 'speakers are often highly skilled and proficient.' Off with his head.

Jessner (2006: 8) says of ELF that 'The level of proficiency and the discourse/ speech type [...] are not very different from native-speaker English,' and then quotes an example from a well-known article by James (2000: 22), from three teenagers in the trilingual Carinthia-Friuli-Slovenia region:

> – I don wanna drink alcohol.
> – Me too.
> – I also not.

While this exchange is perfectly comprehensible, both to the participants and to, shall we say, 'traditional' (i.e. prescriptive) EFL teachers, the latter are less likely to accept that it shows a level of proficiency not very different from native-speaker English. This is an example of the 'conceptual gap' identified by Seidlhofer (2001b). Even so, one assumes that there are contexts in which the speakers in James' example would not be able to function very well in English.

It also needs to be recognized that while letting things pass and making things normal are excellent ways of dealing with or accommodating to *other people's* linguistic eccentricities or shortcomings, they do not enable you to say things for which you cannot find the words. And for many people this is a regular occurrence in an L2. Most recent work on bilingualism contains a paragraph explaining that 'balanced' or 'true' or 'symmetrical' bilinguals scarcely exist. These would be people with absolutely no 'foreign accent,' no propensity to borrow, code-switch or transfer any element from one language to another, and the ability to converse fluently with any interlocutor on any subject in either language. Such a perfect bilingual would in fact resemble 'two monolinguals in one person,' which, as Grosjean (1989) has shown, is precisely what bilinguals are not. Even 'simultaneous' or 'early' bilinguals, who are exposed to two languages from birth or early childhood, and who continue to use them throughout their life, tend to have subjects they generally think and converse about in one language rather than the other. The majority of ELF speakers are 'unbalanced' or 'late' bilinguals who either acquired English at school, or 'naturalistically' (perhaps in a professional setting), and who use their languages with different people in different contexts for different purposes.[19] Consequently, there are likely to be occasions when they are unable to produce a target form, and have to give up, say something else, or switch to another language.

Most research articles about code-switching state, if only in passing, that far from being an indication of deficiency in one or both languages (or of 'semilingualism'), code-switching is in fact a skill, talent or resource requiring considerable pragmatic and grammatical competence in both languages, which is used to achieve various communicative effects and discursive functions, to enact social roles and identities, to accommodate to interlocutors, etc., while obeying both socially and culturally imposed constraints and the morpho-syntactic constraints imposed by both languages. All of this is true, but it is equally true that bilinguals occasionally code-switch because they are unable to express something in a particular language.

Although accommodating to or converging with other people's linguistic uses is indeed an excellent way of establishing goodwill or camaraderie or what Guy Aston (1993: 226) refers to as 'comity' between speaker and hearer, varying your own uses too much is not necessarily cooperative behaviour, as I have already argued in the foregoing chapters. It is one thing to expect your interlocutors to accommodate to your non-standard usages, and another to increase their processing load, however minimally, by not speaking like anyone else. Even if ELF requires fuzziness to be stretched wider than usual, as Mauranen (2012: 42) argues, there comes a point when innovation and creativity, or deliberate variation, collide with the law of diminishing returns. A lack of entrenched memory representations certainly leads to fuzziness, but is it really necessary to describe *every* non-standard item in an ELF corpus in terms of creativity, analogy, coining, innovation, or a 'shift' away from ENL?[20] As opposed, that is, to a symptom of incomplete learning, forgetting, or – heaven forfend – an error or a deviation from the established lexicogrammar or phraseology of English, which most ELF users will encounter in print, if not in speech. Innovating too much does *not* aid hearers who are also familiar with less innovative forms. It is rather like a musician playing all the right notes, though not necessarily in the right order.

It is undeniable that ELF exists as a function of language – a widely-used L2 in which it cannot be assumed that predictable StE norms (of syntax, morphology, lexis, phraseology and pronunciation) will be used. In these circumstances, NES usages are not necessarily ideal. Some forms are regularly simplified, others are changed in the quest for increased explicitness, and so on. Teachers used to teaching native English as a model may wish this was not the case, but it is; lamenting the realities of L2 learning and use is rather like doctors complaining that all their patients are unwell, or criminal lawyers bemoaning the chosen profession of their clients. Furthermore, NESs in ELF interactions can usefully modify their language use in various respects. On the other hand, many L2 speakers of English participate in multifarious 'interactions across Englishes' with inner and outer circle speakers as well as with expanding circle ELF speakers. Some of these people *have* acquired near nativelike syntax, phraseology, etc., and consequently do not use the variable, non-standard syntax of less proficient ELF speakers. While accommodation and convergence are widespread (or universal) traits of language use, neither NESs nor relatively nativelike L2 users of English in ELF settings are likely to imitate too many forms which appear to them to be non-standard.

ELF researchers regularly assert that the kind of English that is appropriate for NESs is not appropriate for ELF speakers. But what is it that *needs* to be different?

- Almost certainly speakers' accents: one cannot reasonably expect (the immense majority of) adolescent or adult learners to master NSs' phonological patterns (and as argued in Chapter 7, I would expect and allow more phonological variation than Jenkins grants in her Lingua Franca Core).
- Where specific communities of ELF speakers share similar L1s, one can expect them occasionally to borrow lexis from those languages, and/or to code-switch into them.
- One would not expect to find much use of opaque, culture-specific idioms and formulaic expressions.
- Given the inherent fuzziness of ELF, one can expect some variation in what for NESs are fixed expressions, e.g. articles and prepositions can be changed without expressions losing their standard meaning.
- One can expect the simplification or regularization of the most obvious grammatical idiosyncrasies and typological oddities of StE.
- One can expect ELF speakers to alter some ENL grammatical constructions and patterns so as to enhance communication by way of various processes including regularization, reducing redundancy, adding explicitness or clarity or prominence, and accommodating to other speakers' uses.

However this list still potentially leaves quite a lot of ENL unchanged (English is English). There is a lot of English lexicogrammar that is *not* obviously 'replete with in-group markers of shared sociocultural identity' (Seidlhofer 2011: 91) or 'references and allusions to shared experience and the cultural background of particular native-speaker communities' (p. 16) which it would be inappropriate or unwise for ELF speakers to conform to. To be precise – a lot of nouns (with or without articles and determiners), adjectives, modal verbs, lexical verbs, verbal patterns or constructions (with or without standard ENL prepositions), adverbs, pronouns, conjunctions, the present and past tenses, etc.

Much of this lexicogrammar can still be taught, even in courses taking an ELF perspective. As Seidlhofer (2007: 316) puts it,

> Of course there still need to be standards in language pedagogy, and this must involve prescribing some model of use that calls for conformity, otherwise both teachers and learners would be in limbo and no teaching or learning would be possible, let alone measurement of learning outcomes.

Quite. This implies that errors can exist, at least in language *learning*, and it seems reasonable to assume, *pace* Cogo and Dewey, that the notion of error consequently extends to ELF *usage* too.

Angels and demons

In most of the work of Jenkins, Cogo and Dewey, however, the only mistakes are made by dim-witted applied linguists and language teachers, who are repeatedly described as suffering from misinterpretations, misunderstandings, misconceptions, 'strongly held ideological positions and/or sociolinguistic naivety,' 'deep-seated concerns and insecurities about language change,' 'irrational fear,' 'deeply entren-ched prejudice,' and so on.[21] The linguistics of ELF does not appear to be a falsi-fiable science, as counter arguments can do nothing but reveal the critic's 'ENL ideology' at work. This form of argumentation has led Alan Maley (2008), bor-rowing from the Indian playwright Girish Kanath, to lament the 'holier than cow' attitude of some proponents of ELF.

Reading many ELF researchers unfortunately reminds me of the physicist Lee Smolin's critique of his fellow string theorists. Smolin accuses them of 'groupthink,' a term coined by the psychologist Irving Janin (quoted in Smolin 2008: 286): 'a mode of thinking that people engage in when they are deeply involved in a cohesive in-group, when the members' strivings for unanimity override their motivation to realistically appraise alternative courses of action.' Of course, when this criticism is applied to linguists one usually needs to substitute 'alternative theories' for 'alter-native courses of action.' Smolin lists various aspects of an academic in-group, including overestimating its high moral stance (p. 287), and tremendous self-confidence, a strong sense of boundary between the group and other experts, a disregard for and disinterest in the ideas, opinions, and work of experts who are not part of the group, a tendency to interpret evidence optimistically, to believe exaggerated or incorrect statements of results, and to disregard the possibility that a theory might be wrong (p. 284). Such criticisms might be levelled at many groups of linguists, including generativists, functionalists, cognitivists, critical discourse analysts, relevance theorists, etc., but they certainly seem pertinent to ELF.[22]

The obverse of the angelizing of ELF and ELF speakers is the demonization of ENL and NESs. One small example: Seidlhofer (2011: 20) complains that ENL corpora, whatever they are designed and used for, 'also have the effect of further enhancing the prestige and authority of English as a native language.' Just as a survey of people's apple-eating habits would implicitly diminish the prestige of oranges. A more likely consequence of ENL corpora would be to reveal how few people actually speak StE and how many non-standard forms are in common use – see David Britain (2007) and the 'Introduction' to David Crystal's *The Stories of English* (2004: 5), in which he states that StE

> is only a small part of the kaleidoscopic diversity of dialects and styles which make up 'the English language.' Indeed, for every person who speaks Standard English, there must be a hundred who do not, and another hundred who speak other varieties as well as the standard.

Not all these native varieties can have prestige and authority.

A related gambit is to disparage the inner circle countries. Speaking in ENL, at a conference in England, run by a UK-based organization (IATEFL), in a session sponsored by a British newspaper (*The Guardian*), Jenkins (2001)[23] stated that her recordings of young European English speakers show that European attitudes towards the British and Americans are becoming negative. Jenkins' gleeful tone seems to reveal what A.A. Phillips, writing about Australia in 1950, famously called 'the cultural cringe' – the ingrained inferiority complex of colonized nations – now transferred back to the colonizer. To imagine that a large percentage of ELF speakers do not also wish to be able to communicate with NESs and use or consume some of their technological and cultural products is almost certainly misguided.

Another frequent trope is to state categorically that there is less native than non-native English use. No-one knows how many NNESs there are, and there is nothing resembling a definition of what 'being able to speak English' actually means, but most estimates are that there are three or four NNESs for every NES.[24] Consequently Seidlhofer (2005a: 339) states that 'the vast majority of verbal exchanges in English do not involve any native speakers of the language at all,' while Mauranen (2006: 125) considers it a 'fact' that 'most of the use of English today is by nonnative speakers.' Yet it seems intuitively obvious that even though they are greatly outnumbered by NNESs, the average (i.e. monolingual) American or British or Australian NES will use English a great deal more than, say, a Chinese chief executive in Chongqing or a Polish plumber in Poznan, who might be very infrequently called upon to use their English for professional or social reasons.

Furthermore, the Chinese or the Pole might well need to use English to communicate with a NES. Unlike Knapp (2002: 221), for whom ignoring the existence of NESs in the composition of ELF 'would simply mean ignoring the reality,' Jenkins (2007: 24) writes about ELF speakers being 'able to understand NSs of English should the need arise,' with the clear implication that it might not. She also (2005a: 207) writes about ELF learners needing weak forms in their receptive repertoires 'if they wish to be able to understand the speech of NSs of English, whether in occasional face-to-face interactions or in films and the like.' The 'if' is wonderful: have you met many English learners who did *not* want to be able to understand ENL films and songs and the like? And the grudging 'occasional' is also loaded: are the chances really that slim of meeting a NES (one of that 'small minority' of English speakers) in Continental Europe, or Latin America, or Asia, or Africa, in business, or a university,[25] or tourism, etc.? And what are the chances of an ELF speaker wanting to visit an inner circle country, or of a young Continental European wanting to spend some time working in Britain? Did *you* ever see a foreigner or a foreign-born resident in London or New York or Sydney? No, I thought not. The attempted erasure of NESs from the present and future story of the English language is a further unnecessary aspect of the angelic view of ELF.

At least the 'occasional [...] films' is an advance on Jenkins' (2000: 148) earlier statement that 'These learners' – i.e. not all learners – 'will still need to work on weak forms […] *receptively* in the classroom […] until the time comes when L1 speakers of English also take lessons in EIL and in accommodating their speech to their international interlocutors.' Leaving aside the fantasies of L1 speakers taking EIL lessons, at least it doesn't presuppose that Hollywood will be putting out movies adhering to the Lingua Franca Core.

As well as the lessons that will teach them not to use weak forms, Jenkins also insists that 'GA speakers will need to master the production of the intervocalic /t/ and RP speakers of rhotic /r/, so that they are able to produce them in EIL settings.'[26] To be precise, inner circle English speakers may require 'reverse training' (Jenkins 2007: 233), because

> The perhaps unpalatable truth for 'NSs' is that if they wish to participate in international communication in the 21st Century, they too will have to learn EIL. For future children, it can be incorporated into the secondary school curriculum as a compulsory component of their existing English studies […] For those who have already reached adulthood, it will be necessary to attend adult EIL classes in the same way that 'NNS' adults do.
>
> *(2000: 227–28)*

To which I can do no better than quote Trudgill's (2005b: 96) response: 'Don't watch this space.'[27]

The future of English

Even if we accept that English is now a truly global language in what Kirkpatrick (2010: 74) calls its 'post-Anglophone stage,' and that its major international role is as a lingua franca which needn't involve any NESs, it is not yet clear whether it will 'develop into a systematically different variety of English,' or indeed that there is a genuine ontological distinction between ELF and English *tout court* (English is English). Graddol (1997: 10) states that 'Those who speak English alongside other languages will outnumber first-language speakers and, increasingly, will decide the global future of the language.' Seidlhofer (2003: 7) trumps this with 'it is the non-native speakers of English who will be the main agents in the ways English is used, is maintained, and changes, and who will shape the ideologies and beliefs associated with it.' Yet this dismissal of the native speaker is both premature and absurdly exaggerated. The 'global' future need not obliterate the 'inner circle' future.

Certainly monolingual NESs are no longer perceived (except perhaps by themselves) to be the ideal English teachers or international businesspeople. Graddol (2006: 66) writes about 'The declining reverence of "native speakers" as the gold standard for English,' and states that 'In organisations where English has become the corporate language, meetings sometimes go more smoothly when no native speakers are present. Globally, the same kind of thing may be happening, on a larger scale' (p. 115). Graddol suggests that 'few native speakers belong to the community of practice which is developing amongst lingua franca users' so that

'Their presence hinders communication.' The second claim may be true, but the first is dubious: is there really an undifferentiated (billion strong?) global 'community of practice' of ELF speakers?

Even if NESs are unlikely to go back to school to learn EIL or ELF, they will increasingly need to function, in international contexts, with speakers who do not follow native English norms, or share 'Anglo' cultural baggage. Jenkins (2007: 196) quotes 'unpublished studies of secondary school students' preferences, in which around a third opt for an international kind of English rather than a British and American variety.' Elizabeth Erling and Tom Bartlett (2006) quote a similar figure for university students in Berlin. However that leaves the other two-thirds. Ironically, Erling and Bartlett's journal article is followed by a contribution by Mollin (2006a) which claims to show that European speakers of English 'stick to native-speaker standard usage' (p. 48).

Jenkins envisages

> the possibility that younger English speakers may at some future stage start to resist ENL regardless of what they are taught. If some of them went on to become teachers of English themselves, ELF might then become the focus of English teaching by default.
>
> *(2007: 196)*[28]

Perhaps, but when I explained the logic of ELF to English Department students at the University of Bern, most of whom were planning to become secondary school English teachers, they looked at me in horror and disbelief, and asserted that they wanted to achieve near-native competence. My multilingual translation students in Geneva, from a range of countries,[29] who collectively display many of the expected tendencies of ELF usage in their written and spoken English,[30] are equally aghast at the notion of endonormative European ELF.

Jenkins (2007) ends with the hopeful conjecture that

> If ELF were to be established and recognized [...] it is reasonable to suppose that the majority of English users in the expanding circle would rethink their attitudes and identities, and choose to learn and use this kind of English because it would be to their advantage to do so.
>
> *(pp. 252–53)*

Soothsayers, rather harshly, have their own corner in the eighth circle of Dante's Inferno, but this may indeed come to pass, though there are also contrary predictions – e.g. by Crystal (1997), Tom McArthur (1998), Gunnel Melchers and Philip Shaw (2003), and Maley (2008) – to which Jenkins gives short shrift. Yet writing about a form of ELF in which ENL norms have no place seems to be a case of what Pol Vandevelde (2005: 31), in another context (hermeneutics and translation), describes as the 'future-perfect fallacy': at a certain future date, X *will have happened* – a new interpretation of this text will have appeared, a new kind of English will have emerged.[31]

At present, most expanding circle ELF speakers have learnt a lot of their English through formal teaching with ENL materials, and continue to have access to ENL publishing and electronic media. For the moment, the language used in educational materials and in published (as opposed to self-published or uploaded) written English in general, contains a huge amount of standard lexicogrammar; as Görlach (2002: 13) puts it, the linguistic norm 'is, and always has been, based on the consent of the learned and guided by the accepted written norm, which has remained surprisingly homogeneous around the globe.'

Trudgill (2004) explains how new colonial dialects (in Australia, New Zealand, South Africa, etc.) were formed from dialect mixing as speakers from different regions of the home country accommodated to each other, given the natural human tendency to coordinate behaviour. Children in such colonies were surrounded by a hugely variable set of models, with no single peer-group model to accommodate to. Eventually, a new dialect appeared consisting of those variants that were most widely shared in the mixture. If it turns out that this model applies to ELF, it will be because there are common elements among the various 'similects' of ELF, or a congruence of simplifications in areas where the grammar of a majority of languages differs from that of native English. As suggested in Chapter 1, this could eventually lead, for example, to a kind of European ELF, despite Görlach's claim that 'For a homogeneous transnational "Euro-English" to develop it would be necessary to have prescriptive school norms discarded and to have a billion-fold increase in international communication conducted in English' (p. 152). The 'billion' is absurdly hyperbolic, and not all prescriptive school norms are respected in everyday usage.

Yet even in the absence of a homogeneous transnational variety there *are* differences between ELF and ENL, as analysed in the previous chapters, and most ELF researchers expect these to impinge on ENL. For example, Cogo and Jenkins (2010: 278) say that 'ELF speakers make frequent and systematic use of certain forms that are not (in some cases, yet) found in native English,' and Mauranen (2012: 33) says that 'It is reasonable to expect the sheer scale of ELF use to have an effect on the English language,' and 'it would be surprising' if ELF did not 'have a significant impact on ENL communities' (p. 57).[32]

But how will this happen? Language change via accommodation and diffusion requires face-to-face interaction,[33] and Leonard Bloomfield (1933: 476) and William Labov (2001: 19) posit a principle of density, such that the diffusion of change can be explained mechanically by the amount and frequency of communication. Yet if the 375 million or so NESs are such a 'small minority' in global ELF usage, presumably most of them must be spending most of their time at home in the inner circle countries. Meanwhile, it is regularly argued that many ELF speakers rarely or never meet NESs. And ELF (or ESL) speakers who do find themselves for any length of time in inner circle countries are more likely to accommodate to the local majority than vice versa. Unfortunately, arguing that ELF will have a major impact on ENL seems to be a case of having your ELF and eating it.

Language change and dialect mixing generally involve a minority adopting majority forms, although a majority can also accommodate to linguistically simpler or more natural and unmarked forms, as argued in Chapter 3. Levelling and simplification – the replacement of marked and opaque synthetic forms by transparent analytic ones, the increase of morphophonemic regularity via the loss of inflections, the increase of invariable word forms, etc. – have been occurring in English for centuries, and Cogo and Jenkins (2010: 277) argue that 'ELF is simply quickening the pace of regularisation processes towards which the English language is predisposed, and which are already underway more slowly in native English.' Yet language change still requires a habituation process: there is a critical threshold, and new forms need to be heard quite frequently. For accommodation by NESs to become permanent, and to turn into diffusion – the use of new features in the absence of ELF speakers – would require frequent, long-term and wide-scale face-to-face interaction, as well as a favourable attitude on the part of the NESs towards the NNESs.

As Trudgill's analyses of the simplification of Old English (or its transformation into 'creoloid' Middle English), and of the absence of the third person singular *-s* in East Anglia show, change resulting from language contact with NNSs requires there to be a critical mass of the latter.[34] Even if NESs were predisposed to accommodate to NNESs and change their 'emergent grammar' by, for example, abandoning uncountable nouns, not marking third person singular verbs, regularizing past tense forms, using articles and prepositions differently, extending the use of the continuous, discarding the present perfect, etc., the number of ELF speakers in inner circle countries (and the percentage of ENL speakers regularly participating in global ELF interactions) is nowhere near the critical mass required to effect such changes. Thus the growth of ELF usage around the world is in no way guaranteed to have a significant impact on ENL usage.

All in all, ELF researchers make far too many extreme claims. ELF exists, with both more and less proficient, competent and innovative speakers. As does ENL, from which ELF differs, not least in the pragmatic strategies its speakers use to counter the effects of variance in language form and proficiency. Some NNESs take ENL as a model, some do not. Some ENL speakers accommodate to ELF speakers, some do not. And vice versa. All of this is likely to continue. Robert Dixon (1997: 67) puts forward a punctuated equilibrium model of language change, borrowed from evolutionary biology, according to which periods of equilibrium are punctuated by cataclysmic events. Increasing numbers of NNESs are indeed using the language around the world in the absence of NESs. This may not be an equilibrium, but neither is it a cataclysm, either for NESs or for speakers of ELF.

Notes

1   Admittedly, one of the Vienna researchers – Breiteneder – has the first name Angelika!
2   Firth and Wagner are in turn re-reinterpreted in Kasper (1997). Both these articles are reprinted in Seidlhofer (ed.) (2003).
3   Kirkpatrick (2010: 14) also states that Laotian and Cambodian delegates remain silent in ASEAN meetings because of their relatively low proficiency in English. Unlike the

European Union, ASEAN operates in a single language – English, now the mother tongue of part of the population of its smallest member, Singapore, and the language of the former colonizers in Brunei, Burma, Malaysia and the Philippines.

4 See also Kaur (2009: 119) on how repetition and reformulation or paraphrase are used to override dysfluencies and ungrammaticalities, compensate for a 'less-than-perfect grasp' of English, and bring about shared understanding. House (2002, 2003) also describes the uses of echoic (or shadowing or mirroring) utterances, which she calls 'Represents.'

5 See also Clyne (1994).

6 Cf. Kasper and Blum-Kulka (1993: 3), who argue that competent bilinguals create an intercultural speech style which draws on both codes but is distinct from either.

7 See House 1996, 1999, 2002, 2003, 2006, 2010, etc. The difference between House's earlier work on EFL, and more recent work on ELF, is that she no longer writes that 'To be rated as pragmatically fluent, nonnative speakers' (NNSs') talk must meet the expectations of the native speakers (NSs) of the foreign language' (1996: 228–29).

8 As mentioned in Chapter 1 in relation to grammatical features, Meierkord's data were recorded in Britain, which is likely to have some impact on speakers' L2 usages.

9 See, e.g. Morizumi (2009) and Honna (2012) on how politeness strategies influence Japanese spoken English.

10 Kirkpatrick (2010: 119ff.) gives further examples of Asian cultural and pragmatic norms. For cross-cultural pragmatics in general, see Blum-Kulka *et al.* (eds) (1989); Clyne (1994); Scollon *et al.* (2012); and Wierzbicka (2003). The conclusions of Kirkpatrick (2010) are summarized in Kirkpatrick (2011). Guido (2008, 2012) studies ELF communication rendered problematic by the transfer of speakers' native language structures, socio-cultural schemata and pragmatic behaviours into English.

11 Voltaire's *Candide* (1759) is probably better known than the target of its satire – Leibniz's 'theodicy,' or the claim that the actual world is the best of all possible worlds.

12 Admittedly this is spoken by a capon – *[ils] n'emploient les paroles que pour déguiser leurs pensées* – in *Le Chapon et la Poularde* (1763).

13 The phrase 'lack of concord and agreement is usual' is to be found in Mauranen (2012: 127) – but it is preceded by 'Syntactically'! The only exception to this rule is Knapp (2002), who reports on teenage NESs and near-natives being uncooperative and ignoring NNESs with lower proficiency.

14 Some of these interactions are what Meierkord calls 'interactions across Englishes,' as one party is speaking ESL, but they can also involve Francophones who pretend not to be and speak English instead; the police are not trained in accent recognition.

15 Marketing textbooks will inform you that marketing is all about identifying or anticipating consumers' needs, developing products and services that have customers clamouring for them, and making a lifelong, loyal customer rather than trying to make a one-off sale. But there still appear to be salespeople who haven't got the message.

16 See also Sperber *et al.* (2010), who claim that humans have (and need) 'a suite of cognitive mechanisms for epistemic vigilance, targeted at the risk of being misinformed by others' (p. 359) and that 'A disposition to be vigilant is likely to have evolved biologically alongside the ability to communicate in the way that humans do' (pp. 360–61).

17 See MacKenzie (2002), which argues at length against deconstructionist accounts of language involving the impossibility of reading and the aberrancy of all cognition and understanding.

18 Mauranen (2012: 16) says of lingua franca speakers that 'With a modicum of a shared code, they will find a way of not only carrying out their business with each other, but also dealing with the subtler aspects of social interaction. In brief, they will bring their linguistic, cognitive, and social resources to bear on the communicative task whatever language they are operating in, to achieve the purposes they have.' This at least leaves open the possibility that the subtler aspects and the communicative purpose might involve dishonesty, but this is probably not what she means. Seidlhofer *et al.* (2006: 17–19)

do at least give an example of a business meeting in which one side uses 'strategic mis-communication' to gain a (minor) advantage over the other.

19 This is known as the 'complementarity principle.' Clearly there are also very competent ELF speakers who were brought up with one or more parents or carers speaking ELF to them.

20 For example, Cogo and Dewey (2012: 57) describe a single 'innovative' use of a preposition – *consequences on (the child)* in place of the standard ENL *consequences for* – as a 'shift away from the existing pattern through the use of a different dependent preposition.' However this isn't exactly a *shift* in the sense of the Great Vowel Shift in England between the fourteenth and seventeenth centuries, or the shift of most of the population of Ireland from Irish to English in the three centuries after that. It is merely a one-off individual usage, or indeed an error if the speaker *was* actually aiming at *consequences for*.

21 These accusations are from Jenkins (2007: 19, 31, 118, 120, 147), parts of which read like a rant with references.

22 To be fair, Smolin is talking about the kind of groupthink that led, e.g. to the US's disastrous invasion of the Bay of Pigs in Cuba in 1961, which isn't really something with which I can reproach the likes of Chomsky, Halliday, Langacker, Fairclough, Sperber or Jenkins. Moreover, the second issue of the new *Journal of English as a Lingua Franca* contains (invited) articles contesting the very notion of ELF, including Mufwene (2012) and Swan (2012), quoted in previous chapters.

23 Jenkins (2001) 'Accents of English in Europe,' http://www.guardian.co.uk/GWeekly/Global_English/0,8458,400340,00.html (click on 'Listen to Audio').

24 Graddol (1997: 11) gives the figure of approximately 375 million L1 speakers. Crystal (1997: 54) estimated 320–80 million NESs, which increases to about 400 million in the second edition (2003: 65–67). This – correctly – includes speakers of English-derived pidgins and creoles: see 'The legitimate and illegitimate offspring of English,' Chapter 4 in Mufwene (2001). Graddol goes for 375 million L2 or ESL speakers in the outer circle while Crystal (2003) gives the higher figure of 430 million. Figures for EFL or ELF speakers vary. Bolton (2008: 7) gives the 'very conservative' figure of 812 million English speakers in Asia, although some of these are NESs. Crystal (2008) accepts that his previous (2003) total figure of 1.5 billion could now be approaching two billion.

25 Jenkins *et al.* (2011: 300) state that native English speakers are 'a tiny minority of global academia'. It's not clear what adjectives are left to describe the number of, say, Luxemburgish or Maltese academics.

26 See Trudgill (1986: 16) on the difficulty speakers of British English have accommodating to American non-prevocalic /r/.

27 Smith (1983c: v) long ago made the obvious point that 'native English speakers should study English as an international language if they plan to interact in English with non-native or with other native speakers who use a different national variety,' but such 'studying' doesn't necessarily require attending formal classes.

28 Or to put it in Yiddish, *Az di bobe volt gehat beytsim volt zi geven mayn zeyde!*

29 Mainly Switzerland, France, Germany, Italy, Spain, Latin America and North Africa.

30 E.g. in a piece of written work: 'I think that ELF is a utopia, which wants to acquire English erasing all its difficulties and mixing it with the other tongue. We have the impression that the English language crumbles and is finally weakened by these deficiencies. […] The ELF idea is like wanting people to sing on a wrong tune, to dress as miserably as they can or to be ignorants.'

31 Seidlhofer (2007: 310) too offers hostages to fortune: 'my prediction is that in ten or twenty years these new concepts will be taken for granted and people will wonder what the fuss was all about.'

32 Specifically, Mauranen (2012: 33) argues that this will take three generations of ELF users, starting from the 1990s. Although English has been spoken as a lingua franca for quite a long time, Mauranen describes current ELF speakers as the 'first generation' following the 'explosive expansion' of English use that coincided with the internet in the

mid-1990s. She suggests that the current 'first-generation hybrid forms are entirely based on cross-linguistic influence (similects in contact).' Consequently the next generation of ELF learners and users will 'have available to them a selection of ELF expressions that results from second-order contact and has diffused into common usage.' Second-generation speakers will use such expressions, 'probably developing them further and adding more, and by the time the third generation learns English, we may expect English already to show clear traces of lingua franca influence.'

33 Electronic media are not very instrumental in the diffusion of linguistic innovations (Trudgill 1986: 40), although speakers can choose to imitate or copy (rather than accommodate to) television, radio, films, etc. Yet the bulk of English language media is still in ENL rather than ELF.

34 Norwich was home to a large group of Flemish weavers and many Protestant refugees from the Low Countries, leading to a high proportion (about 37 per cent) of French and Dutch speakers in the city in 1579. Trudgill (2002: 97) suggests that they used English as a lingua franca among themselves and with the native population, but failed to master the 'non-natural' third person singular marking of the English verb. This coincided with the gradual replacement in Early Modern English of the third person -*th* form (deriving from Old English) with the -*s* form (deriving from Old Norse). Trudgill conjectures that the zero-marking variant of the French and Dutch speakers was competing with equal numbers of NESs using the two native forms, and the non-native form won because it had 'the advantage of linguistic naturalness and simplicity' (p. 98). See also Trudgill (2010, Chapter 2).

9

ELF IN THE CLASSROOM

Practice which is informed by theory in general is very different from practice informed by a theory in particular.

Widdowson (2003: 19)

Students often make comments like, 'I thought I was good at English until I took this course.'

Erling (2002: 11)

There is no thoroughly described – let alone institutionalised – variety of ELF as yet and so it is not possible to teach and learn it. Therefore it seems that teachers as well as learners have to concentrate on the function of ELF and on the structure of an ENL variety for successful international communication.

Gnutzmann and Intemann (2005: 21)

To return to the joke at the beginning of Chapter 1, once upon a time we used to teach English as a foreign language, and learners obligingly learned to speak English like foreigners, even though they might have had coursebooks with names like *Imagine You're English*. And we did it so well in so many countries that suddenly it was noticed that these foreign-sounding non-native speakers hugely outnumbered the natives. Then it was pointed out that they were actually talking to each other more than to the kindly natives who had helped spread the language around the world – using English as a lingua franca. So on the face of it, there are clearly good reasons to teach ELF.

The problem here, however, lies in the ambiguity of the notion of ELF – is it a variety (or a set of varieties) of English, or merely a function of language use? As mentioned in Chapter 1, during the first few years of this millennium, many claims were made for the variety status of ELF. For example, Jenkins (2006c: 142) affirmed that 'lingua franca varieties of English are emerging in their own right and exhibiting shared features which differ systematically from NS English norms, regardless of the ELF speaker's L1.' Then – when it became apparent that such codifiable varieties were somewhat chimerical – there was a sudden functional 'turn' in ELF research, and emphasis was placed on ELF's inherent fluidity, and on pragmatic strategies. Particular 'surface-level' formal features are now only deemed important because of the functions they are symptomatic of in ELF interactions (Ferguson 2009; Firth 2009; Seidlhofer 2009c; Cogo and Dewey 2012), and many ELF researchers look rather pityingly at backward language teachers and course-book writers who still ask what formal ELF features might be presented in the classroom.

In fact, Cogo and Dewey (2012: 166–67) have cannily redefined codification to cater for the fluidity of ELF:

> The codification of ELF can begin to take place without that much stability; we can document emerging trends in the ways in which speakers in ELF select from a 'feature pool' (Mufwene 2001) of linguistic choices available to them. […] We contest that […] codification can only take place when 'endonormative stabilization' (Schneider 2007) occurs. […] We are concerned in our discussion of ELF data not so much with the codification of surface-level linguistic features themselves, but rather the means by which speakers collaboratively achieve communication through accommodative manipulations of an ever-emerging bank of communicative assets […] In other words, it is not so much the codification of form in a conventional sense that matters, but rather a redefined (dynamic) notion of codification concerned more with communicative practices and interactive processes.

Fair enough, but what is the poor English teacher to do? How do you get to the point where learners can manipulate their bank of communicative assets? Gibson Ferguson (2012: 178–79) makes some succinct suggestions. He states that 'teaching ELF is far more than teaching a collection of forms, though this is, of course, still necessary,' and that the forms taught will need to include both those that appear in standard English, and those which have been found to be distinctive of ELF use. Teaching the forms that appear in StE is necessary because the large majority of them are also widely used in World Englishes in Africa, Asia and the Caribbean (especially in their written forms) as well as – necessarily – in ELF. Moreover, most English learners at school around the world probably believe they are learning English rather than ELF.

Ferguson continues:

> Going beyond forms, teaching for ELF will need […] to focus more on processes of communication – that is, on how to adapt what one wishes to say to the needs of the interlocutor through paraphrase, repetition, exploitation of redundancy, through variation in lexis, through the exploitation of shared plurilingual resources (e.g. borrowing, code-switching, cognate lexis),

and so on. In short, what seems required is an increased emphasis on communication strategies and processes, and this lends itself less to a methodology of presentation and practice and rather more to one of awareness-raising. Specifically, awareness of variation in language, awareness of how successful communication of meaning is negotiated in ELF contexts, awareness of crosslinguistic similarities and differences, and awareness that different normative regimes operate in different places and at different scale levels.

This all sounds like fun, but although you can try to teach the various pragmatic skills listed in Chapter 8, you cannot turn all English classes into lectures on variational sociolinguistics and communication strategies: standard (and non-standard) English forms will still have to be presented and practised.

Ferguson's paragraph continues:

> what counts as an effective use of linguistic resources in an ELF context in Bratislava, say, may index something rather different, and attract different, less favourable evaluations, when used, say, in a formal presentation to a mixed American/international audience in New York. For this reason drawing too rigid a distinction between students whose goal is ELF communication on the one hand and those with an EFL orientation on the other may be unhelpful for pedagogy. After all, most students will be, and may well want to be, mobile across locations [...] and their repertoire of linguistic resources, encompassing both L1 standard and ELF variants, may need to reflect this.

Thus Ferguson does not subscribe to the ELF-fundamentalist notion that many NNESs never encounter NESs, and the last sentence of the quotation could stand as a paraphrase of the main argument of this book. I will now look at language forms, communication strategies, language awareness and testing in more detail.

Language forms

Learners of any language need to experience / notice / become aware of / be presented with / learn / acquire (delete as applicable) a repertoire of words, phrases and constructions. ELF is no exception. Even if these forms are then used fuzzily / approximately / wrongly / creatively / with variants / in hybrids resulting from crosslinguistic interaction (delete as applicable), they still need to be encountered in the language syllabus. The input (the 'feature pool') will necessarily include many of the constructions of ENL. As argued in Chapters 3, 4 and 6, if language is conceived as consisting of constructions and phrasal patterns and lots of pre-fabricated phrases (the more easily learnable of which are tokens of particular constructions), it seems somewhat implausible that NNESs would require an entirely different repertoire of these than NESs. English language teaching materials, whether authentic or scripted, whether used in a present-practise-produce paradigm, or task-based learning activities (Skehan 2003), or any other method, will inevitably contain a lot of forms used by both NESs and outer and expanding circle speakers.

ELF does not require teachers to take sides on the authentic vs. contrived, invented or 'unreal' materials debate, but as Widdowson (2003: 105) points out, 'it makes no sense to present learners with "real" examples of text unless they can make them real for themselves.' He also states that 'What makes the language real for its native users is its familiarity, but what is real for learners is the fact that it is unfamiliar, foreign to them' (p. 114), and that 'in the context of the classroom, appropriate language is language that learners can appropriate' (p. 115).[1] Teachers all know that learners appropriate language selectively, and intake never corresponds with teacher input anyway (otherwise EFL learners would all be speaking ENL). Seidlhofer (2011: 186) states that 'What is achieved, and put to use in ELF, is clearly not the English that has been taught, but the English that has been learnt.' This is because learners most readily learn what they 'intuitively recognize as having the greatest inherent valency, the most potential for exploitation' (p. 187). Thus they 'home in on what is most conceptually salient or communicatively usable' (p. 187), while disregarding elements that appear 'surplus to communicative requirement' (p. 188). So 'what is crucial is not so much what language is presented as input but what learners make of it' (p. 198).

Seidlhofer (2001b: 147) says (with a couple of hedges) that we need 'to establish something like an index of communicative redundancy,' because 'certain native-speaker norms might be seen to be in suspense' in ELF. Yet the basic model need not be too different from native English. As Claus Gnutzmann (2005: 117) puts it,

> The standard variety should act as a linguistic model, both in the context of English as a Foreign Language, as well as in the context of English as a Lingua Franca. A model is an idealisation, from which one can diverge. In this sense, the primary function of a model is to offer orientation for the learners and not to act as a frame of reference to signal errors. Consequently, teaching models will have to become as tolerant of errors as possible. And there will be no dogmatic insistence on the norms of the standard language.[2]

Most ELF researchers prefer the notion of variants rather than errors, but even so, ELF must present some kind of model that can or will be diverged from. Even if experience tells us that many learners seem to have little use for the third person -*s* inflection, the countable/uncountable distinction, the *for/since* distinction (or even the present perfect *tout court*), the simple/continuous distinction with stative verbs and verbs with habitual meaning, some irregular past tense forms, fixed (nativelike) preposition use, fixed (nativelike) article use, verb complementation patterns with gerunds, and so on, it is premature – to say the least – to present a model in which these ENL forms are absent. Learners will encounter all these forms in both written and spoken material emanating from inner circle countries – including, perhaps, in content and language integrated learning (CLIL) lessons.[3]

Dewey (2012: 163) suggests that teachers should 'Spend proportionately less time on ENL forms, especially if these are not widely used in other varieties; and thus choose not to penalize non-native-led innovative forms that are intelligible.' There is indeed a difference between spending less time on forms and pretending that they don't exist. Even though Jenkins (2007: xii) calls for 'a reappraisal that will enable ELF, one day perhaps, to be offered as a pedagogic alternative to (but not necessarily a replacement for) traditional EFL,' she concedes that 'It is, of course, too early to talk of "teaching ELF" as such' (p. 238). As she says, 'there is still much to be done before there is any possibility of ELF models being offered even on an equal footing with EFL, let alone as default models' (p. 252). Similarly, Kirkpatrick (2007: 191), who recommends using a lingua franca approach and a local model (see Chapter 7), concedes that 'a major drawback arises if the local model has not been codified and there are no grammars and no textbooks or materials based on the local model,' as is generally the case in the expanding circle.

Seidlhofer (2001b: 151) suggested that ELF could be 'a possible first step for learners in building up a basis from which they can pursue their own learning in directions (ELF or ENL) which it may be impossible, and unwise, to determine from the outset.' More recently (2004: 227), she has implied that the two 'directions' are in fact not so far apart: schools should 'provide a basis that students can learn and can subsequently use for fine-tuning (usually after leaving school) to any native or nonnative varieties and registers that turn out to be relevant for their individual requirements.' It remains to be seen whether in the years to come the majority of students ultimately opt for a native or a non-native variety (or both).

However the elements that learners disregard, such as the usual suspects listed above, actually comprise a relatively small proportion of (native) English grammar (or English constructions) as a whole. The rest remains in place. Learners, as Seidlhofer (2011: 196) puts it, using J.L. Austin's famous phrase (1962), have to 'do things with words,' and you can do a lot – really a lot – in English without using uncountable nouns, the *for/since* distinction, simple aspect with stative verbs, verb complementation patterns with gerunds, and so on.

Echoing Widdowson (2003: *passim*), Seidlhofer (2011: 196–97) argues that learners need to 'develop a capability in English that will enable them to make adaptive and actual use of the virtual language […] no matter how formally "defective."' She is confident that users (beyond the classroom) who find that 'it is in their communicative interests to conform to ENL convention […] will, of course, seek to conform' (p. 199), and indeed 'for certain purposes adherence to canonical norms will be important' (p. 200). For the conceivable future this will probably apply to most people who need to write English for professional purposes, but Seidlhofer insists that this should not be the 'default assumption' as 'most learners have other and far less specific and predictable objectives' (p. 200). For this reason she suggests that 'we might start thinking of learning speaking and writing ENL as ESP – English for Specific Purposes,' and that 'it does not seem reasonable to impose such ESP objectives' on most learners, 'especially as they are unlikely to attain them anyway' (p. 200). What they really need is 'EGP – English for General Purposes – English that can be adapted to any purpose and made appropriate to any context,' and, 'as far as international uses of English are concerned […] it is ELF that is EGP' (p. 200).

On the face of it, it would appear that learning ELF or EGP forms and later unlearning some of them (if necessary or desired) in order to approximate ENL might well require *more* rather than less effort. Being presented with the 'standard variety' but possibly disregarding parts of it in favour of what Dewey calls 'non-native-led innovative forms' might be simpler. Widdowson (2003: 141), however, disagrees, suggesting that there is nothing wrong with teaching forms that are not the ultimate target: 'the claim that students might have to unlearn what they have been taught seems to be unfounded since the chances are they will not have learnt it in the first place'! Moreover,

> learners proceed not by adding items of knowledge or ability, but by a process of continual revision and reconstruction. In other words, learning is necessarily a process of recurrent unlearning and relearning, whereby encoding rules and conventions for their use are modified, extended, realigned, or abandoned altogether to accommodate new language data.
>
> *(pp. 140–41)*

This could just as easily be an argument for beginning with particularly useful ENL forms as for teaching (or encouraging) 'the unrealized resource for meaning which the code provides […] the potential inherent in the language for innovation *beyond* what has become established as well-formed or "correct" encodings' (p. 173). But for Widdowson, input is not a set of examples of fixed conventions to conform to, but rather an adaptable resource for meaning making that you can call your own: 'You are proficient in a language to the extent that you possess it, make it your own, bend it to your will, assert yourself through it rather than simply submit to the dictates of its form' (p. 42). He asserts that

> the kind of encodings that are selected, and the kind of activities devised to present them and put them to use have to be pedagogically appropriate and cannot be simply imported directly from the actually attested texts and contextually appropriate discourses for native speaker users of the language.
>
> *(p. 135)*

Yet ELF corpora reveal that many of the encodings of NESs *are* relevant to ELF users. Taking the contrary perspective to Widdowson, Prodromou (2008: 254) argues that given the presence of L1 users in EIL, and the sheer quantity of StE forms that are shared by indigenized varieties, 'it would be irresponsible to encourage the learners to assume that they can do without standard forms of the language.' He insists that 'a reduced form of ELF' risks bringing L2 users 'stuttering onto the world stage of ELF, i.e. with reduced linguistic capital. The point, as

Caliban failed to realize, is not to "burn" Prospero's books, the source of the master's power, but to appropriate them' (p. 250). Learners need to be exposed to 'an *amplified* form of their own emerging English rather than a *simplified* English' (p. 253). One might add, even though they will diverge from or disregard parts of the amplified model.

Despite the current insistence on 'function not form,' I would suggest that there is no reason not to amplify learners' input even further: why ignore the (few) attested widespread lexicogrammatical ELF forms that do seem to be emerging? If we agree with Dewey's (2012: 163) proposals to 'Increase exposure to the diverse ways in which English is used globally; presenting alternative variants as appropriate whenever highlighting linguistic form,' we could also devise teaching materials that included items such as the pluralization of ENL uncountable nouns (*informations, luggages, childcares, countrysides,* etc.); new prepositional verbs such as *discuss about, emphasise on, return back,* etc.; common lexical items such as *actual* (current), *eventually* (possibly), *the responsible* (the person responsible); and so on. English is a pluricentric language, and learners are regularly told about British and American variants of grammar, lexis, spelling, pronunciation, etc. (*got/gotten, sneaked/snuck, behind/in back of, pavement/sidewalk, trousers/pants, colour/color,* /ʃɛdʒul/ skɛdʒul/, etc.), so they can also be told about regional 'ELF' usages. Learners' input and output could encompass both StE and ELF variants.

Furthermore, rather than producing books inviting learners to *Imagine You're English,* coursebook writers could, as Cook (2002: 337) suggests, include bilingual characters as models:

> L2 users are never shown using the target language as a second language except as tourists or students who ask the way in the street, decipher a res-taurant menu, or try to get from one place to another. They are supplicants to native speakers, not people in their own right who are successful because of their command of a second language.[4]

But NESs and their norms cannot be expunged completely. Jenkins (2007: 244) concedes that 'it would be unreasonable to expect either tests or materials to focus for production on ELF forms before ELF has been fully described, codified, and considered from a range of pedagogic perspectives.' So what is a materials writer to do? It is difficult to find usable authentic *written* ELF materials, and it would be appallingly patronizing, and lead to excruciating results, for a NES author to imitate ELF prose in rubrics, texts, explanations, exercises, etc. So a lot of written material is likely to conform to ENL norms.

Yet listening activities can easily be based on recordings of speakers from all three circles (as in, e.g. MacKenzie 2010),[5] on the principle that learners need to be exposed to as broad a variety of accents as is feasible. In an international language, understanding different accents and dialects is clearly crucial. Courses for schools can (and should) contain listening (or listening and viewing) material with a range of native and non-native accents, with speakers from different parts of the world, or specifically the parts of the world with speakers the learners are likely to find themselves communicating with. Listening material can be scripted as well as authentic, but scripted material still needs to be produced by actors with a variety of accents, which is currently not the case with many courses designed for schools. If listening material is authentic, and contains a variety of native, nativized and ELF forms, the question then becomes which of them should be used as models for production, and which are considered acceptable in assessment and testing, but this will always be a local and contingent decision.

As far as pronunciation is concerned, I outlined my reservations as to the applicability of Jenkins' Lingua Franca Core in Chapter 7. The logic of ELF implies teaching the pronunciation variety that seems most appropriate in a given context. If you believe that the ideal pronunciation model is a local teacher with a local L1 accent, so be it. If, on the other hand, the teacher *is* able to pronounce, e.g. interdental fricatives, and the learners are of an age to learn to produce them effortlessly, then you have to decide whether you agree that substitutions of /th/ sounds are preferable. For the rest, learners are likely to imitate the phonological input they have, as best they can, subject to interference from their L1. Yet as mentioned above, there are good arguments for exposing learners to a broad range of accents right from the start, so choices will have to be made.

Communication strategies and language awareness

Given that ELF is used with varying levels of proficiency by bi- or plurilingual speakers of a multitude of L1s, with somewhat variable or approximate lexico-grammar and phraseology, there is a broad consensus among ELF researchers that pragmatic strategies and accommodation skills are important, if not crucial, to ELF communication. Common cooperative, interactive, pragmatic or discourse strategies were outlined in Chapter 8 – let it pass, make it normal, focus on intelligibility rather than correctness, request repetition or clarification when necessary, signal non-comprehension in a face-saving way, make things explicit (e.g. by fronting), orient towards the hearer, repeat phrases, paraphrase utterances by adjusting their form, make prompts and suggestions, etc. – and language teachers can certainly draw attention to these gambits and try to encourage their use. House (1996, 2010) recommends explicitly teaching discourse strategies to make them more salient, including practising specific utterances for particular speech acts.

Accommodating to or converging with other people's uses, adapting or approximating their speech patterns, and generally showing behavioural congruence or coordination, was described in Chapter 4 as a deeply automatic process and an apparently biologically given drive. Even so, some people are more skilled communicators than others, and Mauranen (2012: 238) concedes that 'To what extent accommodation is a teachable skill is uncertain.' But teachers can try.

If borrowing and code-switching come naturally to bi- and plurilingual speakers, these techniques do not need to be taught. But they do have to be *permitted*: an understanding of the realities of plurilingualism requires abandoning the traditional language teaching practice of banning L1 use because, as Cook (2002: 332) puts it, 'Potentially the classroom is a code-switching situation par excellence since the students all know the two languages.'

Seidlhofer *et al.* (2006: 23) recommend teaching language awareness, so as to 'foster an understanding in learners of how language in general operates in similar or different ways across communities with different languages,' as an alternative to focusing on individual foreign languages linked to their linguacultures.[6] Seidlhofer (2004: 227) suggests that

> it would no longer be self-evident that a subject called English needs to remain in all language teaching curricula – for some contexts, it might be worth considering [notice the hedging devices] whether so-called English courses in secondary school [...] could be replaced by a subject designated *language awareness* which would include instruction in ELF awareness as one element.

There is much to be admired in successful spoken ELF: many speakers respond to its inherent diversity and unpredictability by being prepared to encounter unfamiliar features, by being particularly sensitive to interlocutors' intentions and responses, by making efforts to be clear and explicit, and (occasionally) by being creative, or in short, by showing distinct signs of language awareness. But it has *not* been established that self-developed language awareness (noticing strategies, experiential and inductive learning of language rules, etc.) can totally replace explicit, analytical teaching of forms and metalinguistic rules. It may be the case that only more advanced learners/users can employ language awareness strategies in or across languages. Language awareness training cannot wholly replace more orthodox language teaching and learning in the earlier years of education. The same caveat applies to recommendations like 'highlight the particular environment and socio-cultural context in which English(es) will be used,' and 'Engage in critical classroom discussion about the globalization and growing diversity of English' (Dewey 2012: 163); you can't learn to run before you can walk.

A further difficulty is that even if education authorities and English teachers were to agree to such a radical upheaval of the curriculum, English would still probably be taught differently from other foreign languages. For example, most Europeans learn two languages at school, but the other one (English is almost universal) is nearly always learned with the aim of communicating with the language's native speakers. Consequently, there is less likely to be an ELF-like tolerance of fuzziness, approximation, variation and 'creativity.'[7]

There is also a growing trend not to teach English as such in secondary schools, but to teach other subjects through the medium of English. In CLIL classes, attention is often deflected away from communication strategies *per se* and onto the subject that is being taught in the L2 – maths, physics, geography, or whatever. An alternative to this would be to use English lessons to develop cross-cultural awareness. Writing about South-East Asia, Kirkpatrick (2010: 184) argues that because neighbouring languages are rarely taught in schools, learners should study the culture of neighbouring countries 'in a cross-cultural course which uses English as the medium of instruction.' This seems to be a very reasonable suggestion. John Corbett (2003: 2) says that

> Intercultural communicative competence includes the ability to understand the language and behaviour of the target community, and explain it to members of the 'home' community – and vice versa. [...] This aim effectively displaces the long-standing, if seldom achieved, objective of teaching learners to attain 'native speaker proficiency.'

Yet if the languages of the target communities are not taught, as in the ASEAN countries, English (ELF) can be substituted for them, as Kirkpatrick suggests. On the other hand, European and Latin American learners are closer to an inner circle country, and are often interested in some aspects of its culture. Thus Gnutzmann (2005: 117) states that 'If English was only taught as a "cultureless" language it would probably deprive many of our pupils of cultural encounters they were hoping to have through the medium of English,' which also seems to be a very reasonable argument. Meanwhile, monolingual NESs in inner circle countries could usefully be taught some international communication skills too. As Graddol (2006: 87) puts it (with the hedging that some proponents of ELF specialize in), 'It may be that elements of an ELF syllabus could usefully be taught within a mother tongue curriculum.'

Testing

English as an international auxiliary language is, as Kirkpatrick (2010: 74) puts it, in 'a post-Anglophone stage,' widely used in the absence of NESs. English is also a postcolonial language in the outer circle. Some people try to ally ELF with the hybridity, indeterminacy, pluralism, variety and contingency of postmodernity. And Dewey (2012: 166) advocates 'a postnormative orientation to language learning and use.' But this is perhaps a post too far, in relation to evaluation: norms or not, something has to be taught and learned and tested.

Given the consensus that ELF is all about communicative practices and processes, Mauranen (2012: 239) argues that 'language testing should take place in interaction: the speakers to be evaluated for spoken proficiency should be observed as full participants with other international speakers.' Moreover, monolingual ENL evaluators are not the best judges, as 'What works best for an international context can be a very different matter from what is appropriate in an ENL perspective.' Hüttner's (2009) dialogic conceptualization of fluency – a fluent speaker is more like a skilled musician in a jam session than a virtuoso soloist – is pertinent here. Jenkins (2007: 241) reasonably suggests that examination boards could start 'prioritizing accommodation skills and not penalising forms that are already emerging as frequent, systematic, and intelligible among proficient ELF speakers, regardless of the fact that they differ from the ways in which NSs of English speak to each other.'

In short, in the expanding circle, a measure of sympathy and understanding is due to the crestfallen learners who 'learn English since ten years' and lament that 'I thought I was good at English until I took this course.' Or better still, they should not be made to feel incompetent because they use the present simple rather than the present perfect to indicate a period from past to present, without distinguishing between *for* and *since*, and use the progressive with stative verbs, and fail to distinguish between count and non-count nouns, and so on (Erling 2002). All these uses are perfectly comprehensible to ELF speakers in Europe and beyond. And they would not cause you to fail a thesis defence at the University of Helsinki (see ELFA).

Widdowson (2003: 171) suggests briskly that 'communicative tests are impossible in principle,' but he also has practical suggestions, notably that testing also needs to give credit to nonconformist language which 'showed an ability to exploit the virtual resource, and which therefore provides evidence of investment in capability for further learning' (p. 173).

On the other hand, nonconformist language is (currently) *not* normally acceptable in formal written English. This may change if publishers and the Anglophone world at large begin to accept such uses, but until such time, many advanced learners (or those who will need to write in English) probably also need to learn to use standard English written forms. Furthermore, as Ferguson says, what goes down well in Bratislava may be less favourably received in New York. Consequently many learners may need to be 'mobile across locations' and have a 'repertoire of linguistic resources, encompassing both L1 standard and ELF variants.' As Canagarajah (2006: 201) puts it, we have to 'teach English for shuttling between diverse English-speaking communities worldwide, and not just for joining a single community.' So even though ELF syllabuses should obviously not be designed – in vain – to produce nativelike speakers, and learners should not be treated *de facto* as failed native speakers, evaluation of written English might require targets that are closer to StE than those used to evaluate spoken ELF.

Conclusion

The proponents of ELF have shaken up many 'Anglo-Saxon attitudes' concerning English teaching and the use of the English language in the expanding circle. Seidlhofer, Mauranen and colleagues have done a great service to linguists and language teachers by compiling and publishing sizeable ELF corpora. They have also drawn a number of conclusions from their data, but they do not have a monopoly on wisdom. To insist upon the irrelevance of the native speaker in international communication and the future of the English language seems to me to be unwise. To reify ELF and ELF speakers, as if they were wholly separate from native and nativized Englishes and their users, is tendentious. To insist upon analogies between (heterogeneous, hybrid, indeterminate) ELF and (standardized, codified, endonormative) New Englishes is spurious. To warn ELF speakers against using any ENL idioms seems to me unhelpful. To state that NESs will soon need to go to classes to learn ELF if they wish to communicate in the expanding circle seems to be entirely counter-factual. To describe every last deviation or variation from ENL norms as an act of creativity or a sign of an ongoing language shift, rather than merely a sign of fuzzy processing or partial entrenchment, seems to be quite unnecessary. To claim that non-cooperation and misunderstanding are vanishingly rare in ELF interactions is overstating the case. And so on.

English teachers can learn a lot from ELF researchers, but there are also other things they need to know. In the terms of the fragment from the seventh century BC Greek poet Archilocus, popularized by Isaiah Berlin (1953/1970: 1), 'the fox knows many things, but the hedgehog knows one big thing,' proponents of ELF can sometimes resemble the prickly, defensive hedgehog (even if they hedge some of their wilder claims), while foxes, with their knowledge of many little things, have the better of the argument.[8] The hedgehog-like insistence that ELF speakers all need to have their awareness raised so that they make the informed choice to assert their NNES identities and turn their backs on anything that smacks of the dreaded 'Anglo-American English' is redolent of what Berlin called an 'all-embracing, sometimes self-contradictory and incomplete, at times fanatical, unitary inner vision' (pp.1–2). The needs and interests of many ELF speakers are actually rather more complex than that. Berlin states that 'the fox, for all his cunning, is defeated by the hedgehog's one defence' (p. 1). Maybe so, but this book has at least tried to restore the balance.

Notes

1 Widdowson (2003) is full of pithy apophthegms like this, which really should be collected and published as such, like Oscar Wilde's aphorisms.
2 See also Gnutzmann (1999).
3 For a starry-eyed account of the advantages of CLIL and early immersion schooling, see Van Parijs (2011: 103ff.); for a more sober account of the realities of early English-medium education in South-East Asia, see Kirkpatrick (2010: Part III).
4 Unlike most linguists – including most ELF researchers – Cook began his career as a language teacher. He also remarks (2002: 333) that 'Grammatical structures for teaching are selected from the description of native speech or writing, not that of L2 users. [...] In other words, students are usually supposed to say *I live in France* and not *Me live France* in the classroom.' Yes indeed!
5 Specifically, this course contains speakers from Australia, Britain, France, India, Italy, Greece, Malaysia, Russia, Singapore, South Africa, South Korea and the USA.
6 For a very brief overview of language awareness, see Bolitho *et al.* (2003).
7 An example from Kramsch (1999: 132): 'As one of my former graduate students, a Rumanian studying German in America, said to her fellow students: "With an American passport, you can afford to have sloppy grammar, but when I appear at the German border, grammatical accuracy is what will make me acceptable, not communicative efficiency."'
8 The fox/hedgehog opposition will be familiar to many people in the splendidly bellicose world of Anglophone applied linguistics, as it was referred to in a spat between Rampton and Widdowson, notably in Widdowson (1998). The whole exchange is reprinted as 'Controversy 9, The nature of applied linguistics,' in Seidlhofer (ed.) (2003).

BIBLIOGRAPHY

All websites accessed 30 December 2012.

Abrahamsson, N. and Hyltenstam, K. (2009) 'Age of onset and nativelikeness in a second language: listener perception versus linguistic scrutiny', *Language Learning* 59(2): 249–306.

Achebe, C. (1975) 'The African writer and the English language', in *Morning Yet in Creation Day*, New York: Doubleday.

Adams, D. (1979) *The Hitchhiker's Guide to the Galaxy*, London: Pan Macmillan.

Alderson, J.C. (2007) 'Judging the frequency of English words', *Applied Linguistics* 28(3): 383–409.

——(2009) 'Air safety, language assessment policy, and policy implementation: the case of aviation English', *Annual Review of Applied Linguistics* 29: 168–87.

Alptekin, C. (2010) 'Redefining multicompetence for bilingualism and ELF', *International Journal of Applied Linguistics* 20(1): 95–110.

Altenberg, B. (1998) 'On the phraseology of spoken English: the evidence of recurrent word-combinations', in A.P. Cowie (ed.) *Phraseology: theory, analysis, and applications*, Oxford: Oxford University Press, pp. 101–24.

Andersen, R.W. (1990) 'Models, processes, principles and strategies: second language acquisition inside and outside the classroom', in B. VanPatten and J. Lee (eds) *Second Language Acquisition/Foreign Language Learning*, Cleveland: Multilingual Matters, pp. 45–68.

Anderson, B. (1983/1991) *Imagined Communities: reflections on the origin and spread of nationalism*, London: Verso.

Anzaldúa, G. (1987) *Borderlands = La Frontera: the new mestiza*, San Fransisco: Aunt Lute Books.

Appadurai, A. (1996) *Modernity at Large: cultural dimensions in globalization*, Minnesota: University of Minnesota Press.

Aston, G. (1993) 'Notes on the interlanguage of comity', in G. Kasper and S. Blum-Kulka (eds) *Interlanguage Pragmatics*, New York: Oxford University Press, pp. 224–50.

Auer, P. (1999) 'From codeswitching via language mixing to fused lects: toward a dynamic typology of bilingual speech', *International Journal of Bilingualism* 3(4): 309–32.

Austin, J.L. (1962) *How to Do Things with Words*, Oxford: Clarendon Press.

Baker, P. and Eversley, J. (eds) (2000) *Multilingual Capital: the languages of London's schoolchildren and their relevance to economic, social and educational policies*, London: Battlebridge.

Bakhtin, M.M. (1934–35/1981) 'Discourse in the Novel', in M. Holquist (ed.) *The Dialogic Imagination: four essays by M.M. Bakhtin*, trans. C. Emerson and M. Holquist, Austin: University of Texas Press, pp. 259–422.

Bamgboṣe, A. (1998) 'Torn between the norms: innovations in World Englishes', *World Englishes* 17(1): 1–14.

Barfield, O. (1962) *History in English Words*, London: Faber & Faber.

Barlow, M. and Kemmer, S. (2000) 'Introduction: a usage-based conception of language', in M. Barlow and S. Kemmer (eds) *Usage-Based Models of Language*, Stanford, CA: CSLI, pp. vii–xxvi.

Barnes, J. (1992) *Talking it Over*, London: Picador.

Bate, W.J. (1970) *The Burden of the Past and the English Poet*, Cambridge, MA: Harvard University Press.

Bauman, Z. (1992) 'A sociological theory of postmodernity', in *Intimations of Post-Modernity*, London: Routledge, pp. 187–204.

Becker, A.L. (1983) 'Towards a post-structuralist view of language learning: a short essay', *Language Learning* 33(5): 217–20.

——(1994) 'Repetition and otherness: an essay', in B. Johnstone (ed.) *Repetition in Discourse: interdisciplinary perspectives, Volume 2*, Norwood, NJ: Ablex, pp. 162–75.

——(1995) *Beyond Translation: essays toward a modern philology*, Ann Arbor: University of Michigan Press.

Bellos, D. (2011) *Is That a Fish in Your Ear? Translation and the Meaning of Everything*, New York: Faber & Faber.

Bénabou, M. and Fournel, P. (eds) (2009) *Anthologie de l'Oulipo*, Paris: Gallimard.

Bent, T. and Bradlow, A.R. (2003) 'The interlanguage speech intelligibility benefit', *The Journal of the Acoustical Society of America* 114(3): 1600–610. <http://www.tessabent.com/interlanguage.pdf>

Berlin, I. (1953/1970) *The Hedgehog and the Fox: an essay on Tolstoy's view of history*, New York: Simon and Schuster.

Berman, A. (1985/2004) 'Translation and the trials of the foreign', trans. L. Venuti, in L. Venuti (ed.) *The Translation Studies Reader*, 2nd edn, London: Routledge, pp. 276–89.

Berns, M. (1995a) 'English in Europe: whose language, whose culture?' *International Journal of Applied Linguistics* 5(1): 21–32.

——(1995b) 'English in the European Union', *English Today* 11(3): 3–11.

——(2007) 'The presence of English: sociocultural, acquisitional, and media dimensions', in M. Berns, K. De Bot and U. Hasebrink (eds) *In the Presence of English: media and European youth*, New York: Springer.

——(2008) 'World Englishes, English as a lingua franca, and intelligibility', *World Englishes* 27(3–4): 327–34.

——(2009) 'English as lingua franca and English in Europe', *World Englishes* 28(2): 192–99.

Berthele, R. (2008) 'A nation is a territory with one culture and one language: the role of metaphorical folk models in language policy debates', in G. Kristiansen and R. Dirven (eds) *Cognitive Sociolinguistics: language variation, cultural models, social systems*, Berlin: Mouton de Gruyter, pp. 301–32.

Biber, D., Johansson, S., Leech, G., Conrad, S. and Finegan, E. (eds) (1999) *The Longman Grammar of Spoken and Written English*, London: Pearson Education.

Biermeier, T. (2008) *Word-Formation in New Englishes: a corpus-based analysis*, Münster: LIT.

Birdsong, D. (ed.) (1999) *Second Language Acquisition and the Critical Period Hypothesis*, Mahwah, NJ: Lawrence Erlbaum.

Björkman, B. (2008a) 'English as the lingua franca of engineering: the morphosyntax of academic speech events', *Nordic Journal of English Studies* 7(3): 103–22. <http://ojs.ub.gu.se/ojs/index.php/njes/article/view/154/152>

——(2008b) 'So where are we? Spoken lingua franca English at a technical university in Sweden', *English Today* 24(2): 35–41.

——(2009) 'From code to discourse in spoken ELF', in A. Mauranen and E. Ranta (eds) *English as a Lingua Franca: studies and findings*, Newcastle upon Tyne: Cambridge Scholars Publishing, pp. 225–53.

——(2012) 'Questions in academic ELF interaction', *Journal of English as a Lingua Franca* 1(1): 93–119.

Blackledge, A. and Creese, A. (2010) *Multilingualism: a critical perspective*, London: Continuum.

Blommaert, J. (2010) *The Sociolinguistics of Globalization*, Cambridge: Cambridge University Press.

Bloomfield, L. (1933) *Language*, New York: Holt, Rinehart & Winston.

Blum-Kulka, S., House, J. and Kasper, G. (eds) (1989) *Cross-Cultural Pragmatics: requests and apologies*, Norwood, NJ: Ablex.

Boas, F. (1940) *Race, Language and Culture*, New York: Macmillan.

Bodmer, F. (1944/1985) *The Loom of Language: an approach to the mastery of many languages*, L. Hogben (ed.), New York: Norton.

Bolinger, D. (1976) 'Meaning and memory', *Forum Linguisticum* 1(1): 1–14.

Bolitho, R., *et al.* (2003) 'Ten questions about language awareness', *ELT Journal* 57(3): 251–59.

Bolton, K. (2008) 'English in Asia, Asian Englishes, and the issue of proficiency', *English Today* 24(2): 3–12.

Bourdieu, P. (1991) *Language and Symbolic Power*, trans. G. Raymond and M. Adamson, Oxford: Polity.

Breiteneder, A. (2009) 'English as a lingua franca in Europe: an empirical perspective', *World Englishes* 28(2): 256–69.

Britain, D. (2007) 'Grammatical variation in England', in D. Britain (ed.) *Language in the British Isles*, Cambridge: Cambridge University Press, pp. 75–104.

Bronckart, J-P. and Bota, C. (2011) *Bakhtine démasqué: histoire d'un menteur, d'une escroquerie et d'un délire collectif*, Genève: Droz.

Bruthiaux, P. (2003) 'Squaring the circles: issues in modeling English worldwide', *International Journal of Applied Linguistics* 13(2): 159–78.

Brutt-Griffler, J. (2002) *World English: a study of its development*, Clevedon: Multilingual Matters.

Bryson, B. (1990) *Mother Tongue: the English language*, London: Penguin.

Bühler, K. (1934/1990) *Theory of Language: the representational function of language*, trans. D. Fraser, Amsterdam: John Benjamins.

Bullock, B.E. and Toribio, A.J. (2009) 'Themes in the study of code-switching', in B.E. Bullock and A.J. Toribio (eds) *The Cambridge Handbook of Linguistic Code-switching*, Cambridge: Cambridge University Press, pp. 1–17.

Butler, J. (1990) *Gender Trouble: feminism and the subversion of identity*, London: Routledge.

Butler, S. (1997) 'Corpus of English in Southeast Asia: implications for a regional dictionary', in M.L.S. Bautista (ed.) *English is an Asian Language: the Philippine context*, Sydney: Macquarie Library, pp. 103–24.

Bybee, J.L. (1985) *Morphology: a study of the relation between meaning and form*, Amsterdam: John Benjamins.

——(1998/2007) 'The emergent lexicon', in Bybee, J.L. (ed.) *Frequency of Use and the Organization of Language*, Oxford: Oxford University Press, pp. 279–93.

——(2010) *Language, Usage and Cognition*, Cambridge: Cambridge University Press.

Bybee, J.L. and Hopper, P.J. (2001) 'Introduction to frequency and the emergence of linguistic structure', in J.L. Bybee and P.J. Hopper (eds), *Frequency and the Emergence of Linguistic Structure*, Amsterdam: John Benjamins, pp. 1–24.

Canagarajah, A.S. (1999) *Resisting Linguistic Imperialism in English Teaching*, Oxford: Oxford University Press.

——(2006) 'Interview', in R. Rubdy and M. Saraceni (eds) *English in the World: global rules, global roles*, London: Continuum, pp. 200–11.

——(2007) 'Lingua franca English, multilingual communities, and language acquisition', *Modern Language Journal* 91(5): 921–37.

Cancino, H., Rosansky, E., and Schumann, J. (1978) 'The acquisition of English negatives and interrogatives by native Spanish speakers', in E. Hatch (ed.) *Second Language Acquisition: a book of readings*, Rowley, MA: Newbury House, pp. 207–30.

Carter, R. (2004) *Language and Creativity: the art of common talk*, London: Routledge.

Carter, R. and McCarthy, M. (2006) *Cambridge Grammar of English*, Cambridge: Cambridge University Press.

Cenoz, J. (2001) 'The effect of linguistic distance, L2 status and age on crosslinguistic influence in L3 acquisition', in J. Cenoz, B. Hufeisen and U. Jessner (eds) *Cross-Linguistic Influence in Third Language Acquisition: psycholinguistic perspectives*, Clevedon: Multilingual Matters, pp. 8–20.

Chafe, W.L. (1968) 'Idiomaticity as an anomaly in the Chomskyan paradigm', *Foundations of Language* 4: 109–27.

Chambers, J.K. (2004) 'Dynamic typology and vernacular universals', in B. Kortmann (ed.) *Dialectology Meets Typology: dialect grammar from a cross-linguistic perspective*, Berlin: Mouton, pp. 127–45.

——(2009) 'Cognition and the linguistic continuum from vernacular to standard', in M. Filppula, J. Klemola, and H. Paulasto (eds) *Vernacular Universals and Language Contacts: evidence from varieties of English and beyond*, London: Routledge, pp. 19–32.

Chávez-Silverman, S. (2004) *Killer Crónicas*, Madison: University of Wisconsin Press.

Chomsky, N. (1964) *Current Issues in Linguistic Theory*, The Hague: Mouton.

——(1965) *Aspects of the Theory of Syntax*, Cambridge, MA: MIT Press.

——(1977) *Essays on Form and Interpretation*, New York: North-Holland.

——(1981) 'On the representation of form and function', *The Linguistic Review* 1(1), 3–40.

——(1986) *Knowledge of Language: its nature, origin, and use*, New York: Preager.

——(1995) *The Minimalist Program*, Cambridge, MA: The MIT Press.

Clackson, J. and Horrocks, G. (2007) *The Blackwell History of the Latin Language*, Oxford: Blackwell.

Clifford, J. (1988) *The Predicament of Culture*, Cambridge, MA: Harvard University Press.

Clyne, M. (1994) *Inter-cultural Communication at Work: cultural values in discourse*, Cambridge: Cambridge University Press.

——(2003) 'Towards a more language-centered approach to bilingualism', in J-M. Dewaele, A. Housen and L. Wei (eds) *Bilingualism: beyond basic principles*, Clevedon: Multilingual Matters, pp. 43–55.

Cogo, A. (2009) 'Accommodating difference in ELF conversations: a study of pragmatic strategies', in A. Mauranen and E. Ranta (eds) *English as a Lingua Franca: studies and findings*, Newcastle upon Tyne: Cambridge Scholars Publishing, pp. 254–73.

——(2010) 'Strategic use and perceptions of English as a Lingua Franca', *Poznań Studies in Contemporary Linguistics* 46(3), 295–312. <http://versita.metapress.com/content/t4274578759531p2/fulltext.pdf>

Cogo, A. and Dewey, M. (2006) 'Efficiency in ELF communication: from pragmatic motives to lexico-grammatical innovation', *Nordic Journal of English Studies* 5(2), 59–93. <http://ojs.ub.gu.se/ojs/index.php/njes/article/view/65/69>

——(2012) *Analysing English as a Lingua Franca: a corpus-driven investigation*, London: Continuum.

Cogo, A. and Jenkins, J. (2010) 'English as a lingua franca in Europe: a mismatch between policy and practice', *European Journal of Language Policy* 2(2): 271–94.

Cook, V.J. (1991) 'The poverty-of-the-stimulus argument and multi-competence', *Second Language Research* 7(2): 103–17. <http://homepage.ntlworld.com/vivian.c/Writings/Papers/SLR91.htm>

——(1999) 'Going beyond the native speaker in language teaching', *TESOL Quarterly* 33(2): 185–209.

——(2002) 'Language teaching methodology and the L2 user perspective', in V. Cook (ed.) *Portraits of the L2 User*, Clevedon: Multilingual Matters, pp. 325–44.

——(2009) 'Multilingual Universal Grammar as the norm', in I. Leung (ed.) *Third Language Acquisition and Universal Grammar*, Bristol: Multilingual Matters, pp. 55–70.

Coppieters, R. (1987) 'Competence differences between native and near-native speakers', *Language* 63: 544–73.

Corbett, J. (2003) *An Intercultural Approach to English Language Teaching*, Clevedon: Multilingual Matters.

Coulmas, F. (2005) *Sociolinguistics: the study of speakers' choices*, Cambridge: Cambridge University Press.

Coupland, N. (2008) 'The delicate constitution of identity in face-to-face accommodation: a response to Trudgill', *Language in Society* 37(2): 267–70.

Coupland, N., Giles, H. and Wiemann, J.M. (1991) 'Talk as "problem" and communication as "miscommunication": an integrative analysis', in N. Coupland, H. Giles and J.M. Wiemann (eds) *'Miscommunication' and Problematic Talk*, Newbury Park, CA: Sage, pp. 1–17.

Coxhead, A. (2000) 'A new academic word list', *TESOL Quarterly* 34(2): 213–38.

Croft, W. (2001) *Radical Construction Grammar: syntactic theory in typological perspective*, Oxford: Oxford University Press.

Crystal, D. (1997) *English as a Global Language*, Cambridge: Cambridge University Press.

——(2003) *English as a Global Language*, 2nd edn, Cambridge: Cambridge University Press.

——(2004) *The Stories of English*, London: Allen Lane.

——(2008) 'Two thousand million?' *English Today* 24(1): 3–6.

Cummins, J. (1984) *Bilingualism and Special Education: issues in assessment and pedagogy*, Clevedon: Multilingual Matters.

——(2000) *Language, Power and Pedagogy: bilingual children in the crossfire*, Clevedon: Multilingual Matters.

Dabrowska, E. (2004) *Language, Mind and Brain: some psychological and neurological constraints on theories of grammar*, Edinburgh: Edinburgh University Press.

Dakhlia, J. (2008) *Lingua Franca: histoire d'une langue métisse en Méditerranée*, Arles: Actes Sud.

Dalton, C. and Seidlhofer, B. (1994) *Pronunciation*, Oxford: Oxford University Press.

Daniels, H. (1997) 'Psycholinguistic, psycho-affective and procedural factors in the acquisition of authentic L2 pronunciation', in A. McLean (ed.) *SIG Selections 1997, Special Interests in ELT*, Whitstable: IATEFL, pp. 80–85.

Davies, A. (1996) 'Proficiency or the native speaker: what are we trying to achieve in ELT?' in G. Cook and B. Seidlhofer (eds) *Principle and Practice in Applied Linguistics*, Oxford: Oxford University Press, pp. 145–57.

——(2004) 'The native speaker in applied linguistics', in A. Davies and C. Elder (eds) *Handbook of Applied Linguistics*, Oxford: Blackwell, pp. 431–50.

De Bot, K. (1992) 'A bilingual production model: Levelt's "speaking" model adapted', *Applied Linguistics* 13(1): 1–24.

——(2004) 'The multilingual lexicon: modeling selection and control', *International Journal of Multilingualism* 1(1): 17–32.

Deterding, D. (2012) 'Intelligibility in spoken ELF', *Journal of English as a Lingua Franca* 1(1): 185–90.

Dewey, M. (2007) 'English as a lingua franca and globalization: an interconnected perspective', *International Journal of Applied Linguistics* 17(3): 332–54.

——(2012) 'Towards a *post-normative* approach: learning the pedagogy of ELF', *Journal of English as a Lingua Franca* 1(1): 141–70.

Dixon, R.M.W. (1997) *The Rise and Fall of Languages*, Cambridge: Cambridge University Press.

Dröschel, Y. (2011) *Lingua Franca English: the role of simplification and transfer*, Bern: Peter Lang.

Duhem, P. (1914/1991) *The Aim and Structure of Physical Theory*, trans. P. Wiener, Princeton: Princeton University Press.

Durant, A. (2010) *Meaning in the Media*, Cambridge: Cambridge University Press.

Eckert, P. (2000) *Linguistic Variation as Social Practice*, Oxford: Blackwell.

Eco, U. (1977) *A Theory of Semiotics*, London: Macmillan.

Edwards, J. (2009) *Language and Identity*, Cambridge: Cambridge University Press.

ELFA (English as a Lingua Franca in Academic Settings corpus) <http://www.helsinki.fi/elfa/elfacorpus>

Eliot, T.S. (1963) *Collected Poems, 1909–1962*, New York: Harcourt, Brace & World.

Erling, E.J. (2002) '"I learn English since ten years": the global English debate and the German university classroom', *English Today* 18(2): 8–13.

Erling, E.J. and Bartlett, T. (2006), 'Making English their own: the use of ELF among students of English at the FUB', *Nordic Journal of English Studies* 5(2): 9–40. <http://ojs.ub. gu.se/ojs/index.php/njes/article/view/69/73>

Erman, B. and Warren, B. (2000) 'The idiom principle and the open choice principle', *Text* 20(1): 29–62.

European Council for Cultural Co-operation (2001) *Common European Framework of Reference for Languages: learning, teaching, assessment*, Cambridge: Cambridge University Press.

Extra, G. and Gorter, D. (eds) (2001) *The Other Languages of Europe*, Clevedon: Multilingual Matters.

Færch, C. and Kasper, G. (1983) 'Plans and strategies in foreign language communication', in C. Faerch and G. Kasper (eds) *Strategies in Interlanguage Communication*, London: Longman, pp. 20–60.

Fairclough, N. (2006) *Language and Globalisation*, London: Routledge.

Ferguson, C.A. (1982/1992) 'Foreword to the First Edition', in Kachru, B.B. (ed.) *The Other Tongue: English across cultures*, 2nd edn, Urbana: University of Illinois Press, pp. xii–xvii.

Ferguson, G. (2009) 'Issues in researching English as a lingua franca: a conceptual enquiry', *International Journal of Applied Linguistics* 19(2): 117–35.

——(2012) 'The practice of ELF', *Journal of English as a Lingua Franca* 1(1): 177–80.

Fernando, C. (1996) *Idioms and Idiomaticity*, Oxford: Oxford University Press.

Field, J. (2003) *Psycholinguistics*, London: Routledge.

Fillmore, C.J., Kay, P. and O'Connor, M.C. (1988) 'Regularity and idiomaticity in grammatical constructions: the case of *let alone*', *Language* 64(3): 501–38.

Filppula, M., Klemola, J. and Paulasto, H. (eds) (2009) *Vernacular Universals and Language Contacts: evidence from varieties of English and beyond*, London: Routledge.

Firth, A. (1996) 'The discursive accomplishment of normality: on "lingua franca" English and conversation analysis', *Journal of Pragmatics* 26(2): 237–59.

——(2009) 'The lingua franca factor', *Intercultural Pragmatics* 6(2), 147–70.

Firth, A. and Wagner, J. (1997) 'On discourse, communication, and (some) fundamental concepts in SLA research', *Modern Language Journal* 81(3): 285–300.

Firth, J.R. (1957/1968) 'A synopsis of linguistic theory, 1930–55', in F.R. Palmer (ed.) *Selected Papers of J.R. Firth 1952–1959*, London: Longman, pp. 168–205.

Fishman, J.A. (1992) 'Sociology of English as an additional language', in B.B.Kachru (ed.) *The Other Tongue: English across cultures*, 2nd edn, Urbana: University of Illinois Press, pp. 19–26.

Franceschini, R. (2009) 'The genesis and development of research on multilingualism: perspectives for future research', in L. Aronin and B. Hufeisen (eds) *The Exploration of Multilingualism: development of research on L3, multilingualism and multiple language acquisition*, Amsterdam: John Benjamins, pp. 27–61.

Friedman, T. (2007) *The World is Flat: a brief history of the twenty-first century*, Release 3.0, New York: Picador.

Furiassi, C. (2010) *False Anglicisms in Italian*, Monza: Polimetrica.

Gadamer, H-G. (1960/2004) *Truth and Method*, 2nd edn, trans. J. Weinsheimer and D.G. Marshall, London: Continuum.

Gardner, W.E. and Lambert, R.C. (1972) *Attitudes and Motivation in Second Language Learning*, Rowley, MA: Newbury House.

Gardner-Chloros, P. (1991) *Language Selection and Switching in Strasbourg*, Oxford: Clarendon Press.

——(1995) 'Code-switching in community, regional and national repertoires: the myth of the discreteness of linguistic systems', in L. Milroy and P. Muysken (eds) *One Speaker, Two Languages: cross-disciplinary perspectives on code-switching*, Cambridge: Cambridge University Press, pp. 68–89.

Gellner, E. (1983) *Nations and Nationalism*, Oxford: Blackwell.

Giddens, A. (1984) *The Constitution of Society: outline of the theory of structuration*, Cambridge: Polity.

——(1991) *Modernity and Self-Identity: self and society in the late modern age*, Cambridge: Polity.

Gil, D. (2009) 'How much grammar does it take to sail a boat?' In G. Sampson, D. Gil and P. Trudgill (eds) *Language Complexity as an Evolving Variable*, Oxford: Oxford University Press, pp. 19–33.

Giles, H. (1973) 'Accent mobility: a model and some data', *Anthropological Linguistics* 15: 87–105.

Giles, H. and Byrne, J. (1982) 'An intergroup approach to second language acquisition', *Journal of Multilingual and Multicultural Development* 3(1): 17–41.

Giles, H. and Coupland, N. (1991) *Language: contexts and consequences*, Milton Keynes: Open University Press.

Giles, H., Coupland, N. and Coupland, C. (1991) 'Accommodation theory: communication, context, and consequence', in H. Giles, C. Coupland and N. Coupland (eds) *Contexts of Accommodation*, Cambridge: Cambridge University Press, pp. 1–68.

Giles, H. and Smith, P. (1979) 'Accommodation theory: optimal levels of convergence', in H. Giles and R. St Clair (eds) *Language and Social Psychology*, Oxford: Blackwell, pp. 45–65.

Gladwell, M. (2008) 'The ethnic theory of plane crashes', in *Outliers*, New York: Little, Brown, pp. 177–223.

Glucksberg, S. (1993) 'Idiom meanings and allusional content', in C. Cacciari and P. Tabossi (eds) *Idioms: processing, structure and interpretation*, Hillside, NJ: Lawrence Erlbaum, pp. 3–26.

Gnutzmann, C. (1999) 'English as a global language. Perspectives for English language teaching and for teacher education in Germany', in C. Gnutzmann (ed.) *Teaching and Learning English as a Global Language*, Tübingen: Stauffenburg, pp. 157–69.

——(2005) '"Standard English" and "World Standard English." Linguistic and pedagogical considerations', in C. Gnutzmann and F. Intemann (eds) *The Globalisation of English and the English Language Classroom*, Tübingen: Gunter Narr, pp. 107–18.

Gnutzmann, C. and Intemann, F. (2005) 'Introduction: the globalisation of English. Language, politics, and the English language classroom', in C. Gnutzmann and F. Intemann (eds) *The Globalisation of English and the English Language Classroom*, Tübingen: Gunter Narr, pp. 9–24.

Goethe, J.W. (1883/2012) *Maximen und Reflexionen*, Wiesbaden: Marixverlag.

Goldberg, A.E. (1995) *Constructions: a construction grammar approach to argument structure*, Chicago: University of Chicago Press.

——(2006) *Constructions at Work: the nature of generalization in language*, Oxford: Oxford University Press.

Görlach, M. (1991) *Englishes*, Amsterdam: John Benjamins.

——(1995) *More Englishes*, Amsterdam: John Benjamins.

——(1998) *Even More Englishes*, Amsterdam: John Benjamins.

——(2002) *Still More Englishes*, Amsterdam: John Benjamins.

Gozdawa-Gołębiowski, R. (2008) 'Grammar and formulaicity in foreign language teaching', *Glottodidactica* 34: 75–86.

Graddol, D. (1997) *The Future of English?* London: British Council. <http://www.british council.org/learning-elt-future.pdf>

——(2006) *English Next*, London: British Council. <http://www.britishcouncil.org/learning-research-english-next.pdf>

Granger, S. (ed.) (1998a) *Learner English on Computer*, London: Longman.

——(1998b) 'Prefabricated patterns in advanced EFL writing: collocations and formulae', in A.P. Cowie (ed.) *Phraseology: theory, analysis, and applications*, Oxford: Oxford University Press, pp. 145–60.

Granger, S., Hung, J. and Petch-Tyson, S. (eds) (2002) *Computer Learner Corpora, Second Language Acquisition and Foreign Language Teaching*, Amsterdam: John Benjamins.

Grice, H.P. (1975/1989) 'Logic and conversation', in *Studies in the Way of Words*, Cambridge, MA: Harvard University Press, pp. 22–40.

Grosjean, F. (1985) 'The bilingual as a competent but specific speaker-hearer', *Journal of Multilingual and Multicultural Development* 6(6): 467–77.

——(1989) 'Neurolinguists, beware! The bilingual is not two monolinguals in one person', *Brain and Language* 36: 3–15.

——(1995) 'A psycholinguistic approach to code-switching: the recognition of guest words by bilinguals', in L. Milroy and P. Muysken (eds) *One Speaker, Two Languages: cross-disciplinary perspectives on code-switching*, Cambridge: Cambridge University Press, pp. 259–75.

——(2008) 'The bilingual's language modes', in *Studying Bilinguals*, Oxford: Oxford University Press, pp. 37–66.

——(2010) *Bilingual: life and reality*, Cambridge, MA: Harvard University Press.

Guido, M.G. (2008) *English as a Lingua Franca in Cross-Cultural Immigration Domains*, Bern: Peter Lang.

——(2012) 'ELF authentication and accommodation strategies in crosscultural immigration encounters', *Journal of English as a Lingua Franca* 1(2): 219–40.

Gurevich, O., Johnson, M.A. and Goldberg, A.E. (2010) 'Incidental verbatim memory for language', *Language and Cognition* 2(1): 45–78.

Haiman, J. (1994) 'Ritualization and the development of language', in W. Pagliuca (ed.) *Perspectives on Grammaticalization*, Amsterdam: John Benjamins, pp. 3–28.

——(1998) *Talk is Cheap: sarcasm, alienation, and the evolution of language*, Oxford: Oxford University Press.

Hall, E.T. (1959) *The Silent Language*, New York: Anchor.

——(1966) *The Hidden Dimension*, New York: Anchor.

——(1976) *Beyond Culture*, New York: Anchor.

Halliday, M.A.K. (1968) 'The users and uses of language', in J. Fishman (ed.) *Readings in the Sociology of Language*, The Hague: Mouton.

——(1978) *Language as Social Semiotic*, London: Edward Arnold.

——(1994) *An Introduction to Functional Grammar*, 2nd edn, London: Edward Arnold.

Hamers, J.F. and Blanc, M.H.A. (1989) *Bilinguality and Bilingualism*, Cambridge: Cambridge University Press.

Hannerz, U. (1992) *Cultural Complexity: studies in the social organization of meaning*, New York: Columbia University Press.

——(1996) *Transnational Connections*, London: Routledge.

Harris, R. (1981) *The Language Myth*, London: Duckworth.

——(1997) *Signs, Language and Communication*, London: Routledge.

——(1998) *Introduction to Integrational Linguistics*, Oxford: Pergamon.

Held, D., McGrew, A., Goldblatt, D. and Perraton, J. (1999) *Global Transformations. Politics, economics and culture*, Cambridge: Polity.

Herdina, P. and Jessner, U. (2002) *A Dynamic Model of Multilingualism: perspectives of change in psycholinguistics*, Clevedon: Multilingual Matters.

Hill, J.H. (2008) *The Everyday Language of White Racism*, Chichester: Wiley-Blackwell.

Hockett, C.F. (1958) *A Course in Modern Linguistics*, New York: Macmillan.

Hoey, M. (2005) *Lexical Priming*, London: Longman.

Hoffman, C. (1996) 'Societal and individual bilingualism with English in Europe', in R. Hartmann (ed.) *The English Language in Europe*, Oxford: Intellect Books, pp. 47–60.

Hofstede, G. (1980) *Culture's Consequences: international differences in work-related values*, Beverly Hills CA: Sage Publications.

——(1991) *Cultures and Organizations: software of the mind*, London: McGraw-Hill.

Holliday, A. (2005) *The Struggle to Teach English as an International Language*, Oxford: Oxford University Press.

Honna, N. (2012) 'The pedagogical implications of English as a multicultural lingua franca', *Journal of English as a Lingua Franca* 1(1): 191–97.

Hopper, P.J. (1987) 'Emergent grammar', *Berkeley Linguistics Society* 13: 139–57.

——(1988) 'Emergent grammar and the a priori grammar postulate', in D. Tannen (ed.) *Linguistics in Context: connecting observation and understanding*, Norwood, NJ: Ablex, pp. 117–34.

——(1992) 'Emergence of grammar', in W. Bright (ed.) *International Encyclopedia of Linguistics, Volume 1*, Oxford: Oxford University Press, pp. 364–67.

——(1998) 'Emergent Grammar', in M. Tomasello (ed.) *The New Psychology of Language: cognitive and functional approaches to linguistic structure*, Englewood Cliffs, NJ: Erlbaum, pp. 155–75.

——(2004) 'The openness of grammatical constructions', *Proceedings from the Annual Meeting of the Chicago Linguistic Society* 40(2): 153–75.

Hopper, P.J. and Traugott, E. (2003) *Grammaticalisation*, 2nd edn, Cambridge: Cambridge University Press.

Horkheimer, M. and Adorno, T. (1944/2002) *Dialectic of Enlightenment: philosophical fragments*, trans. E. Jephcott, Stanford: Stanford University Press.

Hornby, A.S. (1954) *A Guide to Patterns and Usage in English*, Oxford: Oxford University Press.

House, J. (1996) 'Developing pragmatic fluency in English as a Foreign Language: routines and metapragmatic awareness', *Studies in Second Language Acquisition* 8(2): 225–52.

——(1999) 'Misunderstanding in intercultural communication: interactions in English as a lingua franca and the myth of mutual intelligibility', in C. Gnutzmann (ed.) *Teaching and Learning English as a Global Language*, Tübingen: Stauffenburg, pp. 73–89.

——(2002) 'Developing pragmatic competence in English as a lingua franca', in K. Knapp and C. Meierkord (eds) *Lingua Franca Communication*, Frankfurt: Peter Lang, pp. 245–67.

——(2003) 'English as a lingua franca: A threat to multilingualism?' *Journal of Sociolinguistics* 7(4): 556–78.

——(2006) 'Unity in diversity: English as a lingua franca for Europe', in C. Leung and J. Jenkins (eds) *Reconfiguring Europe: the contribution of applied linguistics*, London: Equinox, pp. 87–103.

——(2010) 'The pragmatics of English as a lingua franca', in A. Trosborg (ed.), *Handbook of Pragmatics, Volume 7: Pragmatics across languages and cultures*, Berlin: Mouton de Gruyter, pp. 363–87.

Howarth, P. (1998) 'The phraseology of learners' academic writing', in A.P. Cowie (ed.) *Phraseology: theory, analysis, and applications*, Oxford: Oxford University Press, pp. 161–86.

Hüllen, W. (1992) 'Identifikationssprachen und Kommunikationssprachen: über Probleme der Mehrsprachigkeit', *Zeitschrift für germanistische Linguistik* 20(3): 298–317.

Hülmbauer, C. (2009) '"We don't take the right way: we just take the way we think you will understand" – the shifting relationship between correctness and effectiveness in ELF', in A. Mauranen and E. Ranta (eds) *English as a Lingua Franca: studies and findings*, Newcastle upon Tyne: Cambridge Scholars Publishing, pp. 323–47.

——(2011) 'Old friends? Cognates in ELF communication', in A. Cogo, A. Archibald and J. Jenkins (eds) *Latest Trends in ELF Research*, Newcastle upon Tyne: Cambridge Scholars Publishing, pp. 139–61.

Humboldt, W. (1836/1999) *On Language: on the diversity of human language construction and its influence on the mental development of the human species*, M. Losonsky (ed.), trans. P. Heath, Cambridge: Cambridge University Press.

Hunston, S. (2002) *Corpora in Applied Linguistics*, Cambridge: Cambridge University Press.

Hunston, S. and Francis, G. (1999) *Pattern Grammar: a corpus-driven approach to the lexical grammar of English*, Amsterdam: John Benjamins.

Hüttner, J. (2009) 'Fluent speakers – fluent interactions: on the creation of (co)-fluency in English as a lingua franca', in A. Mauranen and E. Ranta (eds) *English as a Lingua Franca: studies and findings*, Newcastle upon Tyne: Cambridge Scholars Publishing, pp. 274–97.

Hymes, D. (1972) 'On communicative competence', in J.B. Pride and J. Holmes (eds) *Sociolinguistics*, Harmondsworth: Penguin, pp. 269–93.

Intemann, F. (2005) '"Taipei ground, confirm your last transmission was in English?" An analysis of aviation English as a world language', in C. Gnutzmann and F. Intemann (eds) *The Globalisation of English and the English Language Classroom*, Tübingen: Gunter Narr, pp. 71–88.

Israel, M. (1996) 'The way constructions grow', in A.E. Goldberg (ed.) *Conceptual Structure, Discourse and Language*, Stanford, CA: CSLI, pp. 217–30.

Jakobson, R. (1953/1971) 'Results of a joint conference of anthropologists and linguists', in *Selected Writings, Volume 2*, Mouton: The Hague, pp. 554–67.

——(1959/2004) 'On linguistic aspects of translation', in L. Venuti (ed.) *The Translation Studies Reader*, 2nd edn, London: Routledge, pp. 138–43.

——(1960) 'Closing statement: linguistics and poetics', in T.A. Sebeok (ed.) *Style in Language*, Cambridge, MA: MIT Press, pp. 350–77.

James, A.R. (2000) 'English as a European lingua franca: current realities and existing dichotomies', in J. Cenoz and U. Jessner (eds) *English in Europe: the acquisition of a third language*, Clevedon: Multilingual Matters.

Jarvis, S. (2003) 'Probing the effects of the L2 on the L1: a case study', in V. Cook (ed.) *The Effects of the Second Language on the First*, Clevedon: Multilingual Matters, pp. 81–102.

——(2009) 'Lexical transfer', in A. Pavlenko (ed.) *The Bilingual Mental Lexicon: interdisciplinary approaches*, Clevedon: Multilingual Matters, pp. 99–124.

Jarvis, S. and Pavlenko, A. (2007) *Crosslinguistic Influence in Language and Cognition*, London: Routledge.

Jenkins, J. (2000) *The Phonology of English as an International Language*, Oxford: Oxford University Press.

——(2001) 'Accents of English in Europe', <http://www.guardian.co.uk/GWeekly/Global_English/0,8458,400340,00.html>

——(2002) 'A sociolinguistically based, empirically researched pronunciation syllabus for English as an International Language', *Applied Linguistics* 23(1): 83–103.

——(2005a) 'Misinterpretation, bias, and resistance to change: the case of the Lingua Franca Core', in K. Dziubalska-Kolaczyk and J. Przedlacka (eds) *English Pronunciation Models: a changing scene*, Bern: Peter Lang, pp. 199–210.

——(2005b) 'Teaching pronunciation for English as a lingua franca: a sociopolitical perspective', in C. Gnutzmann and F. Intemann (eds) *The Globalisation of English and the English Language Classroom*, Tübingen: Gunter Narr, pp.145–58.

——(2006a) 'Current perspectives on teaching World Englishes and English as a Lingua Franca', *TESOL Quarterly* 40(1): 157–81.

——(2006b) 'Global intelligibility and local diversity: possibility or paradox?' in R. Rubdy and M. Saraceni (eds) *English in the World: global rules, global roles*, London: Continuum, pp. 32–39.

——(2006c) 'Points of view and blind spots: ELF and SLA', *International Journal of Applied Linguistics* 16(2): 137–62.

——(2007) *English as a Lingua Franca: attitude and identity*, Oxford: Oxford University Press.

——(2009) '(Un)pleasant? (in)correct? (un)intelligible? ELF speakers' perceptions of their accents', in A. Mauranen and E. Ranta (eds) *English as a Lingua Franca: studies and findings*, Newcastle upon Tyne: Cambridge Scholars Publishing, pp. 10–36.

——(2011) 'Accommodating (to) ELF in the international university', *Journal of Pragmatics* 43(4): 926–36.

Jenkins, J., Cogo, A. and Dewey, M. (2011) 'State-of-the-art article: review of developments in research into English as a lingua franca', *Language Teaching* 44: 281–315.

Jessner, U. (2003a) 'A dynamic approach to language attrition in multilingual systems', in V. Cook (ed.) *Effects of the Second Language on the First*, Clevedon: Multilingual Matters.

——(2003b) 'The nature of cross-linguistic interaction in the multilingual system', in J. Cenoz, B. Hufeisen and U. Jessner (eds) *The Multilingual Lexicon*, Dordrecht: Kluwer, pp. 45–55.

——(2006) *Linguistic Awareness in Multilinguals: English as a third language*, Edinburgh: Edinburgh University Press.

Johnson, K. and Johnson, H. (eds) (1998) *Encyclopedic Dictionary of Applied Linguistics*, Oxford: Blackwell.

Johnstone, B. (1996) *The Linguistic Individual: self-expression in language and linguistics*, Oxford: Oxford University Press.

Jørgensen, J.N. (2008) 'Polylingual languaging around and among children and adolescents', *International Journal of Multilingualism* 5(3): 161–76.

Kachru, B.B. (1985) 'Standards, codification, and sociolinguistic realism: the English language in the outer circle', in R. Quirk and H.G. Widdowson (eds) *English in the World: teaching and learning the language and literatures*, Cambridge: Cambridge University Press, pp. 11–30.

——(1992) 'Models for non-native Englishes', in B.B. Kachru (ed.) *The Other Tongue: English across cultures*, 2nd edn, Urbana: University of Illinois Press, pp. 48–74.

Kachru, Y. and Smith, L.E. (2008) *Cultures, Contexts, and World Englishes*, London: Routledge.

Kahane, H. and Kahane, R. (1976) 'Lingua franca: the story of a term', *Romance Philology* 30(1): 25–41.

Kasper, G. (1997) '"A" stands for acquisition: a response to Firth and Wagner', *Modern Language Journal* 81(3): 318–23.

Kasper, G. and Blum-Kulka, S. (1993) 'Interlanguage pragmatics: an introduction', in G. Kasper and S. Blum-Kulka (eds) *Interlanguage Pragmatics*, New York: Oxford University Press, pp. 3–17.

Kaur, J. (2009) 'Pre-empting problems of understanding in English as a lingua franca', in A. Mauranen and E. Ranta (eds) *English as a Lingua Franca: studies and findings*, Newcastle upon Tyne: Cambridge Scholars Publishing, pp. 107–25.

Kayman, M.A. (2009) 'The lingua franca of globalisation: "Filius nullius in terra nullius", as we say in English', *Nordic Journal of English Studies* 8(3): 87–115. <http://ojs.ub.gu.se/ojs/index.php/njes/article/view/361/354>

Kecskes, I. (2003) *Situation-Bound Utterances in L1 and L2*, Berlin: Mouton de Gruyter.

——(2007) 'Formulaic language in English Lingua Franca', in I. Kecskes and L. Horn (eds), *Explorations in Pragmatics: linguistic, cognitive and intercultural aspects*, Berlin: Mouton de Gruyter, pp. 191–219.

——(2010) 'Dual and multilanguage systems', *International Journal of Multilingualism* 7(2): 91–109.

Kecskes, I. and Papp, T. (2000) *Foreign Language and Mother Tongue*, Mahwah, NJ: Lawrence Erlbaum.

Keller, R. (1994) *On Language Change: the invisible hand in language*, London: Routledge.

Kellerman, E. and Sharwood Smith, M. (eds) (1986) *Crosslinguistic Influence in Second Language Acquisition*, Oxford: Pergamon.

Kemp, C. (2009) 'Defining multilingualism', in L. Aronin and B. Hufeisen (eds) *The Exploration of Multilingualism: development of research on L3, multilingualism and multiple language acquisition*, Amsterdam: John Benjamins, pp. 11–26.

Kirkpatrick, A. (2007) *World Englishes: implications for international communication and English language teaching*, Cambridge: Cambridge University Press.

——(2010) *English as a Lingua Franca in ASEAN: a multilingual model*, Hong Kong: Hong Kong University Press.

——(2011) 'English as an Asian lingua franca and the multilingual model of ELT', *Language Teaching*, 44(2): 212–24.

Klein, W. and Perdue, C. (1997) 'The basic variety (or: couldn't natural languages be much simpler?)', *Second Language Research* 13(4): 301–47.

Klimpfinger, T. (2009) '"She's mixing the two languages together": forms and functions of code-switching in English as a lingua franca', in A. Mauranen and E. Ranta (eds) *English as a Lingua Franca: studies and findings,* Newcastle upon Tyne: Cambridge Scholars Publishing, pp. 348–71.

Knapp, K. (2002) 'The fading out of the non-native speaker. Native speaker dominance in lingua-franca-situations', in K. Knapp and C. Meierkord (eds) *Lingua Franca Communication*, Frankfurt: Peter Lang.

——(2009) 'English as a lingua franca in Europe – variety, varieties or different types of use?' in M. Albl-Mikasa, S. Braun and S. Kalina (eds) *Dimensionen der Zweitsprachenforschung. Dimensions of second language research (Festschrift for Kurt Kohn)*, Tübingen: Gunter Narr, pp. 131–39.

Kortmann, B., Burridge, K., Mesthrie, R., Schneider, E.W. and Upton, C. (eds). (2004) *A Handbook of Varieties of English, Volume 2: Morphology and Syntax*, Berlin: Mouton de Gruyter.

Kramsch, C. (1997) 'The privilege of the nonnative speaker', *PMLA* 112(3): 359–69.

——(1999) 'Global and local identities in the contact zone', in C. Gnutzmann (ed.) *Teaching and Learning English as a Global Language*, Tübingen: Stauffenburg, pp. 131–43.

——(2000) 'Social discursive constructions of self in L2 learning', in J.P. Lantolf (ed.) *Sociocultural Theory and Second Language Learning*, Oxford: Oxford University Press, pp. 133–53.

——(2006) 'The traffic in meaning', *Asia Pacific Journal of Education*, 26(1): 99–104.

Labov, W. (1972a) 'The logic of non-standard English', in *Language in the Inner City: studies in the Black English vernacular*, Philadelphia: University of Pennsylvania Press, pp. 201–40.

——(1972b) *Sociolinguistic Patterns*, Philadelphia: University of Pennsylvania Press.

——(2001) *Principles of Linguistic Change, Volume 2: Social Factors*, Oxford: Blackwell.

Langacker, R.W. (1987) *Foundations of Cognitive Grammar, Volume 1: Theoretical Prerequisites*, Stanford: Stanford University Press.

Langlotz, A. (2006) *Idiomatic Creativity*, Amsterdam: John Benjamins.

Larsen-Freeman, D. (1997) 'Chaos/complexity science and second language acquisition', *Applied Linguistics* 18(2): 141–65.

Larsen-Freeman, D. and Cameron, L. (2008) *Complex Systems and Applied Linguistics*, Oxford: Oxford University Press.

Lass, R. (1997) *Historical Linguistics and Language Change*, Cambridge: Cambridge University Press.

Laufer, B. (2003) 'The influence of L2 on L1 collocational knowledge and on L1 lexical diversity in free written expression', in V. Cook (ed.) *Effects of the Second Language on the First*, Clevedon: Multilingual Matters, pp. 19–31.

Lawrence, D.H. (1960) *Lady Chatterley's Lover*, London: Penguin.

Lederer, M. (2003) *Translation: the interpretive model*, trans. N. Larché, Manchester: St Jerome.

Leech, G., Cruickshank, B. and Ivanic, R. (2001) *An A-Z of English Grammar and Usage*, 2nd edn, Harlow: Pearson.

Lenneberg, E.H. (1967) *Biological Foundations of Language*, New York: Wiley.

Le Page, R.B. and Tabouret-Keller, A. (1985) *Acts of Identity: creole-based approaches to language and ethnicity*, Cambridge: Cambridge University Press.

Levelt, W.J.M. (1989) *Speaking: from intention to articulation*, Cambridge, MA: MIT Press.

Lewis, M. (1993) *The Lexical Approach: the state of ELT and a way forward*, Hove: Language Teaching Publications.

——(1997) *Implementing the Lexical Approach*, Hove: Language Teaching Publications.

Lewis, R.D. (2003) *The Cultural Imperative: global trends in the 21st century*, Yarmouth, Maine: Intercultural Press.

Lipski, J.M. (2004) 'Is "Spanglish" the third language of the South?: truth and fantasy about US Spanish.' <http://www.personal.psu.edu/jml34/spanglsh.pdf>

Lüdi, G. (1987) 'Les marques transcodiques: regards nouveaux sur le bilinguisme', in G. Lüdi (ed.) *Devenir bilingue, parler bilingue*, Tübingen: Niemeyer, pp. 1–21.

McAllister, R. (1997) 'Perceptual foreign accent: L2 users' comprehension ability', in J. Leather and J. Allan (eds) *Second-Language Speech*, Berlin: Mouton de Gruyter, pp. 663–66.

McArthur, T. (1998) *The English Languages*, Cambridge: Cambridge University Press.

MacKenzie, I. (1986) 'Gadamer's hermeneutics and the uses of forgery', *Journal of Aesthetics and Art Criticism*, 45(1): 41–48.

——(1995) *Financial English*, Hove: Language Teaching Publications.

——(1997) *English for Business Studies: Student's Book, Teacher's Book, CDs*, Cambridge: Cambridge University Press.

——(2000a) 'Improvisation, creativity, and formulaic language', *Journal of Aesthetics and Art Criticism* 58(2): 173–79.

——(2000b) 'Institutionalized utterances, literature, and language teaching', *Language and Literature* 9(1): 61–78.

——(2002) *Paradigms of Reading: relevance theory and deconstruction*, Basingstoke: Palgrave.

——(2006) *Professional English in Use – Finance*, Cambridge: Cambridge University Press.

——(2009) 'Negotiating Europe's lingua franca', *European Journal of English Studies* 13(2), 223–40.

——(2010) *English for Business Studies*, 3rd edn: *Student's Book, Teacher's Book, CDs*, Cambridge: Cambridge University Press.

——(2012a) 'English as a lingua franca in Europe: bilingualism and multicompetence', *International Journal of Multilingualism* 9(1): 83–100.

——(2012b) 'Fair play to them: proficiency in English and types of borrowing', in C. Furiassi, V. Pulcini and F. Rodríguez González (eds) *The Anglicization of European Lexis*, Amsterdam: John Benjamins, pp. 27–42.

——(2012c) *Financial English*, 2nd edn, Andover: Heinle.

McLuhan, M. (1962) *The Gutenberg Galaxy: the making of typographic man*, Toronto: University of Toronto Press.

McWhorter, J.H. (2001) 'The world's simplest grammars are creole grammars', *Linguistic Typology* 6: 125–66.

Makkai, A. (1972) *Idiom structure in English*, The Hague: Mouton.

Makoni, S. and Pennycook, A. (2007) 'Disinventing and reconstituting languages', in S. Makoni and A. Pennycook (eds) *Disinventing and Reconstituting Languages*, Clevedon: Multilingual Matters, pp. 1–41.

Maley, A. (2008) 'EIL/ELF: cup half-full or half-empty', *Trends and Directions: proceedings of the 12th English in Southeast Asia conference*, Bangkok: KMUTT, pp. 62–70.

——(2009) 'ELF: a teacher's perspective', *Language and Intercultural Communication* 9(3): 187–200.

Marani, D. (2009) 'Langues et créativité: un parcours à moitié biblique et à moitié fantastique', Conférénce donnée à Expolangues, Paris, janvier. <http://ec.europa.eu/education/languages/news/expolangues17jan09/diego-marani.pdf >

Martinez, R. and Schmitt, N. (2012) 'A phrasal expressions list', *Applied Linguistics* 33(3): 299–320.

Maslow, A.H. (1968) *Toward a Psychology of Being*, 2nd edn, New York: Van Nostrand.

Matras, Y. (2009) *Language Contact*, Cambridge: Cambridge University Press.

Mauranen, A. (2003) 'The Corpus of English as Lingua Franca in Academic Settings', *TESOL Quarterly* 37(3): 513–27.

——(2005) 'English as a lingua franca: an unknown language?' in G. Cortese and A. Duszak (eds) *Identity, Community, Discourse: English in intercultural settings*, Frankfurt: Peter Lang, pp. 269–93.

——(2006) 'Signalling and preventing misunderstanding in English as lingua franca communication', *International Journal of the Sociology of Language* 177: 123–50.

——(2009) 'Chunking in ELF: expressions for managing interaction', *Journal of Intercultural Pragmatics* 6(2): 217–33.

——(2012) *Exploring ELF: academic English shaped by non-native speakers*, Cambridge: Cambridge University Press.

Mauranen, A. and Kujamäki, P. (2004) 'Introduction', in A. Mauranen and P. Kujamäki (eds) *Translation Universals: do they exist?* Amsterdam: John Benjamins, pp. 1–11.

Medgyes, P. (1994) *The Non-Native Teacher*, London: Macmillan.

Meierkord, C. (2000) 'Interpreting successful lingua franca interaction: an analysis of non-native/non-native small talk conversations in English', *Linguistik Online* 5. <http://www.linguistik-online.com/1_00/MEIERKOR.HTM>

——(2002) '"Language stripped bare" or "linguistic masala"? Culture in lingua franca communication', in K. Knapp and C. Meierkord (eds) *Lingua Franca Communication*, Frankfurt: Peter Lang, 109–33.

——(2004) 'Syntactic variation in interactions across international Englishes', *English World-Wide* 25(1): 109–32.

——(2005) 'Interactions across Englishes and their lexicon', in C. Gnutzmann and F. Intemann (eds) *The Globalisation of English and the English Language Classroom*, Tübingen: Gunter Narr, pp. 89–104.

——(2012) *Interactions across Englishes: linguistic choices in local and international contact situations*, Cambridge: Cambridge University Press.

Meisel, J.M. (1983) 'Transfer as a second language strategy', *Language and Communication* 3: 11–46.

Melchers, G. and Shaw, P. (2003) *World Englishes*, London: Edward Arnold.

Mel'čuk, I. (1998) 'Collocations and lexical functions', in A.P. Cowie (ed.) *Phraseology: theory, analysis, and applications*, Oxford: Oxford University Press, pp. 23–53.

Mencken, H.L. (1921) *The American Language*, 2nd edn, New York: A.A. Knopf.

Mesthrie, R. and Bhatt, R.M. (2008) *World Englishes: the study of new linguistic varieties*, Cambridge: Cambridge University Press.

Miller, G.A. (1956) 'The magical number seven, plus or minus two: some limits on our capacity for processing information', *Psychological Review* 63(2): 81–97.

Milroy, J. and Milroy, L. (1985) 'Linguistic change, social network and speaker innovation', *Journal of Linguistics* 21(2): 339–84.

Milroy, L. (1987) *Language and Social Networks*, 2nd edn, Oxford: Blackwell.

Milroy, L. and Muysken, P. (1995) 'Introduction: code-switching and bilingualism research', in L. Milroy and P. Muysken (eds) *One Speaker, Two Languages: cross-disciplinary perspectives on code-switching,* Cambridge: Cambridge University Press, pp. 1–14.

Molière. (1670/2013) *Le bourgeois gentilhomme*, Paris: Flammarion.

Mollin, S. (2006a) 'English as a Lingua Franca: a new variety in the new expanding circle?' *Nordic Journal of English Studies* 5(2): 41–57. <http://ojs.ub.gu.se/ojs/index.php/njes/article/view/67/71>

——(2006b) *Euro-English: assessing variety status*, Tübingen: Gunter Narr.

Moon, R. (1998) *Fixed Expressions and Idioms in English*, Oxford: Clarendon Press.

Morizumi, M. (2009) 'Japanese English for EIAL: what it should be like and how much has been introduced', in K. Murata and J. Jenkins (eds) *Global Englishes in Asian Contexts: current and future debates*, London: Palgrave, pp. 73–93.

Mufwene, S.S. (1994) 'New Englishes and criteria for naming them', *World Englishes* 13(1): 21–31.

——(2001) *The Ecology of Language Evolution*, Cambridge: Cambridge University Press.

——(2010) 'Globalization and the spread of English: what does it mean to be Anglophone?' *English Today* 26(1): 57–59.

——(2012) 'English as a Lingua Franca: myths and facts', *Journal of English as a Lingua Franca* 1(2): 365–70.

Muysken, P. (2000) *Bilingual Speech: a typology of code-mixing*, Cambridge: Cambridge University Press.

Myers-Scotton, C. (1993) *Duelling Languages: grammatical structure in codeswitching*, Oxford: Oxford University Press.

Nation, I.S.P. (1990) *Teaching and Learning Vocabulary*, New York: Newbury House.

——(2001) *Learning Vocabulary in Another Language*, Cambridge: Cambridge University Press.

——(2006) 'How large a vocabulary is needed for reading and listening?' *Canadian Modern Language Review* 63(1): 59–82.

Nattinger, J.R. and DeCarrico, J. (1992) *Lexical Phrases and Language Teaching*, Oxford: Oxford University Press.

Nemser, W. (1991) 'Language contact and foreign language acquisition', in V. Ivir and D. Kalogjera (eds) *Languages in Contact and Contrast: essays in contact linguistics*, Berlin: Mouton de Gruyter, pp. 345–64.

Nerrière, J-P. (2004) *Don't Speak English, Parlez Globish*, Paris: Eyrolles.

Nesselhauf, N. (2009) 'Co-selection phenomena across New Englishes: parallels (and differences) to foreign learner varieties', *English World-Wide* 30(1): 1–26.

O'Laoire, M. and Singleton, D. (2009) 'The role of prior knowledge in L3 learning and use', in L. Aronin and B. Hufeisen (eds) *The Exploration of Multilingualism: development of research on L3, multilingualism and multiple language acquisition*, Amsterdam: John Benjamins, pp. 79–102.

Odlin, T. (1989) *Language Transfer: crosslinguistic influence in language learning*, Cambridge: Cambridge University Press.

Ogden, C.K. (1930/1938) *Basic English: a general introduction with rules and grammar*, London: Kegan Paul.

Ohmae, K. (1990) *The Borderless World*, New York: Harper Business.

Orwell, G. (1946/1968) 'Politics and the English language', in S. Orwell and I. Angus (eds) *The Collected Essays, Journalism and Letters of George Orwell, Volume IV, In Front of Your Nose, 1945–1950*, London: Secker & Warburg, pp. 127–39.

Oxford Advanced Learner's Dictionary, 7th edn (2005), Oxford: Oxford University Press.

Oxford Advanced Learner's Dictionary, 8th edn (2010), Oxford: Oxford University Press.

Parrott, M. (2010) *Grammar for English Language Teachers*, 2nd edn, Cambridge: Cambridge University Press.

Paul, H. (1886) *Prinzipien der Sprachgeschichte*, 2 Aufl., Halle: Max Niemayer.

Pavlenko, A. (2005) *Emotions and Multilingualism*, Cambridge: Cambridge University Press.

——(2009) 'Conceptual representation in the bilingual lexicon and second language vocabulary learning', in A. Pavlenko (ed.) *The Bilingual Mental Lexicon: interdisciplinary approaches*, Clevedon: Multilingual Matters, pp. 125–60.

——(2011a) 'Introduction: bilingualism and thought in the 20th century', in A. Pavlenko, (ed.) *Thinking and Speaking in Two Languages*, Bristol: Multilingual Matters, pp. 1–28.

——(2011b) '(Re-)naming the world: word-to-referent mapping in second language speakers', in A. Pavlenko (ed.), *Thinking and Speaking in Two Languages*, Bristol: Multilingual Matters, pp. 198–236.

Pavlenko, A. and Blackledge, A. (2004) 'Introduction: new theoretical approaches to the study of negotiation of identities in multilingual contexts', in A. Pavlenko and A. Blackledge (eds), *Negotiation of Identities in Multilingual Contexts*, Clevedon: Multilingual Matters, pp. 1–33.

Pawley, A. and Syder, F.H. (1983) 'Two puzzles for linguistic theory: nativelike selection and nativelike fluency', in J.C. Richards and R.W. Schmidt (eds) *Language and Communication*, London: Longman, pp. 191–225.

Peal, E. and Lambert, W.E. (1962) 'The relation of bilingualism to intelligence', *Psychological Monographs* 76: 1–23.

Pei, M. (1967) *The Story of the English Language*, London: George Allen & Unwin.

Peirce, C.S. (1931–58) *Collected Papers*, C. Hartsthorne and P. Weiss (eds), Cambridge, MA: Harvard University Press.

Peng, L. and Ann, J. (2001) 'Stress and duration in three varieties of English', *World Englishes* 20(1): 1–27.

Pennycook, A. (1994) *The Cultural Politics of English as an International Language*, Harlow: Longman.

——(1998) *English and the Discourses of Colonialism*, London: Routledge.

——(2007) *Global Englishes and Transcultural Flows*, London: Routledge.

——(2009) 'Plurilithic Englishes: towards a 3D model', in K. Murata and J. Jenkins (eds) *Global Englishes in Asian Contexts: current and future debates*, Basingstoke: Palgrave Macmillan, pp. 194–207.

——(2010a) *Language as a Local Practice*, London: Routledge.

——(2010b) 'Popular cultures, popular languages, and global identities', in N. Coupland (ed.) *The Handbook of Language and Globalization*, Oxford: Wiley-Blackwell, pp. 592–607.

Peters, A.M. (1983) *The Units of Language Acquisition*, Cambridge: Cambridge University Press.

Phillips, A.A. (2006) *A.A. Phillips on the Cultural Cringe*, Melbourne: Melbourne University Press.

Phillipson, R. (1992) *Linguistic Imperialism*, Oxford: Oxford University Press.

——(2008) '*Lingua franca* or *lingua frankensteinia*? English in European integration and globalisation', *World Englishes* 27(2): 250–67.

——(2009) *Linguistic Imperialism Continued*, London: Routledge.

Piirainen, E. (2012) *Widespread Idioms in Europe and Beyond: toward a lexicon of common figurative units*, New York: Peter Lang.

Pinker, S. (1994) *The Language Instinct*, London: Penguin.

Pitzl, M-L. (2009) '"We should not wake up any dogs": idiom and metaphor in ELF', in A. Mauranen and E. Ranta (eds) *English as a Lingua Franca: studies and findings*, Newcastle upon Tyne: Cambridge Scholars Publishing, pp. 298–322.

——(2012) 'Creativity meets convention: idiom variation and re-metaphorization in ELF', *Journal of English as a Lingua Franca* 1(1): 27–55.

Pitzl, M-L., Breiteneder, A. and Klimpfinger, T. (2008) 'A world of words: processes of lexical innovation in VOICE', *Vienna English Working Papers* 17(2): 21–46. <http://anglistik.univie.ac.at/fileadmin/user_upload/dep_anglist/weitere_Uploads/Views/views_0802.pdf>

Plag, I. (2003) *Word-Formation in English*, Cambridge: Cambridge University Press.

Platt, J. and Weber, H. (1980) *English in Singapore and Malaysia: status, features, functions*, Kuala Lumpur: Oxford University Press.

Platt, J., Weber, H. and Ho, M.L. (1984) *The New Englishes*, London: Routledge and Kegan Paul.

Poplack, S. (1980) 'Sometimes I'll start a sentence in Spanish y termino en español': toward a typology of code-switching', *Linguistics* 18(7–8): 581–618.

Poplack, S., Sankoff, D. and Miller, C. (1988) 'The social correlates and linguistic processes of lexical borrowing and assimilation', *Linguistics* 26(1): 47–104.

Poulisse, N. (1997) 'Some words in defense of the psycholinguistic approach: a response to Firth and Wagner', *Modern Language Journal* 81(3): 324–28.

Pride, J. (1982) *New Englishes*, Rowley, MA: Newbury House.

Prodromou, L. (2008) *English as a Lingua Franca: a corpus-based analysis*, London: Continuum.

Quine, W.V.O. (1953) 'Two Dogmas of Empiricism', in *From a Logical Point of View*, Cambridge, MA: Harvard University Press, pp. 20–46.

Quirk, R. (1982) 'International communication and the concept of Nuclear English', in C. Brumfit (ed.) *English for International Communication*, Oxford: Pergamon, pp. 15–28.

——(1985) 'The English language in a global context', in R. Quirk and H.G. Widdowson (eds) *English in the World: teaching and learning the language and literatures*, Cambridge: Cambridge University Press, pp. 1–6.

——(1990) 'Language varieties and standard language', *English Today* 6(1): 3–10.

Quirk, R., Greenbaum, S., Leech, G. and Svartvik, J. (1972) *A Grammar of Contemporary English*, London: Longman.

Rampton, B. (1987) 'Stylistic variability and not speaking "normal" English: some post-Labovian approaches and their implications for the study of interlanguage', in R. Ellis (ed.) *Second Language Acquisition in Context*, Englewood Cliffs, NJ: Prentice Hall, pp. 47–58.

——(2005) *Crossing: language and ethnicity among adolescents*, 2nd edn, Manchester: St. Jerome.

Ranta, E. (2006) 'The "attractive" progressive – Why use the *-ing* form in English as a lingua franca?' *Nordic Journal of English Studies* 5(2): 95–116. <http://ojs.ub.gu.se/ojs/index.php/njes/article/view/64/68>

——(2009) 'Syntactic features in spoken ELF: learner language or spoken grammar?' in A. Mauranen and E. Ranta (eds) *English as a Lingua Franca: studies and findings*, Newcastle upon Tyne: Cambridge Scholars Publishing, pp. 84–106.

Ravage, M. (1917) *An American in the Making: the life story of an immigrant*, New York: Harper & Brothers.

Reich, R. (1991) *The Work of Nations*, New York: Knopf.

Reithofer, K. (2010) 'English as a lingua franca vs. interpreting: battleground or peaceful coexistence?' *The Interpreters' Newsletter* 15: 143–57. <http://hdl.handle.net/10077/4755>

Remiszewski, M. (2005) 'Lingua Franca Core: picture incomplete', in K. Dziubalska-Kolaczyk and J. Przedlacka (eds) *English Pronunciation Models: a changing scene*, Bern: Peter Lang, pp. 293–308.

Ringbom, H. (1987) *The Role of the First Language in Foreign Language Learning*, Clevedon: Multilingual Matters.

——(2001) 'Lexical transfer in L3 production', in J. Cenoz, B. Hufeisen and U. Jessner (eds) *Cross-Linguistic Influence in Third Language Acquisition: psycholinguistic perspectives*, Clevedon: Multilingual Matters, pp. 59–68.

——(2007) *Cross-Linguistic Similarity in Foreign Language Learning*, Clevedon: Multilingual Matters.

Rorty, R. (1989) *Contingency, Irony, and Solidarity*, Cambridge: Cambridge University Press.

——(1991) 'Postmodernist bourgeois liberalism', in *Objectivity, Relativism, and Truth: philosophical papers, Volume 1*, Cambridge: Cambridge University Press, pp. 197–202.

Rosten, L. (2001) *The New Joys of Yiddish*, New York: Crown.

Sapir, E. (1921*) Language: an introduction to the study of speech*, New York: Harcourt, Brace & Co.

——(1929/1949) *Selected Writings in Culture, Language and Personality*, D.G. Mandelbaum (ed.), Berkeley: University of California Press.

Schell, M. (2008) 'Colinguals among bilinguals', *World Englishes* 27(1): 117–30.

Schmied, J. (1991) *English in Africa: an introduction*, London: Longman.

Schmitt, N. (2010) *Researching Vocabulary: a vocabulary research manual*, Basingstoke: Palgrave.

Schneider, E.W. (2003) 'The dynamics of New Englishes: from identity construction to dialect birth', *Language* 79(2): 233–81.

——(2007) *Postcolonial English: varieties around the world*, Cambridge: Cambridge University Press.

——(2008) 'Accommodation versus identity? A response to Trudgill', *Language in Society* 37(2): 262–67.

——(2011) *English around the World*, Cambridge: Cambridge University Press.

——(2012) 'Exploring the interface between World Englishes and Second Language Acquisition – and implications for English as a Lingua Franca', *Journal of English as a Lingua Franca* 1(1): 57–91.

Schneider, E.W., Burridge, K., Kortmann, B., Mesthrie, R. and Upton, C. (eds) (2004) *A Handbook of Varieties of English, Volume 1: Phonology*, Berlin: Mouton de Gruyter.

Schrijver, P. (2006) 'What Britons spoke around 400 AD', in N.J. Higham (ed.) *Britons in Anglo-Saxon England*, Woodbridge: Boydell, pp. 165–71.

Scollon, R., Scollon, S.W. and Jones, R.H. (2012) *Intercultural Communication: a discourse approach*, 3rd edn, Oxford: Blackwell.

Seidlhofer, B. (2001a) 'Brave New English?' *European English Messenger* 10(1): 42–48.

——(2001b) 'Closing a conceptual gap: the case for a description of English as a lingua franca', *International Journal of Applied Linguistics* 11(2): 133–58.

——(2002) 'The shape of things to come? Some basic questions about English as lingua franca', in K. Knapp and C. Meierkord (eds) *Lingua Franca Communication*, Frankfurt: Peter Lang, pp. 269–302.

——(2003) 'A concept of "international English" and related issues: from "real English" to "realistic English"?' Strasbourg: Council of Europe. <http://www.coe.int>

——(ed.) (2003) *Controversies in Applied Linguistics*, Oxford: Oxford University Press.

——(2004) 'Research perspectives on teaching English as a lingua franca', *Annual Review of Applied Linguistics* 24: 209–39.

——(2005a) 'English as a lingua franca', *ELT Journal* 59(4): 339–41.

——(2005b) 'English as a lingua franca', in A.S. Hornby (ed.) *Oxford Advanced Learner's Dictionary of Current English*, 7th edn, Oxford: Oxford University Press, p. R92.

——(2007) 'English as a lingua franca and communities of practice', in S. Volk-Birke and J. Lippert (eds) *Anglistentag 2006 Halle Proceedings*, Trier: Wissenschaftlige Verlag Trier, pp. 307–18.

——(2009a) 'Accommodation and the idiom principle in English as a lingua franca', *Journal of Intercultural Pragmatics* 6(2): 195–215.

——(2009b) 'Common ground and different realities: World Englishes and English as a lingua franca', *World Englishes* 28(2): 236–45.

——(2009c) 'ELF findings: form and function', in A. Mauranen and E. Ranta (eds) *English as a Lingua Franca: studies and findings*, Newcastle upon Tyne: Cambridge Scholars Publishing, pp. 37–59.

——(2010) 'Lingua franca English: the European context', in A. Kirkpatrick (ed.), *The Routledge Handbook of World Englishes*, London: Routledge, pp. 355–71.

——(2011) *Understanding English as a Lingua Franca*, Oxford: Oxford University Press.

Seidlhofer, B., Breiteneder, A. and Pitzl, M-L. (2006) 'English as a lingua franca in Europe: challenges for applied linguistics', *Annual Review of Applied Linguistics* 26: 3–34.

Seidlhofer, B. and Widdowson, H.G. (2007) 'Idiomatic variation and change in English. The idiom principle and its realizations', in U. Smit *et al.* (eds) *Tracing English through Time: explorations in language variation (Festschrift for Herbert Schendl, Austrian Studies in English 95)*, Vienna: Braumüller, pp. 359–74.

——(2009) 'Conformity and creativity in ELF and learner English', in M. Albl-Mikasa, S. Braun and S. Kalina (eds), *Dimensionen der Zweitsprachenforschung. Dimensions of second language research (Festschrift for Kurt Kohn)*, Tübingen: Gunter Narr, pp. 93–107.

Seiler, W. (2009) 'English as a lingua franca in aviation', *English Today* 25(2): 43–48.

Selinker, L. (1972) 'Interlanguage', *International Review of Applied Linguistics* 10(3): 209–31.

Sharifian, F. (2011) *Cultural Conceptualisations and Language: theoretical framework and applications*, Amsterdam: John Benjamins.

Simpson, R.C., Briggs, S.L., Ovens, J. and Swales, J.M. (2002) The Michigan Corpus of Academic Spoken English, Ann Arbor, MI: The Regents of the University of Michigan. <http://micase.elicorpora.info>

Sinclair, J. (1991) *Corpus, Concordance, Collocation*, Oxford: Oxford University Press.

——(2004) *Trust the Text: language, corpus and discourse*, London: Routledge.

Sinclair, J. and Mauranen, A. (2006) *Linear Unit Grammar*, Amsterdam: John Benjamins.

Skehan, P. (2003) 'Task-based instruction', *Language Teaching* 36(1): 1–14.

Skutnabb-Kangas, T. (1984) *Bilingualism or Not: the education of minorities*, Clevedon: Multilingual Matters.

Slobin, D.I. (1996) 'From "thought and language" to "thinking for speaking,"' in J.J. Gumperz and S.S. Levinson (eds) *Rethinking Linguistic Relativity*, Cambridge: Cambridge University Press, pp. 70–96.

Smith, A. (1776/1976) *An Inquiry into the Nature and Causes of the Wealth of Nations*, R.H. Campbell and A.S. Skinner (eds), Oxford: Oxford University Press.

Smith, L.E. (1983a) 'English as an international auxiliary language', in L.E. Smith (ed.), *Readings in English as an International Language*, Oxford: Pergamon, pp. 1–5.

——(1983b) 'English as an international language: No room for linguistic chauvinism', in L.E. Smith (ed.) *Readings in English as an International Language*, Oxford: Pergamon, pp. 7–12.

——(1983c) 'Preface', in L.E. Smith (ed.), *Readings in English as an International Language*, Oxford: Pergamon, pp. v–vi.

——(1988) 'Language spread and issues of intelligibility', in P.H. Lowenberg (ed.) *1987 Georgetown Round Table on Languages and Linguistics: language spread and language policy*, Washington, DC: Georgetown University Press, pp. 265–82.

——(1992) 'Spread of English and issues of intelligibility', in B.B. Kachru (ed.) *The Other Tongue: English across cultures*, 2nd edn, Urbana: University of Illinois Press, pp. 75–90.

——(2009) 'Dimensions of understanding in cross-cultural communication', in K. Murata and J. Jenkins (eds) *Global Englishes in Asian Contexts: current and future debates*, Basingstoke: Palgrave Macmillan, pp. 17–25.

Smith, L.E. and Bisazza, J.A. (1983) 'The comprehensibility of three varieties of English for college students in seven countries', in L.E. Smith (ed.) *Readings in English as an International Language*, Oxford: Pergamon, pp. 59–67.

Smith, L.E. and Nelson, C.L. (1985) 'International intelligibility of English: directions and resources', *World Englishes* 4(3): 333–42.

Smith, L.E. and Rafiqzad, K. (1983) 'English for cross-cultural communication: the question of intelligibility', in L.E. Smith (ed.) *Readings in English as an International Language*, Oxford: Pergamon, pp. 49–58.

Smith, L.P. (1925) *Words and Idioms: studies in the English language*, London: Constable.

Smolin, L. (2008) *The Trouble with Physics*, London: Penguin.

Snell-Hornby, M. (2000) '"McLanguage": the identity of English as an issue in translation today', in M. Grosman *et al.* (eds) *Translation into Non-Mother Tongues in Professional Practice and Training*, Tübingen: Stauffenburg, pp. 35–44.

Sobkowiak, W. (2005) 'Why not LFC?' in K. Dziubalska-Kolaczyk and J. Przedlacka (eds) *English Pronunciation Models: a changing scene*, Bern: Peter Lang, pp. 131–49.

Sperber, D., Clément, F., Heintz, C., Mascaro, O., Mercier, H., Origgi, G. and Wilson, D. (2010) 'Epistemic Vigilance', *Mind & Language* 25(4): 359–93.

Sperber, D. and Wilson, D. (1986/1995) *Relevance: communication and cognition*, Oxford: Blackwell.

Sridhar, S.N. (1994) 'A reality check for SLA theories', *TESOL Quarterly* 28(4): 800–805.

Stavans, I. (ed.). (2008) *Spanglish*, Westport, CN: Greenwood Press.

Steiner, G. (1998) *After Babel: aspects of language and translation*, 3rd edn, Oxford: Oxford University Press.

Stern, H.H. (1983) *Fundamental Concepts of Language Teaching*, Oxford: Oxford University Press.

Swales, J.M. (1990) *Genre Analysis: English in academic and research settings*, Cambridge: Cambridge University Press.

Swan, M. (2005) *Practical English Usage*, 3rd edn, Oxford: Oxford University Press.

——(2012) 'EFL and ELF: are they really different?' *Journal of English as a Lingua Franca* 1(2): 379–89.

Swan, M. and Smith, M (eds) (2001) *Learner English: a teacher's guide to interference and other problems*, 2nd edn, Cambridge: Cambridge University Press.

Szmrecsanyi, B. (2009) 'Typological parameters of intralingual variability: grammatical analyticity vs. syntheticity in varieties of English', *Language Variation and Change* 21(3): 319–53.

——(2012) 'Analyticity and syntheticity in the history of English', in T. Nevalainen and E.C. Traugott (eds) *The Oxford Handbook of the History of English*, Oxford: Oxford University Press, pp. 654–65.

Szmrecsanyi, B. and Kortmann, B. (2009) 'Vernacular universals and Angloversals in a typological perspective', in M. Filppula, J. Klemola, and H. Paulasto (eds) *Vernacular Universals and Language Contacts: evidence from varieties of English and beyond*, London: Routledge, pp. 33–53.

——(2011) 'Typological profiling: Learner Englishes versus indigenized L2 varieties of English', J. Mukherjee and M. Hundt (eds) *Exploring Second-Language Varieties of English and Learner Englishes: bridging a paradigm gap*, Amsterdam: John Benjamins, pp. 167–87.

Szpyra-Kozlowska, J. (2005) 'Lingua Franca Core, phonetic universals and the Polish context', in K. Dziubalska-Kolaczyk and J. Przedlacka (eds) *English Pronunciation Models: a changing Scene*, Bern: Peter Lang, pp. 151–76.

Tagliamonte, S.A. (2009) 'There was universals; then there weren't: a comparative socio-linguistic perspective on "default singulars"', in M. Filppula, J. Klemola, and H. Paulasto (eds) *Vernacular Universals and Language Contacts: evidence from varieties of English and beyond*, London: Routledge, pp. 103–29.

Tajfel, H. (1974) 'Social identity and intergroup behaviour', *Social Science Information* 13: 65–93.

——(ed.) (1978) *Differentiation between Social Groups: studies in the social psychology of intergroup relations*, London: Academic Press.

——(1981) *Human Groups and Social Categories*, Cambridge: Cambridge University Press.

Talmy, L. (1991) 'Path to realization: a typology of event conflation', *Proceedings of the Seventeenth Annual Meeting of the Berkeley Linguistics Society*, pp. 480–519.

Tannen, D. (1989) *Talking Voices: repetition, dialogue, and imagery in conversational discourse*, Cambridge: Cambridge University Press.

Teubert, W. (2009) 'Sinclair, pattern grammar and the question of *hatred*', in R. Moon (ed.) *Words, Grammar, Text: revisiting the work of John Sinclair*, Amsterdam: John Benjamins, pp. 59–84.

Theroux, P. (1986) *Sunrise with Seamonsters*, Harmondsworth: Penguin.

Thomason, S.G. (2001) *Language Contact: an introduction*, Edinburgh: Edinburgh University Press.

Thomason, S.G. and Kaufman, T. (1988) *Language Contact, Creolization, and Genetic Linguistics*, Berkeley: University of California Press.

Thornbury, S. (1998) 'The Lexical Approach: a journey without maps?' *Modern English Teacher* 17(4): 7–13.

Timmis, I. (2002) 'Native-speaker norms and International English: a classroom view', *ELT Journal* 56(3): 240–49.

Tomasello, M. (2003) *Constructing a Language: a usage-based theory of language acquisition*, Cambridge, MA: Harvard University Press.

Toolan, M. (1996) *Total Speech: an integrational linguistic approach to language*, London: Duke University Press.

Tristram, H. (2004) 'Diglossia in Anglo-Saxon England, or what was spoken Old English like?' *Studia Anglica Posnaniensia* 40: 87–110.

Trompenaars, F. (1993) *Riding the Waves of Culture: understanding cultural diversity in business*, London: Nicolas Brealey.

Trudgill, P. (1974) *The Social Differentiation of English in Norwich*, Cambridge: Cambridge University Press.

——(1986) *Dialects in Contact*, Oxford: Blackwell.

——(1989) 'Contact and isolation in linguistic change', in L.E. Breivik and E.H. Jahr (eds) *Language Change: contributions to the study of its causes*, Berlin: Mouton de Gruyter, pp. 227–37.

——(1995) 'Linguistic oppression and the non-native speaker', *Journal of Pragmatics* 24(3): 314–17.

——(1999) 'Standard English: what it isn't', in T. Bex and R.J. Watts (eds), *Standard English: the widening debate*, London: Routledge, pp. 117–28.

——(2002) *Sociolinguistic Variation and Change*, Edinburgh: Edinburgh University Press.

——(2004) *New-Dialect Formation: the inevitability of colonial Englishes*, Edinburgh: Edinburgh University Press.

——(2005a) 'Finding the speaker-listener equilibrium: segmental phonological models in EFL', in K. Dziubalska-Kolaczyk and J. Przedlacka (eds) *English Pronunciation Models: a changing scene*, Bern: Peter Lang, pp. 213–28.

——(2005b) 'Native speaker segmental phonological models and the English Lingua Franca Core', in K. Dziubalska-Kolaczyk and J. Przedlacka (eds) *English Pronunciation Models: a changing scene*, Bern: Peter Lang, pp. 77–98.

——(2008a) 'Colonial dialect contact in the history of European languages: on the irrelevance of identity to new-dialect formation', *Language in Society* 37(2): 241–80.

——(2008b) *In Sfakiá: passing time in the wilds of Crete*, Athens: Lycabettus Press.

——(2009) 'Sociolinguistic typology and complexification', in G. Sampson, D. Gil and P. Trudgill (eds), *Language Complexity as an Evolving Variable*, Oxford: Oxford University Press, pp. 98–109.

——(2010) *Investigations in Sociohistorical Linguistics: stories of colonisation and contact*, Cambridge: Cambridge University Press.

——(2011) *Sociolinguistic Typology: social determinants of language complexity*, Oxford: Oxford University Press.

Trudgill, P. and Hannah, J. (2008) *International English: a guide to the varieties of standard English*, 5th edn, London: Hodder Arnold.

Ullman, M.T. (2001) 'The neural basis of lexicon and grammar in first and second language: the declarative/procedural model', *Bilingualism: Language and Cognition* 4(1): 105–22.

——(2007) 'The biocognition of the mental lexicon', in M.G. Gaskell (ed.) *The Oxford Handbook of Psycholinguistics*, Oxford: Oxford University Press, pp. 267–86.

Urry, J. (1995) *Consuming Places*, London: Routledge.

Valdés, G. (1988) 'The language situation of Mexican-Americans', in S.L. McKay and S-L.C. Wong (eds) *Language Diversity: problem or resource?*, New York: Newbury House, pp. 111–39.

Van den Doel, R. (2008) 'The blind spots of Jenkins' "Lingua Franca"', in E. Waniek-Klimczak (ed.) *Issues in Accents of English*, Newcastle upon Tyne: Cambridge Scholars Publishing, pp. 140–49.

——(2010) 'Native and non-native models in ELT: advantages, disadvantages, and the implications of accent parallelism', *Poznań Studies in Contemporary Linguistics* 46(3): 349–65. <http://versita.metapress.com/content/l31lv278483458t8/fulltext.pdf>

Vandevelde, P. (2005) *The Task of the Interpreter: text, meaning and negotiation*, Pittsburgh: University of Pittsburgh Press.

Van Parijs, P. (2011) *Linguistic Justice for Europe and the World*, Oxford: Oxford University Press.

VOICE (Vienna-Oxford International corpus of English) <http://www.univie.ac.at/voice>

Voloshinov, V.N. (1929/1973) *Marxism and the Philosophy of Language*, trans. L. Matejka and I.R. Titunik, New York: Seminar Press.

Voltaire. (1759/2012) *Candide*, Paris: Flammarion.

——(1763/1837) 'Le Chapon et la Poularde', in *Oeuvres complètes de Voltaire, Tome 6, Philosophie. Dialogues*, Paris: Furne, pp. 645–47.

Vonnegut, K. (1973) *Breakfast of Champions*, London: Jonathan Cape.

Vygotsky, L.S. (1934/1962) *Thought and Language*, trans. E. Hanfmann and G. Vakar, Cambridge, MA: MIT Press.

Walker, R. (2010) *Teaching the Pronunciation of English as a Lingua Franca*, Oxford: Oxford University Press.

Wallace, A.F.C. (1961) 'On being just complicated enough', *Proceedings of the National Academy of Sciences* 47 (1961): 458–64.

Weaver, W. (1949) 'Recent contributions to the mathematical theory of communication', in C.C. Shannon and W. Weaver (eds) *The Mathematical Theory of Communication,* Urbana: University of Illinois Press, pp. 31–125.

Weber, A. and Cutler, A. (2004) 'Lexical competition in non-native spoken-word recognition', *Journal of Memory and Language* 50(1): 1–15.

Weinreich, U. (1953/1968) *Languages in Contact: findings and problems*, The Hague: Mouton.

——(1969) 'Problems in the analysis of idioms', in J. Puhvel (ed.) *Substance and Structure of Language*, Berkeley: University of California Press, pp. 23–81.

Weinreich, U., Labov, W. and Herzog, M.I. (1968) 'Empirical foundations for a theory of language change', in W.P. Lehmann and Y. Malkiel (eds) *Directions for Historical Linguistics*, Austin: University of Texas Press, pp. 95–195.

Wells, J.C. (1982) *Accents of English, Volume 1: An Introduction*, Cambridge: Cambridge University Press.

Wenger, E. (1998) *Communities of Practice: learning, meaning and identity*, Cambridge: Cambridge University Press.

West, M. (1953) *A General Service List of English Words*, London: Longman, Green.

Whorf, B.L. (1956) *Language, Thought, and Reality*, J. Carroll (ed.), Cambridge, MA: MIT Press.

Widdowson, H.G. (1983) *Learning Purpose and Language Use*, Oxford: Oxford University Press.

——(1990) *Aspects of Language Teaching*, Oxford: Oxford University Press.

——(1998) 'Positions and oppositions: hedgehogs and foxes', *International Journal of Applied Linguistics* 8(1): 147–51.

——(2003) *Defining Issues in English Language Teaching*, Oxford: Oxford University Press.

——(2004) 'A perspective on recent trends', in A.P.R. Howatt and H.G. Widdowson, *A History of English Language Teaching*, 2nd edn, Oxford: Oxford University Press, pp. 353–72.

——(2012) 'ELF and the inconvenience of established concepts', *Journal of English as a Lingua Franca* 1(1): 5–26.

Wierzbicka, A. (1985) 'Oats and wheat: the fallacy of arbitrariness', in J. Haiman (ed.) *Iconicity in Syntax*, Amsterdam: John Benjamins, pp. 311–42.
——(1988) *The Semantics of Grammar*, Amsterdam: John Benjamins.
——(2003) *Cross-Cultural Pragmatics: the semantics of human interaction*, 2nd edn, Berlin: Mouton de Gruyter.
——(2006) *English: meaning and culture*, New York: Oxford University Press.
Wilde, O. (1894/2000) *The Major Works*, Oxford: Oxford University Press.
Williams, J. (1987) 'Non-native varieties of English: a special case of language acquisition', *English World-Wide* 8(2): 161–99.
Williams, R. (1965) *The Long Revolution*, Harmondsworth: Penguin.
Wilson, D. (2004) 'Relevance and lexical pragmatics', *UCL Working Papers in Linguistics* 16: 343–60.
Wilson, D. and Carston, R. (2007) 'A unitary approach to lexical pragmatics: relevance, inference and ad hoc concepts', in N. Burton-Roberts (ed.) *Pragmatics*, Basingstoke: Palgrave, pp. 230–59.
Winford, D. (2003) *An Introduction to Contact Linguistics*, Oxford: Blackwell.
Wolf, H-G and Polzenhagen, F. (2009) *World Englishes: a cognitive sociolinguistic approach*, Berlin: Mouton de Gruyter.
Wray, A. (2002) *Formulaic Language and the Lexicon*, Cambridge: Cambridge University Press.
——(2008) *Formulaic Language: pushing the boundaries*, Oxford: Oxford University Press.
——(2009) 'Conclusion: navigating L2 collocation research', in A. Barfield and H. Gyllstad (eds), *Researching Collocations in Another Language: multiple interpretations*, Basingstoke: Palgrave, pp. 232–44.
Wray, A. and Grace, G.W. (2007) 'The consequences of talking to strangers: evolutionary corollaries of socio-cultural influences on linguistic form', *Lingua* 117(3): 543–78.
Yano, Y. (2001) 'World Englishes in 2000 and beyond', *World Englishes* 20(2): 119–31.
——(2009) 'English as an international language: from societal to individual', *World Englishes* 28(2): 246–55.
Yorio, C.A. (1989) 'Idiomaticity as an indicator of second language proficiency', in K. Hyltenstam and L.K. Obler (eds) *Bilingualism across the Lifespan: aspects of acquisition, maturity, and loss*, Cambridge: Cambridge University Press, pp. 55–72.
Zenner, E., Speelman, D. and Geeraerts, D. (2010) 'What makes a catchphrase catchy? Possible determinants in the borrowability of English catchphrases in Dutch', Pre-published paper for the Laud Symposium on Cognitive Sociolinguistics, Landau, Germany, 15–18 March.
Zobl, H. (1992) 'Prior linguistic knowledge and the conservation of the learning procedure: grammaticality judgements of unilingual and multilingual learners', in S. Gass and L. Selinker (eds) *Language Transfer in Language Learning*, Amsterdam: John Benjamins, pp. 176–96.

INDEX

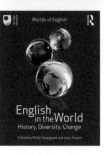